CHASING SHADOWS

SHELLEY BOWEN HATFIELD

Chasing Shadows

INDIANS ALONG THE UNITED STATES-MEXICO
BORDER 1876–1911

✠ ✠ ✠

University of New Mexico Press Albuquerque

Map 1 cartography by Nancy Lamm, © *1997 by the University of New Mexico Press.*

Map 2 courtesy of the Arizona Historical Society/Tucson, Don Bufkin map.

Library of Congress Cataloging-in-Publication Data

Hatfield, Shelley Ann Bowen, 1947–

[Indians of the United States-Mexico border during the Porfiriato, 1876–1911]

Chasing shadows: Indians along the United States-Mexico border,

1876–1911 / Shelley Bowen Hatfield. — 1st ed.

p. cm.

Originally presented as the author's thesis (Ph. D. — University of

New Mexico, 1983) under title: Indians of the United States-Mexico

border during the Porfiriato, 1876–1911.

Includes bibliographical references and index.

ISBN 0-8263-1853-3 (cloth)

ISBN 0-8263-2146-1 (paper)

1. Indians of Mexico — Government relations.   2. Indians of North

America — Government relations — 1869–1934.   3. Apache Indians — Wars.

4. Mexico — Foreign relations — United States.   5. United States —

Foreign relations — Mexico.   I. Title.

F1219.3.G6H37   1998

328.1′197072 — DC21   97-13403

CIP

To Bob and Berry

Contents

Illustrations

+

�֏

Preface

Comparative studies of United States and Mexican Indian policies are lacking for the period 1848–1911. This study, based on newspapers and correspondence in the Colección Porfirio Díaz and the Archivo Histórico Genaro Estrada at the Secretaría de Relaciones Exteriores in Mexico City, focuses on U.S. and Mexican Indian policies along the border between 1876 and 1911. Investigated is indigenous policy within the broader policies of societal development.

Most studies of Native Americans on the border during this period written in the United States have relied on English language sources. Mexican studies of Indians during the second half of the nineteenth century have concentrated on either the Yaquis or the Mayas. Few scholars in either Mexico or the United States have extensively consulted the Díaz papers, and no other researcher has explored this topic in the Relaciones Exteriores archive. An important contribution is to separate myth from reality and to elucidate the Mexican perception of these problems.

The study concludes that Porfirian Indian policy demanded maximum economic exploitation of Indians for the capitalistic modernization of the nation. During the regime of Porfirio Díaz, rapid commercial expansion and population growth created new demands for Indian land and labor, especially in the north and south. Indians such as the Mayas and Yaquis reacted with rebellion to forced labor and usurpation of their land, and their resentment played a major role in the social revolution that abruptly ended the Porfiriato.

Economic exploitation of Indian land and labor did not apply to border Indians like the Chiricahuas. Extermination policies, like that of scalp bounties in Chihuahua and Sonora, did not exist in the United States. Blaming United States reservation Indians for border raids, Mexico criticized the reservation system and the American use of Indian scouts.

Mexico combined federal and state forces in efforts to make frontier states safe for economic development. Díaz's correspondence reveals that he allowed governors in border states to direct their Indian campaigns in conjunction with federal military commanders with special federal subsidies. In contrast, United States Indian policy was consistently one of federal control with federal troops.

In spite of differing Indian policies, Mexico and the United States cooperated to end Indian raids on the border and signed an agreement allowing regular troops of both nations to cross the border in "hot pursuit" of hostile Indians. Although both nations cited peaceful assimilation of Native Americans as the ultimate goal of their policies, in reality economic exploitation took precedence. In both countries, economic development policies requiring a peaceful environment decreed that hostile border Indians be fought until they either surrendered or were exterminated. Removal of raiding Indians from the frontier was practiced in both nations, but only Mexico formulated a deportation policy designed to exploit Indian labor.

Acknowledgments

Numerous debts have been incurred in the preparation of this study. The University of New Mexico Latin American Institute/Tinker Foundation generously provided grants for summer research in Mexico in 1980 and 1981. I owe a special debt of gratitude to my professors: the late Edwin Lieuwen; and Richard Ellis, David Maciel, Peter Bakewell, Michael Conniff, and Karl Schwerin. Their encouragement and guidance were invaluable. Above all, I wish to thank the following for their support: my husband Robert D. Hatfield, my parents Annis and Jack Bowen, and my mother-in-law Virginia Hatfield.

The present study would not have been possible without the friendly cooperation of Robert Marín Maldonado, Francisco Bustamante Martínez, Aurora Contreras Huerta, and the staff of the Archivo Histórico Genaro Estrada at the Secretaría de Relaciones Exteriores in Mexico City. Special thanks are due Lucrecia de la Torre and María Cristina Torrales at the Universidad Iberoamericana in Mexico City for patiently offering guidance and for facilitating my access to the Colección Porfirio Díaz.

I should like to acknowledge suggestions received from the following scholars in Mexico City: Ernesto de la Torre Villar, Dr. Enrique Cárdenas de la Peña, María de la Luz Parcero, Colonel Leopoldo Martínez Caraza, Enrique Florescano, Gustavo A. Pérez Trejo, Antonio Pompa y Pompa, and Oscar Zambrano. I wish to thank Moisés González Navarro, Josefina Vásquez, Anne Staples, and Roberto Salazar at the Colegio de México for their constructive criticism. At the Biblioteca Nacional, María del Carmen Ruiz Castañeda enabled me to consult the Colección Lafragua, and Ana María Rosa Carreón Arias Maldonado contributed fresh insights to my research. At the Archivo General de la Nación, Alejandra Moreno Toscano, Ana Laura Delgado, and Stella María González Cicero guided me to regional archives.

In Hermosillo, the following gave their help and advice: Cynthia Radding de Murieta, Armando Quijada, and Ana Sylvia Laborín Abascal. In Chihuahua, Francisco R. Almada, José Fuentes Mares, and Víctor M. Mendoza generously gave suggestions. In Mexico City, Jorge Ortiz González, Luz and Bibiano F. Osorio-Tafall, and Jorge Lozoya offered friendship and support. In addition, special thanks are due Richard E. Greenleaf at Tulane University, Robert Delaney at Fort Lewis College, and Evelyn Hu-Dehart at Washington University for advice and encouragement.

In Tucson, I wish to thank Jean Bock and the staff of the Arizona Historical Society and Laurie and Tom Pew. Russ Davidson and the library staff of the University of New Mexico provided bibliographical assistance. Catherine Conrad and others at Fort Lewis College, Durango, Colorado, gave valuable help. I owe thanks to Jeanne Willson and the Barker Texas History Center staff and to Jane Garner and the staff of the Nettie Lee Benson Latin American Collection at the University of Texas at Austin. Constance Potter of the National Archives genealogy staff provided assistance.

Finally, I owe a debt of gratitude to Richard Ellis and Duane Smith at Fort Lewis College, Spencer Wilson at New Mexico Tech, the late Myra Ellen Jenkins, and Maurene Keilty for reading the manuscript and making valuable suggestions. I wish also to thank Elaine Slade for proofreading and Paula Seay for typing the revised manuscript. To all these persons I wish here once more to express my gratitude.

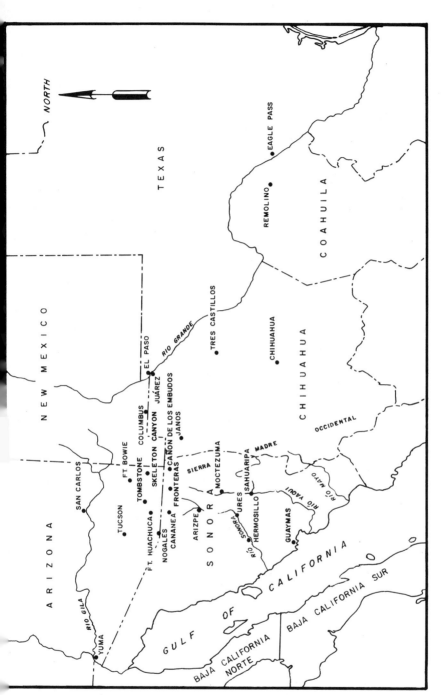

Map 1. The U.S.–Mexico Border
(*Cartography by Nancy Lamm.*)

Prologue

*Their knowledge of country; their powers of observation and deduction; their
watchfulness, endurance and ability to take care of themselves under all circumstances, made them seem at times like superior beings from another world. No
wonder our soldiers could not catch people like these.*

SECOND LIEUTENANT W. E. SHIPP, TENTH CAVALRY.

Before the Indian campaigns had ended, Mexico and the United States had
sacrificed unknown numbers of Indians and soldiers and had spent millions
of dollars in the name of order and progress. Most of Mexico's resources
went toward Indian pacification. In the United States, however, more expenditures were directed in a conscious effort to "civilize" Native Americans through education. In both countries, economic development policies
required a peaceful environment, which ensured that Indians would be
fought until they either surrendered or were exterminated.

During the regime of Porfirio Díaz (1876–1911), maximum economic
exploitation of Indians to foster the country's capitalistic modernization
was one of the tenets of government domestic policy. The Díaz regime's
usurpation of land and enslavement of Indians intensified the Mayo, Yaqui,
and Maya rebellions. Seminomadic border Indians, including Apaches,
provided capitalists with neither land nor labor. Mexico's deportation policy directed toward maximum exploitation of Indian labor was not applicable to border Indians, and different policies were needed to defeat Indians
in the frontier states. Mexico's policies eventually led to joint military action with the United States to defeat the Apaches.

In 1848 Apaches and other rebellious Indians on the southwest frontier
became a United States responsibility under provisions of the Treaty of
Guadalupe Hidalgo, which ended the war with Mexico. The United States
expected to make peace treaties with Indians, permitting American settlement anywhere in the acquired territory while prohibiting raids into Mexico. Apaches could not understand the U.S. government assumption that it
now owned Apache land because it had conquered the Mexicans. Unable to

end border raids into Mexico, the United States abrogated the responsibility of restraining Indian raids into Mexico with the 1853 Gadsden Purchase and Treaty.

Continued failure to prevent Indian raiding led to a U.S. reservation policy of peace through isolation. In 1871 humanitarian Vincent Colyer's urging led to the Department of the Interior's effort to gather Indians of New Mexico and Arizona on reservations to learn farming and livestock raising. Concurrently, military action against Indians increased with General George Crook's appointment as commander of the Department of Arizona.

Although the United States increased military pressure against Mescalero Apaches from Fort Stanton, New Mexico, in 1870–71, Mescaleros continued to raid in Sonora and Chihuahua. Brigadier General Oliver O. Howard's 1872 pact with Chiricahua chief Cochise temporarily ended Chiricahua Apache raiding in the United States, but did not prevent the Apaches from continuing hostilities in Mexico. Comanches no longer threatened the border after their decisive defeat in 1874–75. Kickapoo Indian depredations diminished after 1873, but Texas continued to protest raids by Kickapoos and Lipan Apaches receiving protection in Coahuila. Mexico found it difficult to reconcile Texas complaints of raids from Coahuila with U.S. Indian policy aimed at protecting Arizona and New Mexico at Mexico's expense.

Mexico blamed American Indians for the continued raids, and the United States was convinced that Mexican Indians were responsible for the plunder of the frontier. Unauthorized border crossings by troops from both nations in pursuit of Indians were quietly settled until 1877, when the United States declared, through Brigadier General Edward Ord's order, that American troops would give chase across the border. Mexico resented Ord's order and only agreed to cooperate with the United States to defeat the Indians when the order was revoked in 1880 after conditions had improved on the Rio Grande. After abrogation of the order, Mexico agreed to sign an agreement for reciprocal troop crossing. This pact was directed against the Chiricahua menace, which had grown significantly in the late 1870s.

The area of conflict shifted west to Chihuahua, Sonora, Arizona, and New Mexico, where Chiricahua Apaches raided unhindered. Apaches became pawns in a struggle between the army and the Indian Bureau for their control.[1] The concentration of Apaches on the San Carlos Reservation in Arizona territory exacerbated problems, and in 1877 Chiricahua and Warm Springs Apaches fled the reservation. The United States began a formal campaign against the Warm Springs Apaches in 1879. Victorio, the able leader of the Warm Springs band, was killed by Mexican forces in 1880, but the Apache threat was not over. Mescaleros fled New Mexico to join the remnants of Victorio's band in Chihuahua.

This renewed threat reconfirmed Mexico's position that the U.S. policy isolating Indians on reservations as wards of the federal government was not viable. Mexico, in contrast, offered Indians citizenship and continued to strive for their assimilation. Although assimilation was the professed goal of the Díaz regime, Indians remained at the bottom of society. They formed villages apart and lived in separate barrios of cities. Mexican Indians were kept in a servile position during the Porfiriato through the system of debt peonage. *Hacendado* landowners justified forced labor on their large estates on the grounds that the Indian was allegedly too lazy to work without coercion.

During the Porfiriato, or Díaz period, population growth and rapid commercial expansion, especially in the northernmost and southernmost parts of Mexico, created new demands for Indian land and labor. Capitalism required liquidation of encumbering social and cultural institutions. Human beings became means in the production of goods for profit.

Economic callousness during the Porfiriato was a major cause of the social revolution that would follow. Díaz's *científico* advisors were in the mainstream of world opinion when they claimed Mexico's drive to modernize required more roads, railroads, and bridges. The regime's efforts to transform Mexico into a modern, industrial nation heightened the capitalist confrontation with noncapitalistic Indian societies.

Not benefiting from Díaz's modernization policy, Indians developed a resentment that was transformed into mass revolutionary movements seeking to change the entire social structure. Indian rebellions played a major part in the social revolution that abruptly ended the Porfiriato.

During the Díaz regime, many Mexican intellectuals felt that Indians only needed civilizing to progress. They suggested induction into the army as the most efficient way to educate Indians. Some looked to education for the Indians' regeneration. Others doubted the Indians' ability to learn and improve their status. During the Díaz presidency, Indian education was primarily limited to the teaching of Spanish to Indians.

Interest in Indian education was primarily intellectual rhetoric. Just as ephemeral were the precursors of *indigenismo*, which glorified Mexico's indigenous cultures. The first Indianist societies began during the Porfiriato, and archaeological work started in earnest; but, ironically, this incipient indigenismo began in a society that did little to better the deplorable socioeconomic conditions of the Indians. There were few attempts to protect Indians from economic exploitation during the Porfiriato, a period when no federal indigenista legislation was enacted. A Chihuahua law designed to protect Tarahumara Indians was never implemented.[2]

Porfirian Mexico did not concern itself with social welfare. Its positivist leaders, whose beliefs were based on survival of the fittest, condemned welfare as antiliberal and unscientific. Mexico's capitalist elite created defensive stereotypes to justify exploitation of "inferior" Indians. In Mexico the fittest were the upper classes. The "unfit" Indians did not merit public charity. Governmental obligations to the masses were strictly limited, and charity was considered an individual duty. Church activism was largely limited to speeches during the Porfiriato, and the Catholic church was far more concerned with combating paganism than with promoting social welfare.

During this time, when both church and government were unconcerned with the Indians' miserable living conditions, the percentage of Indians in the Mexican population steadily declined. They represented only 32 percent by 1910, although they increased in absolute numbers. In 1877, an estimated 39 percent of the population spoke Indian languages, but in 1910, the percentage was estimated at only 13 percent. Indian population was concentrated in southern Mexico, whereas the mestizo predominated from northern Mexico to the capital.[3]

As the percentage of those defined as Indians by their linguistic and cultural heritage decreased, some Mexican leaders expressed the hope that the Indians would become extinct through miscegenation. Many educated Mexicans believed that mestizos would eventually absorb the Indians and thereby unify the nation.

Francisco Bulnes, an engineer and politician, wrote in 1899 that a tropical climate, alcohol, and a poor diet kept the Indian at a subhuman level. He added that the Indian was degenerating further and that extinction was inevitable. Bulnes based his theory of the Indian's inherent inferiority on a corn diet, theorizing that white wheat eaters were superior to oriental rice eaters, who, in turn, were superior to Indian corn eaters.[4]

The Indian's capacity as a worker in the industrialization process was considered limited, and education would take time. Mexico needed to modernize, and the fastest way to do so would be the importation of foreigners to hasten Mexico's industrialization. As early as 1864, Francisco Pimentel, historian and student of Indian languages, suggested that European immigration be encouraged to foster *mestizaje* and increase the productivity of Mexican agriculture.[5]

The first efforts to attract foreigners began in 1877. Land was offered as an inducement. The only restriction was that citizens of nations sharing a boundary with Mexico were not allowed to purchase land within frontier states. The lesson of Texas independence had not been forgotten. Large numbers of foreigners never came, but Díaz did not give up on the colonization scheme. Private companies surveyed so-called unoccupied lands, or *terrenos baldíos*, in return for one-third of the land surveyed. The federal government allowed individuals to denounce claims to lands lacking clear titles and, as a result, Indian communal lands were divided.

Seizure of Indian communal lands, or *ejidos*, was based on the Ley Lerdo of 1856, but most Indian lands remained intact until the Porfiriato. Colonizing laws passed between 1883 and 1894 accelerated the growth of large estates. Railroad development from 1877 to 1884 was closely linked to the denouncing and seizure of Indian ejidos. Indian pueblos lost their communal holdings when they failed to produce titles to their lands.[6]

Social Darwinism justified exploitation of Indian labor and seizure of communal land. Property belonged to those strong enough to obtain it. Wealth, an instrument of social progress, merited state protection, and the fact that the Indian lost his land suggested that he was less than deserving.

Indian communities resorted to any means to prove title to their lands. In 1892 Oaxacan Indians presented the Lienzo de Zacatepec, a pre-Columbian Mixtec manuscript painting, to the secretary of development as evidence of their land possession, yet more than three hundred years of possession was not considered sufficient evidence of ownership. Entire Indian towns were demolished; large estates grew without limits.

A Kickapoo chief called on Díaz to protest loss of land to adjoining haciendas. Taking his seat next to Díaz on a bench, the Indian gradually pressed against the president, causing him to fall to the floor. The Kickapoo then said to Díaz that in this very way hacendados deprive Indians of their lands.[7]

Indians refused to view their lands as a commodity fostering national development, and they reacted violently against usurpation of their homelands and the resultant social dislocations that alienated them from their social ties and roots. Indian rebellions had a long history in Mexico, antedating the Díaz dictatorship. Rapid economic development during the Porfiriato only increased the number of such revolts.

The Díaz regime's plan for development and modernization of Mexico required that the positivist motto of "order and peace" become a reality. In order to achieve internal peace in Mexico and to integrate the nation, it was necessary to control hostile tribes. The Mayas of Yucatán were the first to create serious problems for the Díaz government. Mayan rebellions began many years before the Porfiriato, however.

A general Mayan insurrection against all whites and mestizos, termed a *guerra de castas*, or racial war, began in 1847 and lasted four years. Fearing that Indians might take over the entire peninsula, the white elite appealed to the federal government for aid; but Mexico was involved in war with the United States and had no resources for isolated Yucatán. Remaining neutral during the war, the government of Yucatán asked the United States for protectorate status.

After the United States rejected Yucatán's plea, the decision to sell Mayan prisoners into Cuban slavery was justified on grounds that the federal government had abandoned the peninsula, and the state had no other way to obtain funds to pay troops engaged in the campaign against the Mayas. This slave traffic continued from 1849 to 1861, when President Benito Juárez, himself an Indian, terminated it.[8]

During the Porfiriato only the *cruzoob*, Mayan inhabitants of the rebel capital of Chan Santa Cruz, remained hostile. There, in what would become the Mexican territory of Quintana Roo, some seven thousand Mayas maintained their independence, making guerrilla raids into Mérida with arms and ammunition obtained in Belize. The insurgents' territory was increasing, and in 1886, Yucatán asked the federal government for three thousand soldiers to put down the revolt.

An all-out campaign would not take place for nine more years, when General Ignacio A. Bravo began the battle that would lead to the defeat of the Mayas. The campaign was officially declared closed on June 1, 1904. Fighting did not terminate, however, and rebellions recurred in 1907, 1909, and 1912.[9]

Usurpation of land and enslavement of Indians for henequen, or sisal hemp, cultivation provided the motivation for intensification of the Maya *guerra de castas*. During the Porfiriato, fortunes could be made in henequen fiber, which was used to weave rope and rugs, but plantations required excessive acreage and a large labor supply. Systematic deportation of Mayas to Cuba, as well as warfare, had greatly reduced the Indian population. The acute labor shortage gave rise to debt peonage, but indebted peons failed to meet hacendados' labor demands. Therefore, when Yaqui rebellion threatened Sonora's mining interests, Governor Rafael Izábal deported Yaquis, considered superior workers by all accounts, to work on Yucatán's henequen plantations.

Yaqui revolts during the Porfiriato, resulting in deportation of unknown numbers of Indians to Yucatán and other parts of the nation, were caused primarily by the Yaquis' determination to keep their lands. Yaqui refusal to submit to government laws conflicted with the Mexican government's attempts to end all regional hegemony. The regime had hoped to take Yaqui lands peacefully, but this the Yaquis prevented. Therefore, Díaz resorted to the use of force with his policy of *pan* or *palo*, "bread or the club." The bloody fight against the Yaquis and Mayos cost the government enormous sums and some of its best manpower.

Although Yaqui insurrections were continuous from 1825 to 1901, the revolts had an earlier history. Fiercely independent, Yaquis remained autonomous under Spanish rule. Jesuit missions maintained an uneasy peace in Yaqui territory from 1617 until 1740, when the first major revolt occurred. A government study published in 1905 cited 270 instances of Yaqui and Mayo warfare between 1529 and 1902, excluding eighty-five years of relative peace between 1740 and 1825.[10]

Yaquis fought to defend what they considered their land since time immemorial. The longest periods of Yaqui peace occurred when they were allowed to resettle their river bottomlands. Rich Yaqui and Mayo valley lands possessed a soil and climate capable of growing almost any crop. Therefore, it was considered in the best national interest to open these lands to commercial development and foreign investors.

Division of the Yaqui and Mayo valleys began in 1880 when the first railroad reached Sonora and Governor Luis E. Torres began to encourage development of mining and foreign investment. Yaqui and Mayo lands were declared terrenos baldíos and, because the Indians were unable to produce recorded titles to their property, their lands were surveyed and sold. By this method the federal government hoped to take Yaqui and Mayo lands peacefully, but the Indians reacted violently against the loss of their homelands in 1880.

Only the use of force gave Indians a breathing spell from the despoliation of their land. Between three and four thousand Yaquis and Mayos under the leadership of José María Leyva, alias Cajeme, fought both state and federal troops. Cajeme was apprehended in 1887 and executed on orders of Governor Torres in an application of *ley fuga*, in which a prisoner was shot while allegedly trying to escape. The Mayos remained peaceful after Cajeme's death, but the Yaquis continued fighting under their new leader, Juan Maldonado, alias Tetabiate. The death of Tetabiate in July 1901 encouraged the government to officially declare the campaign closed.[11]

The government's declaration of peace was premature, however. In September 1901, a new rebellion began. In April 1902 Luis Torres and Sonora's governor, Rafael Izábal, announced a new policy concentrating Yaqui laborers in guarded ranchería settlements. In 1904 Izábal prohibited the hiring of any Yaqui without a passport. Izábal reported to the Sonoran Congress that between 1903 and 1907 some two thousand Yaquis had been deported to Yucatán, Quintana Roo, and Oaxaca. The majority were sent to henequen haciendas to meet a severe labor shortage. In 1907 Izábal issued orders to rid Sonora of all Yaquis in the areas north of Hermosillo. Because guerrillas were elusive, the government focused its attention on the accessible Yaqui peon; even those with passports were now arrested and deported.[12]

The Yaqui problem came to symbolize government policies in direct conflict with local interests. American investors in Sonora protested the deportation of hard-working Yaqui laborers, and Arizona eagerly offered Yaquis jobs until the 1907–09 depression reduced the labor demand. The depression lessened demand for Yaquis in mining and railroads, but Sonora hacendados' needs continued unabated. Resenting the fact that good workers were being taken from Sonora, the state's hacendados were more concerned with the loss of Yaqui labor than with rebellions. Deportation ended in 1908, probably because the depression caused a drop in the price of henequen, reducing the demand for labor in Yucatán. In 1909 Yaqui leader Luis Bule surrendered, but a small force held out in the Sierra de Bacatete until 1918, and Yaquis continued their disturbances until 1936.[13]

Indians on the United States–Mexico border caused the Díaz government as much consternation as had the Yaquis. These Indians, including the superior Apache warriors, were defeated only when Mexico and the United States agreed to joint military action. The American and Mexican desire to work together to subjugate this enemy resulted in the 1882 reciprocal crossing agreement, allowing regular troops of both nations to cross the border in "hot pursuit" of Indians. Allowed to lapse when Geronimo surrendered in 1886, the agreement, slightly changed, was revived in 1890, 1892, and 1896. Although not renewed again, the crossing agreement was cited by Venustiano Carranza as a precedent for General John J. Pershing's 1916 punitive expedition against Pancho Villa.[14]

Although the United States and Mexico were forced to sign the reciprocal crossing pact because it was their only hope for a successful campaign against the Apaches, distrust and recrimination characterized the two countries' relations. Neither country committed enough resources to effectively pacify the border area. Each nation blamed the other for the failure to bring peace to the frontier region. Mexico believed that United States reservation Indians received passes to raid in Mexico.

Chiricahuas, however, fled the San Carlos reservation in resistance to corruption, the concentration policy, demoralizing rationing, white encroachment on their land, and conflicts between the War Department and the Bureau of Indian Affairs. Anglo miners disregarded reservation boundaries and pieces of the reservation were sliced off for Anglo use as mines went into operation. At the same time, Mormon settlements expanded into

Arizona. Their farmers pressed onto the reservation from the west and north, and on the southeast they diverted Gila water from Indian irrigation projects.

Never accepting the U.S. reservation system, Mexico employed a spy on the San Carlos reservation to monitor movements of Apaches and U.S. troops. Mexico's criticism of American reservations increased when Geronimo and his band were allowed to return to the United States with stolen Mexican stock in 1884. Mexico also disliked the Americans' use of Apache scouts, accusing them of depredation in its territory. Claiming scouts were in violation of the 1882 crossing agreement, Mexico blamed Captain Emmet Crawford's 1886 death on United States scouts having been mistaken for hostiles. The subsequent crossing pacts specified that only two scouts could accompany each company as guides.[15]

Both Mexico and the United States took Indian lands that were valuable for farming or mining. In the United States, western as well as eastern votes passed the 1887 Dawes Act, which was designed to break up Indian reservations via land allotment. Between 1883 and 1894, Mexico passed colonizing laws, accelerating the growth of large estates at the expense of Indian communities. Land-grabbing hacendados received Mexican government protection, defended on the grounds that the state should not intervene in private enterprise.

Removal of Indians from their lands was practiced in both nations, but only in Mexico was this deportation policy directed toward maximum exploitation of Indian laborers such as the Yaquis. Although Mexico did not consider the United States reservation policy viable, Sonora attempted to concentrate Yaquis in guarded ranchería settlements. Yaqui labor continued to be of primary importance, and the Indians were permitted to leave their confinement in order to work in mines and on haciendas.

In contrast to the Yaquis, seminomadic Apaches provided capitalists with neither land nor labor. Although never a federal policy, Chihuahua and Sonora had Apache extermination policies that carried scalp bounties. Such policies did not exist in the United States. An official Mexican publication dated 1905 listed extermination, deportation, and colonization of Indians as policies of the Díaz government.[16]

United States policy was consistently one of federal control with federal troops, and Indian reservations remained under federal jurisdiction. In contrast, in Mexico both federal and state troops were used. Federal presidios and *colonias militares* proved ineffective on the frontier, so Díaz allowed border states to direct their Indian campaigns with special federal subsidies. As commander of the army, Díaz made the ultimate decisions, giving orders through the secretary of war to commanders of Mexico's twelve military zones. After ridding Mexico of local caudillos, Díaz controlled the country with loyal governors, a large percentage of them generals.[17]

When governors and commanders of military zones quarreled over policy decisions, Díaz mediated disputes. The division and overlapping of supreme authority in the states worked to Díaz's advantage, because governors and commanders were eager to show their loyalty by reporting any infractions on the part of their rivals. Díaz granted considerable autonomy to the states but was quick to reprimand abuses, such as Sonora's governor's hiring of an American soldier of fortune to direct the Yaqui campaign.[18]

In fact, Mexican troops and officers served as well in the joint Apache campaign as did American forces, having notable successes against Victorio, Juh, and Nana. Mexican officials cooperated with their U.S. counterparts. Generals Geronimo Treviño and Edward Ord worked together to end Rio Grande raids in the 1870s, and Brigadier General Nelson A. Miles and Sonora's Governor Luis E. Torres acted in close alliance to effect Geronimo's surrender. Only when both nations combined their efforts were they finally able to defeat warring border Indians. Both the United States and Mexico cited peaceful regeneration of Indians as their ultimate goals. Mexico sought political incorporation of Indians, but United States reservation policy kept Indians isolated and provided little experience in local U.S. government. In reality, the primary goal of Indian policy in both countries was economic exploitation. Indians lost their traditional ranges on both sides of the border as settlers encroached on their lands.

Mexican railroad development was closely linked to the denouncing and seizure of Indian communal lands. The U.S. federal government granted railroads a right of way through Indian reservations. Individual Indian assimilation and detribalization resulted from policies of infiltration and colonization in both nations. Solidarity of Native American groups such as the Yaquis and Chiricahuas, however, intensified through warfare. Because both nations were insensitive to the consequences of their actions, the social ills that their policies created or exacerbated haunt present generations.

ONE

The Failure of The Treaty of Guadalupe Hidalgo, 1848–1876

✠

Failure to bring peace to the border was indicative of the failure of both nations to effectively pacify the entire region. In addition to hostile Indians, the United States and Mexico had to contend with frontier outlaws and rustlers such as Robert Martin and Catarino Garza. Mexico did not defeat the Yaquis until 1909, and the United States did not defeat the southern Plains tribes until 1874–75 and conflict with Apaches continued to 1886.

The United States defeated the Comanches, Kiowas, and Cheyennes in 1874–75 only after launching a major offensive. General William T. Sherman advised the secretary of war that ten thousand cavalry would be needed to give defensive protection to the Southwest. However, Sherman added, only a thousand cavalry would be needed to punish the Indians offensively, and on July 20, 1874, he received permission "to turn loose the troops."[1] In spite of this force commitment, in 1874 the United States still placed only a small portion of the total 30,520 officers and men in the Southwest.

This lack of commitment to the border area relative to total military strength was a decisive factor in the continuation of Indian hostilities until the turn of the century. Warfare continued in spite of the fact that, as early as 1865, the United States had placed a line of forts within Apache territory, with lesser posts in between. The forts did not prevent raids into Mexico, however, or provide effective protection for settlers in Apache country.[2] The Geronimo campaign did not end until 1886, and, as late as 1896, both the United States and Mexico feared depredations by Apache Kid, a former Indian scout turned outlaw.

Via the Treaty of Guadalupe Hidalgo, the United States inherited the border Indian problem in 1848 along with Mexico's ceded territory. Indian disturbances have a much longer history on Mexico's northern frontier. Apache raids beginning in the mid seventeenth century pushed back the established frontier, nearly depopulating Sonora and Chihuahua. Spain began to establish presidios to defend the frontier in the sixteenth century, and these military garrisons became the colonial precedents for nineteenth-century colonias militares settlements of soldier-farmers.[3]

In 1786 Mexican viceroy Bernardo de Gálvez initiated a system of reservations called *establecimientos de paz*. By 1793 there were eight Apache establecimientos along the northern frontier, six of them under presidio protection. Approximately two thousand Apaches were placed on reservations, where they were encouraged to farm. The Apaches were allowed to leave their reservations to hunt to supplement their issued rations. It was the Spanish establecimiento that served as a model for subsequent Anglo-American Indian reservations in the borderlands.[4]

Due to the maintenance of establecimientos, Apache raids had diminished by 1800, to the point that Spanish frontier settlement could resume. Spain lacked funds to maintain reservations and presidios during the War for Independence of 1810–21. Apaches, now deprived of rations on a regular schedule because of the war, resumed raiding. Rations were completely terminated in 1831, and in 1833 Apache chief Juan José Compá fled his establecimiento at Janos, Chihuahua, precipitating a revolt throughout Apachería.

An estimated five thousand Mexicans on the frontier died at the hands of Apaches between 1820 and 1835. Apaches raided Sonora, Chihuahua, and New Mexico, even striking as far south as Durango.[5]

Sonora and Chihuahua adopted Apache extermination policies. Extermination of Apaches was attempted because the Mexicans believed that Apaches lacked the desired qualities of other Indians, such as valuable labor skills and land ownership. Sonoran Ramón Corral wrote that the Apaches had always been nomadic, existing primarily by raiding, forming no permanent settlements, and having no occupations.

Because Apache labor was not valuable, as early as 1835, Sonora paid 100 pesos (a peso was roughly equivalent to a dollar) for an adult male Apache's scalp. Sonora set aside 4,000 pesos for the purchase of scalps between 1871 and 1873, raising the amount to 9,620 pesos in 1874.[6] Some fur trappers became mercenary scalp hunters, such as John Johnson, who turned Apaches against Americans when he killed chief Juan José Compá in 1837.

The most notorious scalp hunter was James (Santiago) Kirker, an Irish trapper. Kirker became a naturalized Mexican citizen and settled in Janos, Chihuahua, where he guarded mines and mule trains from Apache attacks.

He also acted as an intermediary for Apache traders with Mexicans and Americans in El Paso, Santa Fe, and other towns. In December 1839, Chihuahua's governor José María Irigoyen signed a four-month contract with Kirker authorizing him to fight Apaches with a force of two hundred men. Kirker's band, composed of Americans, Mexicans, Indians, and runaway blacks, received a salary and a bounty for Indians killed or captured.[7]

The following year, Chihuahua's new governor, Francisco García Conde, did not renew Kirker's contract, believing that it was unpatriotic, dishonorable, and a dangerous precedent for a foreigner to direct the Indian campaign. The governor's suspicions were proven when Kirker joined the invading forces of the United States in 1847. Chihuahua had invited Kirker to organize another expedition against the Apaches in 1846, but after Kirker's betrayal, the state placed a bounty on Kirker's head instead.[8]

In 1846 Chihuahua offered 50 pesos for each dead Indian, and in 1849 paid 200 pesos for a warrior's scalp, 250 pesos for an adult male prisoner, 100 pesos for a dead woman or a child under fourteen, and 150 pesos for a captured woman or child. According to one report, 7,896 pesos were paid out for scalps in 1849. The bounty was actually paid for any scalp, adult or child, male or female, Indian or non-Indian.[9]

Chihuahua increased the bounty to 300 pesos in 1860. Chihuahua and Durango offered a scalp bounty of 200 to 250 pesos in 1873. Instead of ending depredations, scalp bounty policies ultimately served only to make Apaches fight more desperately.[10]

In addition to scalp bounties, individual Mexican states made their own separate peace with Apaches. This lack of a federal policy led Apaches to think in terms of partial peace often in conflict with neighboring states rather than a peace with all of Mexico. When pursued, they fled with their stolen stock to the state they were at peace with at that moment, knowing that they would not be attacked or forced to return their plunder.

There were numerous periods of partial peace in Chihuahua between 1834 and 1856. Sonora twice invaded Chihuahua to attack Apaches allegedly guilty of raiding and killing in Sonora before seeking sanctuary in Janos, Chihuahua, under a peace treaty. Lieutenant Colonel José María Elias González led Sonora forces into Chihuahua in 1844, and in 1851 Colonel José María Carrasco commanded the Sonoran troops attacking Apaches when they reported for rations at Janos. Geronimo's family may have been massacred during Carrasco's attack. The state of Chihuahua protested this incident to the federal government without success, and the case was closed when Carrasco died of cholera a few months later.[11]

The Apaches also found a safe haven and an outlet for their plunder across the border in what is now Arizona. In 1848, Apaches and other hostile Indians on the frontier fell under United States jurisdiction under provisions of the Treaty of Guadalupe Hildago. Through Article XI of the treaty, the United States assumed responsibility for preventing border Indians from making incursions into Mexico. The treaty also declared it unlawful for United States citizens to purchase Mexican captives or stolen property.

This article was accepted by the United States to justify its claims to Mexican territory and to make the treaty more acceptable to the Mexicans. In his presidential message of December 7, 1847, James K. Polk maintained that if New Mexico belonged to the United States, Indian depredations would end. American negotiator Nicolas Trist declared that assumption of Indian responsibility was "indispensable to make the treaty acceptable to the northern states [of Mexico]."[12] Trist added that Article XI did not differ substantially from the obligation assumed by the thirty-third article of the 1831 Treaty of Amity, Commerce, and Navigation. This 1831 treaty required both countries "to restrain by force all hostilities and incursions on the part of the Indian nations living within their respective boundaries" and provided for the return of captives.[13]

Article XI received United States approval only after the Senate added a modification allowing Indians to possess firearms and ammunition. Secretary of State James Buchanan defended the Senate's action on humanitarian grounds because "these Indians must live by the chase; and without firearms they cannot secure the means of subsistence." Buchanan added that lack of arms might drive Indians through hunger to commit further depredations.[14]

Buchanan asserted that the United States possessed the ability and desire to prevent Indians from raiding Mexico. When dealing with border Indians, the United States continued a policy of making treaties with "dependent domestic nations." Apaches considered the United States' demands unreasonable. The United States insisted that Apaches accept treaties denying their right to raid into Mexico and requiring them to deliver up Mexican captives. The Apaches, however, maintained that their Mexican raiding was legitimized because they were now at peace with the United States.

In spite of such differences, the United States did manage to sign Indian treaties in the 1850s. For example, a Gila Apache treaty of July 1852 pledged the Indians to desist from raiding and taking captives in Mexico. On at least three occasions, New Mexico Indian agents managed to return captives to Mexico.

Apache territory was another source of conflict. United States citizens believed that they were free to settle anywhere in territory acquired in

1848. Apaches viewed this as an unreasonable position because the Mexicans had never defeated the Apaches and, hence, the United States could not lay claim to Apache land. Apaches considered the border an artificial barrier because their land use area had always ranged on both sides of the boundary.[15]

Ignoring Apache protests, the United States determined to protect inhabitants of the newly gained territory and to restrain Indians from making incursions into Mexico. The perplexing question was how to reduce military expenses while providing protection. One historian suggests "exasperated Whigs considered the new territory a white elephant on the government's hands and were not unwilling to return it to Mexico and even to give that country a few millions to take it back."[16] In spite of misgivings, the United States began attempts to police the border in September 1850, when $30,000 was set aside for the collection of Bureau of Indian Affairs statistics, the implementation of Indian treaties, and the provision of gifts for border Indians.

A bill introduced into the House of Representatives in February 1850 to increase army enlistments relied on two arguments: the dangerous conditions on the western frontier and treaty obligations to Mexico. While attempts were made to increase enlistments, Congress tried to cut War Department expenses. Instructions for new military posts in 1851 stated that Mexico was to be protected from incursions, but the secretaries of war and interior continued to complain of inadequate resources.[17]

The Bureau of Indian Affairs also lacked money, although an appropriation was made to send four Indian agents to New Mexico in 1851. In 1852 Texas and New Mexico received $85,000 to establish Indian reservations. That same year, Texas was urged to set aside public land for state reservations, but this was not done until 1854. Texas lacked a superintendent of Indian affairs and had no defined Indian policy during this period.[18]

United States attempts to protect the border were slow in coming, and the frontier remained insecure. Mexico did make an effort to protect the northern frontier during the 1840s and 1850s, but it failed because of lack of means rather than indifference. Mexico passed a law to create colonias militares on the frontier in 1846. Land and tools would be given to soldiers for cultivation, and voluntary enlistment was to be for six years. Civilian settlers were encouraged. When the colony had attained a prescribed size, it was to have a civilian government.

There were to be seven colonias militares in Sonora, seven in Chihuahua, four in Nuevo León, four in Durango, six in Coahuila, and two in Baja California. Each would have one hundred well-armed cavalry, half regulars

and half volunteers. The government planned to borrow from the states to
establish the colonias. An 1849 appropriation provided for four thousand
Mexican national guardsmen in addition to colonias militares and regulars
on the frontier. An 1851 report listed 1,093 soldiers and 689 horses and
mules in the colonias. The few colonias actually created in 1849–50, however, disappeared by 1857. Apaches continued raiding in Sonora, Chihuahua, and Coahuila, while Comanche depredations plagued Coahuila and
Nuevo León. Mexican Indian policy proved ineffective because of the lack
of funds in the national treasury, poverty on the frontier, internal disturbances, epidemics, and the California gold rush (which attracted Sonora's
population).[19]

Border raids continued unabated. Coahuila, Sonora, and Chihuahua suffered most from hostile Indians. During 1849–53, Comanche and Apache
raids in Coahuila resulted in 191 deaths. Between 1848 and 1851, the *El
Sonoriense* newspaper listed thirty to forty raids in Sonora. An 1848 report
blamed Apaches for the depopulation of twenty-six mines, thirty haciendas,
and ninety ranches in Sonora. In 1849 Apaches raided as far south as Ures,
killing 181. The prefect of Ures asked the governor for aid, reporting that
Fronteras, Cocóspera, Tubac, and three other towns had been completely
abandoned.[20]

Mexico was convinced that depredations between 1848 and 1853 were
largely caused by Apaches and Comanches from the United States, though
it could not prove these allegations. A defense plan published in Mexico in
1852 suggested that Mexico obtain United States permission to cross the
Rio Grande in pursuit of hostiles, while at the same time demanding fulfill-
ment of the Treaty of Guadalupe Hidalgo and indemnification for losses.
Congress had already stated that Mexico would probably seek indemni-
ties.[21] Mexico believed the only beneficial article in the Guadalupe Hidalgo
Treaty was that protecting Mexico from Indian raids, and that article was
not being followed.

When the United States accepted the responsibility in 1848 to end Indian raids into Mexico, the number and nature of tribes in the acquired
territory, as well as the cost of subduing them, were unknown. It was six
years before the United States adopted a well-defined policy and, meanwhile, raids continued. The United States was also unable to pacify its own
territory. In order to prevent Mexico from demanding reclamations, the
United States determined to abrogate Article XI of the Treaty of Guadalupe Hidalgo.

As late as August 1852, Mexico's minister of foreign relations requested
the governor of Sonora to send a detailed statement of raids in order to file

claims against the United States. But in November of 1853, James Gadsden informed Mexico that the United States objected to Article XI. The Gadsden Treaty of December 30, 1853, declared the eleventh article of the Treaty of Guadalupe Hidalgo null and void, while still providing that it would be illegal for United States citizens to buy or receive stolen Mexican stock. The Gadsden Treaty also provided that Mexico would be paid $10 million for ceding the Mesilla Valley to the United States and for relieving the United States of Indian responsibilities.[22]

Now that the United States was released from liability for border raids in Mexico, both nations blamed each other for continued hostilities. Mexico was convinced that the raiding Indians were from U.S. reservations, while the United States claimed depredations were the work of Indians living in Mexico. Meanwhile, Indians raided both sides of the border. It became evident to the United States that the only way to catch these hostile bands would be to pursue them across the border.

United States troops crossed the border in 1855, without Mexico's permission, in pursuit of hostile Lipan Apaches. The Lipans were a small group of about three hundred Indians living in Texas. After 1848 they emigrated to Mexico, establishing good relations with local authorities and citizens. Lipans continued to cross the Rio Grande to raid in the United States, and in October 1855 Texas Rangers under Captain James H. Callahan entered Piedras Negras to pursue and punish the raiders.[23]

After resorting to this unauthorized border crossing, the United States requested permission to cross the Rio Grande in 1856, but Mexico refused. Napoleon III's intervention in Mexico under Emperor Maximilian von Hapsburg and the United States Civil War prevented the two nations from signing any formal pact for border crossings in pursuit of hostile Indians during the 1860s.[24]

The United States, still believing that only border crossings by troops in pursuit of Indians could end raids, continued to seek informal agreements for crossings. In 1861, the Fort Bliss, Texas, commander proposed a reciprocal crossing of as many as fifty officers and two hundred men to Chihuahua's Governor Luis Terrazas. In 1863 Brigadier General James H. Carleton, commander of the Department of New Mexico, invited Governor Terrazas to send Mexican troops into the United States in pursuit of outlaws.[25]

According to Mexican historian José Fuentes Mares, Benito Juárez, president of Mexico's government in exile, did not understand why it was more important to Governor Terrazas to kill Indians than to kill the French invaders. In January 1866, however, Captain David H. Brotherton, commander of Fort Bliss, wrote to Juárez, requesting permission to cross the border in pursuit of hostiles. That same month, Sebastián Lerdo de Tejada, Mexico's minister of foreign affairs, granted Captain Brotherton's request.[26]

Cooperation in dealing with hostile Indians did not result, however, and both nations continued recriminations. Historian Luis González writes that Apaches raided Sonora equipped with United States army rifles and saddles, causing Mexicans to mistake them for Yankees with suntans, often with fatal consequences. Texas, in turn, complained in 1868 of raids by Indians given protection in Coahuila.[27] In response to Texas's complaints of repeated depredations, a U.S. congressional commission was authorized to investigate Rio Grande raids. In June 1873 the commission listed property losses of more than $48 million and reported that in 1872 the Texas border region possessed only one-tenth the livestock extant in 1865. The losses accounted for in 1873 occurred in spite of the fact that more than eight hundred soldiers guarded the Arizona and New Mexico border region, and twenty-five hundred policed the Texas Rio Grande area. Kickapoos received most of the blame for the raids, although Mescalero and Lipan Apaches were also implicated. A Mexican commission reported in 1873 that Texas exaggerated the losses. Mexico, in turn, complained of Texas horse thieves, adding that Texas was only seeking a pretext to annex northern Mexico.[28]

Texas complaints of raids by Kickapoos harbored in Mexico originated in 1850, when the Indians left Kansas after receiving permission to settle in Mexico. About one thousand Kickapoos were given land in Santa Rosa, Coahuila, in 1859 and, in return, were expected to protect Mexico from Comanches, Kiowas, and Apaches. The Kickapoos, traditional enemies of Apaches, were more successful than colonias militares against hostile Indians in Tamaulipas, Nuevo León, and Coahuila. Thus the Kickapoos protected Mexico but raided Texas. After being attacked by Texans in 1862 and 1865 while peacefully emigrating to Mexico, the Kickapoos had declared open war on Texas in retaliation.[29]

The United States wanted Mexico to return the Kickapoos to their U.S. reservation. In 1871 Colonel Joseph J. Reynolds, a colonel in the Third Cavalry, complained to the adjutant general that, because Mexico refused to allow the Kickapoos to return, raids could only be "permanently stopped by pursuing marauding bands into Mexico with troops accompanied by owners of the stock and records of the brands."[30] In 1873 Mexico was persuaded to aid a U.S. commission coming to Mexico to coerce the Kickapoos to return to their United States reservation. Meanwhile, Texas cattlemen continued to accuse Kickapoos of rustling, so United States troops crossed the border without permission to punish the Indians before the arrival of the authorized commission.[31]

On May 17, 1873, Colonel Ranald S. Mackenzie began his march into Mexico with six companies of the Fourth Cavalry and Seminole scouts led by First Lieutenant John L. Bullis in pursuit of Kickapoos and affiliated Lipans, Potawatomis, and Mescaleros. Mackenzie had no orders to cross the border, but commanding Lieutenant General Philip H. Sheridan gave Mackenzie the freedom to end raids in his own way, advising him to be bold and enterprising. Sheridan added, "Let it be a campaign of annihilation, obliteration, and complete destruction."[32]

Mackenzie traveled about fifty-five miles into Mexico, attacking a Kickapoo camp near Remolino early on the morning of May 18. Mackenzie's men killed nineteen, apprehended one elderly chief, took forty women and children captives, and captured sixty-five horses. Mackenzie's force suffered three wounded, one mortally, before returning to Texas at dawn on May 19. In a joint resolution of the state legislature Texas thanked Mackenzie for "inflicting well-merited punishment upon these scourges of our frontier." Sheridan now decided "to tighten up a little on Colonel Mackenzie" and ordered him not to cross again into Mexico without further provocation.[33] After Remolino, the Kickapoos began to negotiate seriously with the U.S. commissioners for a return to the United States. Some Kickapoos returned to the United States during the next two years.

While Texas praised the raid, Mexico protested by claiming that the raid was "but little less than murder, and that the band attacked was a harmless, peaceful group of Indians."[34] Mexico viewed Mackenzie's raid as a violation of international law, especially because Mexico had previously agreed to demands that Coahuila and Nuevo León aid the U.S. commissioners who were seeking the Kickapoos' return.[35] When Mexico protested the raid, Mackenzie cited Mexican precedents for his crossing.

Mexican troops had entered the United States from Chihuahua in 1872 in pursuit of hostile Indians. Although U.S. border authorities had received an order to capture and imprison Mexican troops entering the United States, the incident had been quietly settled. Lieutenant Colonel William R. Shafter maintained that this 1872 crossing was the second Mexican invasion in six months, Mexican forces having stayed in the United States forty-five days in one case. In reference to Mexican troops crossing the border, Brigadier General Edward Ord, commander of United States troops in Texas, testified that he had no objections. In fact, he admitted to once having given Mexican troops a two-week supply of rations when they crossed the border in pursuit of Apaches.[36]

Although Ord said he welcomed Mexican troops on American territory to aid in the fight against Apaches, he had no instructions for United States troops to cross the border. Nevertheless, contradictory orders were issued. The October 2, 1874, *New York Herald* reported that the governor of Texas ordered state militia to cross the Rio Grande in pursuit of cattle thieves, saying that Texas must act in self-defense, since neither the federal government nor Mexico would prevent the raids.[37] Then, on November 16, 1875, Colonel Potter of Fort Brown, Texas, gave Captain James F. Randlett, Eighth Cavalry, Edinburgh, Texas, the following order: "If you come up with them (cattle thieves) while they cross the river follow them into Mexico."[38] Two days later, however, Ord sent a telegram to Adjutant General William Steele in Austin, advising that "our troops are under orders not to cross."[39]

United States troops, officially under orders not to cross the border, could not protect it. Sheridan's 1875 annual report complained of Mexican raids across the Rio Grande, saying that it was almost impossible to defend because of its low water level and its length, between 1,200 and 1,500 miles.[40]

Mexico had a different version of border raids. The governor of Chihuahua reported in 1875 that U.S. reservation Indians received United States arms and were allowed to leave to hunt, which often meant raids in Mexican territory.[41]

In spite of Mexican complaints, the United States still hoped to decrease border raids by returning Kickapoos and Lipans residing in Mexico to their U.S. reservations. Mexico allowed United States officials to have councils with Kickapoos, Lipans, and Mescaleros in 1875. United States investigator H. M. Atkinson reported to the Department of Interior's Bureau of Indian Affairs that he had councils in Mexico with the tribes in question, but that Mexican authorities were not helpful. He doubted that the seventy Lipans would return to the United States. One hundred Kickapoos at Mapimí, Durango, allegedly wanted to return to their U.S. reservation, but Atkinson lacked money to send them and suspected that Mexico was secretly preventing their removal.[42]

The governor of Coahuila wrote Mexico's minister of foreign relations in January 1876 that it would be a good idea to remove the Kickapoos to the interior of the United States because some were raiding Texas from Mexico, while Lipans raided Coahuila and Chihuahua. The next month, United States minister in Mexico, John W. Foster, asked Mexico to return Kickapoos raiding Texas to U.S. reservations. That same month a United States commissioner appointed to secure removal of Coahuila's Kickapoos warned Foster that the Coahuila Kickapoos might join the Comanches in raids.[43]

Texas continued to complain of incursions of marauding Mexicans, Kick-apoos, and Lipans.[44]In February the sheriff of Hidalgo County, Texas, complained to Brigadier General Ord that Mexicans sold stolen Texas stock and that the federal and state governments failed to provide protection. Faced with mounting protests, Ord asked Chihuahua's governor for reciprocal troop crossing in April 1876, admitting that raiders were from both sides of the border. Mexico's secretary of war forwarded Ord's request to Foreign Relations and received a reply on May 30, 1876, saying that the Mexican Senate would need to approve any agreement.[45]

Meanwhile, Texas suffered more incursions, causing Congress to authorize an increase in the number of cavalry on the Texas frontier in July. By December 1876, General W. T. Sherman could report to the House that Texas forces consisted of two cavalry and three infantry regiments numbering 3,229 enlisted men and about 110 officers, "a larger fraction of the army of the United States than is allotted to a like extent of frontier anywhere else in the country."[46] Texas protests resulted in this large allocation, which was a significant portion of the total 1876 U.S. army numbering 26,312.

The United States not only increased forces on the Rio Grande but also resorted to border crossings to strike at hostile Indians. On July 30, 1876, First Lieutenant John L. Bullis, Fourth Cavalry, with forty men, struck a Lipan and Kickapoo camp near Zaragoza, Mexico, killing ten, capturing four, and taking one hundred horses.[47]

Such unauthorized crossings were settled quietly by both nations until a year later when the United States openly declared its "right" to cross, uninvited, into Mexico in pursuit of raiders. Mexico suspected that the United States hoped to provoke a conflict that might lead to annexation of Mexico. While the United States and Mexico engaged in mutual recriminations, Indian raids continued in both countries.

TWO

The Yankee Peril, 1877–1880

✞

Raids by hostile Indians continued on both sides of the Rio Grande border throughout the 1870s. It was difficult to determine the guilty parties, and both Mexico and the United States denied responsibility. Mexican rustlers, disguised as Indians to confuse the issue further, depredated Texas. On July 18, 1877, the *New York Sun* blamed West Texas raids on Mexican outlaws and Indians. The *Sun* editorial charged that Kickapoo and Lipan Apaches lived in Mexico, stole in Texas, and sold their plunder in Mexico. Kickapoo raids had diminished after the lesson of Mackenzie's Remolino raid, however, and the Comanches received a decisive defeat in 1874–75. Not only Comanches but also Mescaleros from the Fort Stanton, New Mexico, reservation gave Texas the most trouble.[1] Mexico denied that its Mescaleros were responsible for border raids.

Mexico's minister of war Pedro Ogazón reported to Mexico's foreign minister Ignacio L. Vallarta in December 1877 that peaceful Mescaleros had asked Chihuahua's governor for land. Vallarta replied that a 1874–75 joint commission had invited Mescaleros to return to their U.S. reservation, but that they preferred to reside in Mexico, where they had lived peacefully in Chihuahua for two years. Vallarta wanted to know how far from the border they wished to settle. While the central government considered giving Mescaleros a permanent home in 1877, General Gerónimo Treviño, commander of Mexico's northern frontier, ordered the Lipans apprehended for robbery. He wanted to move these Apaches farther inland in order to educate them.

The United States agreed that not only the Lipans but also the Chiricahuas were responsible for raids. In 1876 governor of Arizona Territory

Anson Peacely-Killen Safford asked Sonora's governor Carlos R. Ortiz to join forces to defeat the Chiricahuas. In April 1877 Sonora's governor agreed to cooperate with Arizona's troops, but without crossing the border. In May, however, Safford sent his volunteer militia into Mexico as far as Fronteras in pursuit of the Chiricahuas.

The United States made one border crossing that especially outraged Mexico because the crossing was not to trail Indians but to rescue two Mexicans from Mexican authorities. Governor of Coahuila Hipólito Charles reported that on April 3, 1877, Lieutenant Colonel William R. Shafter had crossed the border into Piedras Negras with one cavalry and two infantry companies. Charles stated that U.S. forces entered Mexico in order to free two Mexicans who had been jailed because they had served as guides for U.S. troops illegally entering Mexico. The Mexicans hid the prisoners and after an hour the U.S. troops retired across the border. Mexico's consul in San Antonio went in person to protest to General Ord, who justified the raid on the grounds that the Mexican guides were in danger. Ord expressed surprise at Mexico's protest; no shots had been fired. Mexico sought damages, however, because U.S. troops had returned home with Mexican livestock.[2]

The United States ignored Mexico's protests, and on April 22, Second Lieutenant Louis A. Craig, Sixth Cavalry, reported that, just two weeks after Shafter's raid, he had crossed into Sonora in pursuit of Indians. Secretary of State William Evarts explained to United States minister in Mexico John W. Foster that Shafter believed the only way to end depredations was to follow the raiders into Mexico. "As the authorities of that country seem to be unable or unwilling to check the depredations, the President may soon have to take into serious consideration the expediency of acting pursuant to Colonel Shafter's opinion." As a result of this turmoil, President Rutherford B. Hayes, through his secretary of war to General William T. Sherman, issued the following order, dated June 1, 1877:

General Ord will at once notify the Mexican authorities along the Texas border, of the great desire of the President to unite with them in efforts to suppress this long-continued lawlessness. At the same time he will inform those authorities that if the Government of Mexico shall continue to neglect the duty of suppressing these outrages, that duty will devolve upon this government, and will be performed, even if its performance should render necessary the occasional crossing of the border by our troops. You will, therefore, direct General Ord that in case the lawless incursions continue he will be at liberty, in the use of his own discretion, when in pursuit of a band of the marauders, and when his troops are either in sight of them or upon a fresh trail, to follow them across the Rio Grande, and to overtake and punish them, as well as retake stolen property taken from our citizens and found in their hands on the Mexican side of the line.[3]

President Hayes defended the Ord order and his denial of recognition to the Díaz government in his annual message to Congress on December 3, 1877, saying that "incursions into our territory by armed bands from the Mexican side of the line, for the purpose of robbery, have been of frequent occurrence" and, therefore, "official recognition has been deferred." Hayes added:

> While I do not anticipate an interruption of friendly relations with Mexico, yet I cannot but look with some solicitude upon a continuance of border disorders as exposing the two countries to initiations of popular feeling and mischances of action which are naturally unfavorable to complete amity.[4]

As further proof of Mexico's lack of cooperation, when Ambassador Foster conferred with the Mexican Foreign Office on June 22, 1877, to justify the Ord order, he maintained that the United States had requested an agreement for reciprocal crossing of troops from 1871 to 1877, but that Mexico declined.

As early as June 1875, Foster had warned Mexico that unless raids ceased, instructions such as those given to General Ord should be anticipated. Foster continued his defense of the U.S. position, declaring that depredations during the last four years had not been common to both sides of the border. Foster claimed that Mexico failed to furnish a single instance when raids originated on the American side, adding that the Mexican border commission only investigated raids dating from before 1873. Foster justified the Ord order, saying, "Mexico has taken no adequate measures to prevent the depredations or punish the outlaws," and adding that depredations in Texas could no longer be tolerated. He went on: "It is only after invitation to cooperate, and after Mexico has declined and continues to neglect its duty, that General Ord is granted discretion to follow the outlaws across the border when in hot pursuit."[5]

Mexico's minister in Washington, Ignacio Mariscal, sent his foreign relations minister U.S. newspaper articles dated June 4 and 5. The articles alleged that protection of the Rio Grande frontier was only a pretext for the Ord order, which in reality allowed acts of war to be committed without congressional consent. The newspapers suggested that President Hayes's scheme to take northern Mexico, using the Ord order, was similar to provocations of President James K. Polk leading to the Mexican-American War. Mexico's minister of foreign relations Vallarta told Foster that United States policy appeared to have changed with President Hayes, who refused to recognize the Díaz government. Vallarta suggested that the United States believed "a war with Mexico would consolidate the government and heighten respect for the Hayes administration now suffering from lack of support." He added that "for this reason, General Ord, who was an annexationist, had been ordered to violate Mexican territory — a breach of international relations equal to war."[6]

Mexico's official reaction to Ord's order was not long in coming. On June 7, 1877, Mexico issued a formal protest, which contained a brief report of the history of so-called Mexican depredations in Texas. Mexico's minister Mariscal first mentioned the investigating commission Mexico had sent to the border in 1872, which concluded that United States claims were exaggerated and that robberies were mutual. Mariscal alleged that depredations in Texas were usually caused by U.S. Indians or those of doubtful nationality, and that the few raids by Mexicans were organized by Texans. A new United States commission sent to the frontier acknowledged that Texas had exaggerated claims. Congress authorized additional cavalry on the frontier and raids diminished.

Mariscal expressed surprise that the Ord order was adopted just when raids had decreased. He also protested giving Ord such great responsibility because Ord recently had ordered U.S. troops to invade Piedras Negras. After Mariscal's official protest, Mexico's minister of war Pedro Ogazón issued his own order to General Gerónimo Treviño on June 18, instructing him to repel any invasion with force. Ogazón declared: "The Government of Mexico cannot allow a foreign force to enter the national territory without the consent of the congress of the Union," adding that Colonel Shafter's report giving rise to the Ord order contained errors.[7]

Colonel Shafter's recommendation that hostile Indians must be pursued into Mexico was cited as a justification for the Ord order. Shafter expressed criticism of the order before a military committee, however, saying that he always worked well with Mexican authorities when he crossed the border. Shafter cited examples of Mexican troops crossing the Rio Grande into Texas, saying that General Anacleto R. Falcon had crossed twice after bandits. He added that he did not believe either government disapproved; cordial relations continued to exist between commanders on both sides of the river. Shafter mentioned General Francisco Naranjo as one Mexican who desired friendship, sending Shafter letters and a campaign chest as a gift.[8]

London papers doubted that the Ord order would lead to United States expansion into Mexico, although they mentioned the possibility that the United States might drift into the necessity of annexation without intending to do so. A *London Times* editorial called the order "not standard diplomacy," and suggested that the United States should have given Mexico more time.[9] Rumors continued in Mexico and the United States that the latter was hoping to provoke a conflict that might lead to annexation.

United States filibuster Dalrymple's expedition into Mexico in February 1877 did nothing to alleviate Mexico's suspicions. Another ominous incident involved the appearance in Mexico of California citizens who were hoping to purchase the northern states. There was evidence that citizens on both sides of the border hoped that the northern Mexican states would change hands. United States citizens wanted minerals, and Mexicans with border property planned to enrich themselves. According to a Mexican source, Secretary of State William Evarts definitely desired annexation of Mexico. As late as 1909, one Mexican writer listed the "Yankee peril" as Mexico's principal problem.[10]

While the Ord order outraged Mexico, it caused the government to consider additional funds and forces to invigorate the 1877 Indian campaign. In a congressional debate that year, a deputy from Yucatán defended the federal system of colonias militares, proposing that 600,000 pesos be allocated to strengthen the colonias as follows: 120,000 to Sonora; 60,000 each to Chihuahua, Nuevo León, Coahuila, and Durango; the remainder was to be reserved for Yucatán. Northern representatives, however, preferred state control of the campaign.

However, Sonora deputy Ismael S. Quiroga criticized the system of presidios and colonias militares, saying that the still extant presidios only guarded the towns where they were located, and seldom saw active service. He added that Apaches were raiding Moctezuma and Sahuaripa before going to Ures and Hermosillo. He complained that the Apache war was in the East, but that all the colonias militares were to the north, leaving exposed a large portion of the Sierra Madre dividing Sonora from Chihuahua at the district of Sahuaripa. The deputy suggested establishing two military forts where Indians entered the state. He concluded that good relations with Arizona were useful in order to keep each other abreast of Apache movements and advised that towns must be armed and ready to aid in their own defense.

In addition, Deputy Quiroga said that state governments should wage the Indian campaign because the war was neither a foreign war nor an internal revolution, and claimed that the constitution gave frontier states responsibility for their own defense. Reasoning that the Indian wars were an exceptional case not subject to rules of military theory, he said that it would be inefficient to direct the campaign from military headquarters in Mexico City. Campaigns varied from state to state, and principles used in Sonora did not necessarily apply to Coahuila or Chihuahua.[11]

Although there was disagreement over the best way to conduct the Indian campaign, Mexico devoted more resources to it. United States minister Foster credited the Ord order with creating this new Mexican concern with border defenses, saying "no effort was made by Mexico to suppress the outlaws until after the instructions to General Ord were issued." Foster said Mexico's president would suppress outlaws on the Texas frontier and Secretary of War George W. McCrary confirmed that Mexico would cooperate with General Ord on the border.[12]

Mexico's minister of war reported to the Foreign Relations Ministry that on June 30 General Ord had suggested reciprocal crossing of troops to General Treviño, citing the example of the Sonora troops he had allowed to enter the United States, and whom he had supplied with rations and reinforcements. Treviño replied that both generals lacked authority to make such an agreement. He added that he would try to prevent raids, and Ord replied that he did not intend any hostility toward Mexico. The United States had taken an extremely volatile position, but violence was averted, largely because of the cordial relationship between Ord and Treviño, exemplified by the marriage of Ord's daughter to Treviño.

Ord further avoided an international incident by tactfully seeking cooperation with Treviño and prohibiting U.S. forces from crossing the border in places where they would have encountered Mexican troops. The Ord order was further modified in July to say that when Mexican troops were prepared to pursue raiders, United States forces should not cross the boundary line.[13]

Mexico not only increased forces on the border in response to the Ord order, but also considered whether Indians living in Mexico should be returned to United States reservations. President Díaz sent a questionnaire dated July 19, 1877, to the governors of Tamaulipas, Coahuila, Nuevo León, Chihuahua, Durango, and Sonora asking the following questions: (1) What tribes are in your state? (2) Have the tribes always lived in Mexico? If they are from the United States, when did they move to Mexico? (3) How many people are in each tribe? (4) Is it advantageous for the tribes to remain in your territory? We have no hostile Indians was the response to the presidential inquiry from the governors of Nuevo León and Tamaulipas.

Coahuila's governor referred only to Kickapoos in his response, saying that they protected the frontier from Lipans, Mescaleros, and Comanches. He added that the United States wanted their return because their value was well-known.

The governor of Durango replied that some eighty Kickapoos in his state refused to work and should be sent back to the United States. The governors of Durango and Chihuahua accused U.S. reservation Indians of raiding Mexico. Chihuahua's governor complained that he could not catch the raiders because he was prohibited from crossing the border, adding that he was unable to extradite guilty Indians because he could not prove his allegations. He also reported that Mescaleros living in his state had never belonged to a United States reservation. Sonora's governor reported Yaquis, Mayos, Papagos, and Yumas in his state, adding that U.S. reservation Apaches were a problem.

While Mexico considered what to do with Indians in its territory, the United States asked again in November for the return of Kickapoos to their United States reservation. On December 29, Mexico replied that it was waiting for additional reports before adopting a general policy on resettlement and, therefore, could not act on the United States request.[14]

While Mexico exercised restraint, the United States continued border crossings using the Ord order as justification. In September 1877, Lieutenant John L. Bullis attacked Lipans near Zaragoza, Mexico, capturing four women, one boy, twelve horses, and two mules. In November, Bullis and thirty-seven Seminole scouts surprised an Apache camp near the Carmen Mountains in Mexico, capturing seventeen horses and six mules.[15]

In October, Colonel Edward Hatch, Headquarters, District of New Mexico, wrote to the assistant adjutant general defending such crossings as necessary to defeat Chiricahuas living in Sonora and Chihuahua. Hatch declared: "I am informed that there is no objection to our troops pursuing raiding parties . . . I see no other way of compelling these Indians to come to terms other than by punishing them in their strongholds."[16]

Hatch was mistaken when he said Mexico did not object to U.S. troops crossing the border, as the following incident, which took place in December 1877, illustrates. Lieutenant Ward was in pursuit of horse thieves when a Mexican officer invited him to cross the border to join Mexican troops in the chase. This action was reported by General Ord to the secretary of war and favorably commented on in the United States press. The day before

Foster could thank the Mexican authorities, however, Mexico's minister of war issued orders to ascertain the identity of the officer who had permitted American troops to cross in order to punish him severely as an example.[17]

While the United States complained that Mexico refused to cooperate with American forces, Texas accused the federal government of neglect. In 1878 Governor Richard B. Hubbard of Texas complained to Hayes that the federal government was not curtailing depredations. That same year Texas asked Congress for reimbursement for expenses incurred in repelling Indian and Mexican invasions during the years 1854–77.

Not only Texas complained to the federal government; in 1878, the governors of Coahuila and Chihuahua protested raids by U.S. Indians. Mexico complained specifically of United States Mescaleros raiding Chihuahua between 1874 and 1877, and in 1878 Mexico declared that there was now proof that raids were originating on both sides of the border.[18]

Díaz emphasized that Mexico suffered as much as its northern neighbor from incursions by unfriendly Indians. He added that he had reinforced the frontier by placing two divisions of federal troops on the border in 1877–78, composed of 4,792 men and 2,000 reinforcements. The president noted that Mexico definitely desired to prevent raiding, pointing out that even the United States, with far greater resources, had been unable to prevent incursions. General Francisco Naranjo agreed that Texas charges were unjust, calling forces on both sides of the border insufficient. He claimed that Mexicans on the frontier had made peace with Mescaleros and Lipans; he also admitted that some Kickapoos had joined hostiles and, therefore, should be sent to the interior and carefully watched.[19]

In spite of Mexican denials, Texas continued to complain of Lipan, Mescalero, and Kickapoo raids from Mexico. In response to Mexico's contention that raids were mutual, the United States reported "all the raids from Mexico into Texas, except one, were for purposes of robbery; all those from Texas into Mexico were in pursuit of robbers." The one exception referred to was Díaz's troops' pursuit of President Sebastián Lerdo de Tejada's forces into Texas during the 1876 Revolution of Tuxtepec. Referring to this incident, the House report claimed this "grave international offense" could not be compared with the pursuit of cattle thieves because "no country can honorably offer an asylum for robbers and criminals. Every country, however, can rightfully offer an asylum to political refugees."[20]

The United States further stated that, because Mexican authorities failed to use their troops on the Rio Grande to prevent depredations, it felt justified in continuing to deal with raiders as it saw fit. Because raids of Mexican Indian camps had not ended incursions, the United States again

determined to attempt removal of Mexico's Kickapoos to its own reservations. Ord requested permission to employ an agent to go to Chihuahua
and facilitate the return of Kickapoos who had gone to Mexico from Texas
during the Civil War.[21]

While the United States anticipated difficulty in effecting the removal of
the Kickapoos, the Lipans were another matter. Lipans were denied permission to establish themselves in Coahuila, and the governor suggested
handing them over to the United States. Colonel Mackenzie said that the
United States would accept the Lipans as prisoners if Mexico offered them.
In contrast to the Lipans, some three hundred peaceful Mescaleros lived in
Chihuahua, and that state's subinspector of colonias militares requested
land and rations for them. He added that Mexican troops could keep an eye
on them, but that if refused aid, their misery would force them into crime.[22]

Although Mexico admitted aiding peaceful Indians, it denied giving protection to Indians raiding Texas. Mexico was incensed by a *New York Times*
dispatch dated July 1878, which claimed that Mexican authorities were
giving shelter in Santa Rosa, Coahuila, to Kickapoos and Lipans raiding the
United States. In August the Mexican consul in San Antonio forwarded a
pamphlet to the Foreign Relations ministry. The pamphlet was an appeal
from Texans for protection from Indian raiders given protection in Coahuila. The Texans provided affidavits as proof, claiming that some Mexicans gloated over the fact that vandals were destroying homes in Texas
because they had wanted revenge ever since the Texas revolt.[23]

The citizens of Santa Rosa drafted a declaration of innocence in response,
sending copies to newspapers in Texas, Coahuila, and other parts of the
United States and Mexico. Coahuila's governor said he would send more
proof of innocence if necessary, admitting that Lipans were given rations by
Mexican authorities, but only to entrap them. One American living in Santa
Rosa, however, was accused by Mexican officials of dealing in contraband
goods and trading with rebel Indians, especially Lipans. In September,
Mackenzie complained to Colonel Jesús Nuncio in Piedras Negras that he
had learned that United States residents of Santa Rosa were forced to sign
documents stating Indians from the pueblo did not raid Texas.[24]

Mackenzie said he was also informed that Kickapoos were given passes
to hunt on the way to Laredo. Mexico's minister of war responded to
this accusation by saying that he would order Santa Rosa authorities not
to give passports to Kickapoos. In November 1878 Ord reported to General Servando Canales, commander of the Rio Bravo border, that Mexican
Lipans and Kickapoos raiding Texas were buying arms in Nuevo Laredo
and showing a pass from General Treviño. Canales asked Colonel George

Sykes, commander of the United States Rio Grande district, to obtain information regarding the people trafficking with Kickapoos near Laredo. Mexico's minister of war said that the Indians referred to disappeared into Mexico's interior, and the pass they carried was a hoax.[25]

In an attempt to locate the raiders, Colonel Price accompanied Colonel Francisco Estrada and three companies of men to a Mexican Kickapoo camp. General Canales ordered Estrada to allow Price to inspect the seventy Indians and their one hundred horses. Price asserted that these were the Indians who had raided Texas in April and that they were hiding the horses they had then stolen. Price claimed that Estrada agreed that these Kickapoos were guilty, but that, without proof, Estrada would not arrest and punish them. In December, Canales wrote Sykes that it would be impossible for the Kickapoos to hide Texas horses, and Colonel Price must furnish proof of his allegations.[26]

By the end of 1878, raids had not diminished, and Mexico and the United States continued mutual recriminations. Mexico maintained that the raids were exaggerated and "the number of those crimes committed by Mexican citizens living in Mexico territory is so small that it could be called insignificant." Mexico also declared that Texas raids were, for the most part, committed not by Mexican citizens, but by United States citizens of Mexican origin. Foster responded to this accusation, saying "the citizenship of the thieves and raiders is of very little consequence. It should be enough for the Mexican Government to be informed that its territory is being thus used for criminal purposes."[27]

Foster complained to Secretary of State Evarts in December 1878 "that during my residence in Mexico (more than five years), notwithstanding repeated complaints, not a single punishment had followed the long list of raids and crimes." In response to Mexico's request for detailed proof of events, dates, and persons involved in raids, Foster replied: "The government of the one ought not to be required by the other to assume the role of public prosecutor, and be expected to present a penal indictment, or the facts necessary to constitute a formal arraignment of criminal raiders."[28]

When Mexico sought reclamations, however, the United States required proof that U.S. Indians committed raids. Mexico, in turn, accused the United States of not punishing guilty Indians. Such recriminations did nothing to end depredations on either side of the border.

In response, however, the United States resolved to increase frontier military expenditures. Congress recommended an additional appropriation for the erection of posts to protect the Rio Grande frontier. As early as December 1877, Secretary of War George W. McCrary claimed a considerable expenditure was needed to protect Texas, because "it is also vastly important that every cause of difficulty between this country and Mexico should be removed." In February 1879 McCrary recommended an appropriation of $200,000 for at least four additional posts on the Rio Grande so that posts could be increased to be situated within forty or fifty miles of each other.[29]

In March, General Ord, commanding the Department of Texas, said he had sixteen companies without quarters and asked for three new posts. Ord estimated it would take an average of $13,000 to quarter each company. General William T. Sherman, commanding the army, said: "I certainly will favor any proposition to build suitable posts along the Rio Grande frontier, because it forms a national boundary and is likely to be permanent." He added that, if more were needed, he preferred "small blockhouses connected with the larger posts by the telegraph, which would give prompt notice of the coming of any raiding party."[30]

In Congress, the Committee of Military Affairs recommended the new posts because "murder, robbery, and arson have been carried on along the border with a high hand by Mexican and Indian raiders." Congress supported more posts because "adequate protection of the frontier is the best security for peace," and once raids end, "commerce along the border between the two countries will spring up, and commerce itself is a handmaid[en] of peace."[31] Because of additional congressional appropriations, Ord was able to state in his annual report dated October 1, 1879, that he had a large reserve of troops ready to cross the border in accordance with the June 1 order.[32]

Realizing that increased expenditures and the Ord order were not satisfactory solutions to the frontier issue, the United States continually urged that an agreement be reached. Mexico was aware that a formal agreement might control invasions of Mexican soil and make Mexico's protests against such violations more viable. Because the U.S. government had finally extended diplomatic recognition to his regime, Díaz announced on September 16, 1878, that he had requested and received the necessary Senate authorization in May to sign a reciprocal crossing agreement with the United States. In accord with general sentiment in Mexico, however, Díaz stressed that no agreement could be realized as long as the Ord order remained in effect.[33] Hayes announced in his December 1, 1879, message to Congress:

Through the judicious and energetic action of the military commanders of the two nations on each side of the Rio Grande, under the instructions of their respective governments, raids and depredations have greatly decreased . . . I entertain a confident expectation that the prevalence of quiet on the border will soon become so assured as to justify a modification of the present orders to our military commanders as to crossing the border, without encouraging such disturbances as would endanger the peace of the two countries.[34]

Ten days after Hayes made his address, the customs official of Janos, Chihuahua, complained that Chiricahua Apache Juh had fled his United States reservation to raid Chihuahua and Sonora. Later that month, the official of the Piedras Negras *aduana*, or custom house, reported Lipans raiding Coahuila. Mexican authorities complained of Texas rustlers in January 1879, specifically referring to John Martin, the notorious bandit of Texas and New Mexico. In February the Janos customs officer reported that the New Mexican newspaper the *Mesilla Valley* termed the raids reciprocal, praising Mexico for allowing Kickapoos to live peacefully in Mexico. The Chihuahua official also complained of a gang of horse rustlers composed of three Americans and one Mexican, saying that the United States was not concerned with their capture.[35]

Throughout the spring of 1879, both countries continued blaming each other for border disturbances. Chihuahua and Sonora complained of raids by Apaches from U.S. reservations; Texas continued to protest depredations attributed to Mexican Lipans. General Servando Canales wrote to Díaz from Matamoros informing him of a Comanche invasion of Tamaulipas in March, adding that he had advised Colonel Sykes of Fort Brown that they headed for Texas. The Janos customs officer complained in May that Juh and his Chiricahua Apache band could buy arms and ammunition freely at the San Carlos Reservation, getting an unlimited supply if they had a hunting license. The governor of Nuevo León reported to Mexico's Department of the Interior that Indians raiding his state were from Texas.[36]

The United States responded equivocally to Mexico's accusations. Ord claimed in May 1879 that the Indians raiding the border were Kickapoos and Lipans from Mexico, living near Santa Rosa, Zaragoza, and El Nacimiento. He explained that it only appeared they were U.S. Indians because they may have raided inside the United States before carrying out depredations in Mexico. Colonel Edward Hatch added an endorsement, saying that Chihuahua raids were caused by Mexican Indians living in Chihuahua and Sonora and not by Indians from United States reservations. Hatch claimed that Indians got arms from traders, usually Mexicans. Hatch concluded that the Indian "trouble" could be ended in one year if the United States, Chihuahua, and Sonora each had one hundred Indian scouts "with a liberal offer of so much per capita for the Indians captured or killed."[37]

Ord and Hatch continued to deny that Indians from Arizona and New Mexico were raiding Mexico; but by the end of May, the U.S. Department of the Interior admitted to the secretary of state that reservation Indians were in fact raiding Mexico. Mescaleros unhappy at their Fort Stanton, New Mexico, reservation continued to raid Chihuahua. They were reacting to squatter encroachment and corrupt reservation officials. The federal government failed to provide either adequate funds or a consistent policy on the reservation.[38]

Chiricahuas from Arizona escalated depredations in both Sonora and Chihuahua, while promising to leave the United States in peace. It was difficult for Mexico to reconcile U.S. Indian policies aimed at protecting Arizona and New Mexico at Mexico's expense with the constant Texas complaints of Coahuila raids. In June, Coahuila reported incursions of Comanches from Texas, saying they had previously raided Tamaulipas and Nuevo León. During this same month, the Janos customs officer again complained of raids by Chiricahua Apache leader Juh.[39]

Mexico had complained of Chiricahua raids since the Treaty of Guadalupe Hidalgo of 1848, but depredations were now escalating. Trouble increased after 1875 when nearly five thousand Western Apaches were concentrated on the White Mountain and San Carlos reservations in Arizona. Chiricahuas resisted removal, and the Bureau of Indian Affairs's decision to concentrate most of the Apaches revived Apache warfare more than anything else.

Brigadier General George Crook was placed in charge of the Arizona Apaches in 1871, and if Crook had remained in charge of them for ten years he might have ameliorated Apache conditions. In 1874, however, jurisdiction over Apaches was transferred from the War Department to the Bureau of Indian Affairs. "The Apaches became pawns in unfortunate struggles between the Army and the Indian Bureau, for control, and between the contractors of Tucson and New Mexico, for profits."[40] Intrusions of white settlers and miners, graft, fraud, and lack of supplies continuously plagued the reservation.

Apaches left the San Carlos Reservation because they were badly treated, did not get enough food, and were placed with hostile tribes, according to Colonel August V. Kautz, commander of the Department of Arizona. In August 1877, First Lieutenant Lemuel A. Abbot, Sixth Cavalry, San Carlos Indian Agency, reported to the assistant adjutant general, Department of Arizona, that William Vandever, the Indian inspector at San Carlos, was negligent and that fraud, theft, and robbery were rampant. Kautz maintained that the accusations against Vandever were confirmed the following month when the majority of the Warm Springs and Chiricahua Apache Indians fled San Carlos to raid New Mexico.[41]

Treviño complained in July 1879 of invasions by U.S. Indians, but Foster said Ord believed that to be improbable since no U.S. Indians were found in the alleged area of incursions; he added that it probably had been the work of Mexican Apaches living in Coahuila and Chihuahua.

Foster asserted that U.S. troops had been unable to capture Juh's band because Mexico would not permit border crossings. He also said that New Mexico commander Hatch reported that the United States patrolled the entire border, unlike Mexico.[42]

The *New York Daily Tribune* took the United States position in an editorial on July 23, 1879, when discussing Díaz's recent message to Congress in which the Mexican president had said that the United States owed Mexico either an apology or money in reparation for United States border crossings. The editorial suggested that a formal withdrawal of the Ord order was probably all that was expected, adding that U.S. actions were justified by the decrease in raids in Texas. The *Tribune* also said that because Mexico had placed troops along the border Ord's cavalry had crossed into Mexico only three times.[43]

While the United States continued to defend the Ord order, Mexico's commander of the northern division declared in August that he had positive proof that the raiders were from the United States. That month the municipal president of Janos complained of more Apache depredations in Chihuahua and Sonora. According to him, both North Americans and Mexicans were in league with Apaches, buying their plunder and selling them arms. He requested a permanent federal force of at least two hundred men, saying that his small force of colonias militares had been removed. He added that the United States was establishing a fort on the border, and United States soldiers in pursuit of Apache rustlers had been seen in Janos. The following month, Mexico's minister of foreign relations complained to the minister of war that conditions had deteriorated.[44]

Governor of Sonora Carlos Ortiz warned in early September that U.S. troops might invade Chihuahua and Sonora in pursuit of Apaches. Later that month, Chihuahua's governor telegraphed the minister of war to advise him that six hundred United States troops had invaded his state, following Apaches.[45]

While Mexico protested these invasions, Ord said that in August Mexican citizens were granted permission to cross into the United States in pursuit of raiders and to recover stolen property. Ord wrote Treviño on September 29, 1879, to respond to the accusation that U.S. reservation Indians were raiding Mexico. He confirmed that Mescaleros from the Fort Stanton reservation were raiding West Texas.[46]

It would be six months before the House Committee on Indian Affairs acknowledged that reservation Indians allowed to hunt in Texas were committing depredations. Ambassador Foster concurred, admitting in 1879 that all evidence from Mexico, Texas, and New Mexico indicated that the Indians giving the most trouble were escapees from United States reservations who were crossing the border into Chihuahua.[47]

Chihuahua began to fear Victorio, the able leader of the Warm Springs Apaches, who declared war on September 4, 1879, after failing to find a satisfactory home in New Mexico. Major Albert P. Morrow followed Victorio and his band and some Mescaleros into Mexico. Victorio easily held off the U.S. force when overtaken at Corralitos, Chihuahua, on October 27, and Morrow returned to Fort Bayard, New Mexico, with his Indian scouts and detachments from the Sixth and Ninth Cavalry companies. In spite of this defeat, the United States told Mexico on November 7, 1879, that a concerted effort was being made to protect Mexico from New Mexican Indians. Finally, on December 11, 1879, Ord advised Treviño that he would cooperate with Mexico against hostile Indians.[48]

Treviño told Ord that he was mounting a major campaign in Chihuahua with both federal and auxiliary troops. Treviño reported on December 20 that Victorio and his band were raiding Chihuahua, and that they had killed more than 150 Mexicans and taken about five thousand head of cattle to the United States. The Janos customs officer complained to Mexico's foreign relations ministry that Victorio could get all the arms he wanted in the United States. Mexico reported that U.S. reservation Apaches were also raiding Moctezuma and Sahuaripa, Sonora, in 1880.[49]

Victorio caused both the United States and Mexico to focus their attention on Indian hostilities on the New Mexico, Arizona, Chihuahua, and Sonora frontier. Fear of Victorio led both nations to try again to reach an agreement, formal or unofficial, for reciprocal crossing of the border in pursuit of raiders. A controversy arose when the governor of New Mexico, Lew Wallace, extended an invitation to Chihuahua's governor Luis Terrazas for Mexican troops to cross the border. Mexico's minister in Washington, M. de Zamacona, wrote the Ministry of Foreign Relations that this invitation was very different from the order of June 1, 1877, and seemed to deviate from the previous two years' policy that had each government policing its own territory.[50]

The minister of war replied in early February that under no circumstances would Mexican troops be allowed to cross the border while the Ord order was in effect; Chihuahua's governor nonetheless accepted the American invitation, which had been approved by the U.S. War Department. When informed that the Mexican government disapproved, Governor Terrazas said he had not yet crossed the border, pending the Mexican presidential response to the issue. Meanwhile, in March, Victorio invaded Chihuahua and Sonora. The *Monitor Republicano* declared that "the neighboring republic, day by day, becomes possessed of greater elements than we have to fight the savages, and this is proven by the fact that the raids of the different tribes are made with preference upon Mexican territory."[51]

While Mexico continued to complain of Apache raids, conditions were improving in Texas, prompting General Ord to recommend abrogation of the order of June 1, 1877, as early as October 1879. Improvement in Rio Grande border conditions made it possible to revoke the Ord order without giving offense to Texas, and on February 24, 1880, the Department of War announced that General Ord, commander of the Department of Texas, had determined that conditions leading to the original promulgation of the order no longer existed. Mexico had demonstrated the ability to end incursions into the United States. With the Rio Grande frontier relatively peaceful, both governments turned their attention to Chiricahua hostilities on the border west of El Paso, where the boundary "was an imaginary surveyor's line about which the Apaches knew nothing."[52]

Díaz expressed distress over Victorio's raids in Chihuahua and Coahuila, while praising abrogation of the Ord order in his April 1, 1880, address to Congress. In September 1880, in another congressional address, Díaz alluded to further Apache raids, adding that he had ordered Mexican troops to cooperate with the Americans with the stipulation that no forces would be permitted to cross the border. The United States continued to seek a limited reciprocal crossing agreement, one that would last for ninety days, in order to pursue Victorio's band. Mexico's minister of foreign affairs José Fernández reported on September 21, 1880, that Díaz had agreed to ask the Senate for the necessary authorization to concede to the United States request.[53]

On October 13, 1880, *El Monitor Republicano* wrote: "Long and violent has been the discussion caused in the Senate by the note of the executive asking permission for American troops to cross the frontiers." An editorial printed two days later in the same paper stated: "We dare to hope that the permission has been granted upon a basis of strict reciprocity and limited to cases when it is necessary for American troops to cross into our territory in pursuit of the Indian Victorio, his tribe and allies." The following week *El Monitor Republicano* suggested that U.S. troops would cross the border even if permission were denied.[54]

In secret session, the Mexican Senate approved the reciprocal, ninety-day, crossing agreement on May 28, 1880. This agreement specified that only troops in close pursuit of hostile Indians could cross the border, that they would retire to their own country when the pursued band was defeated, the trail lost, or when a national force picked up the chase. Crossings were to be permitted only in desert regions at least two leagues from any settlement. The commander of the force crossing the dividing line was constrained to give notice to the nearest civilian and military authorities of the country entered. Mexico agreed that the pact could be extended in case the time allotted was not sufficient to capture Victorio.[55]

In late August, Victorio was still raiding Chihuahua. P. H. Sheridan admitted that the Fort Stanton, New Mexico, Mescalero reservation served as a supply and recruit base for Victorio's band. He agreed to disarm and dismount the Indians there. Attempts to disarm the Indians, however, were unsuccessful, and a large number escaped to join Victorio. On August 29, 1880, Colonel Eugene Carr explained his inability to prevent raids into Sonora as follows:

I have cordially, promptly, and assiduously made every possible effort to prevent any hostile operations from our Territory against our sister republic but, of course, my first duty was to protect our inhabitants against hostile Indians, and the inadequacy of the force at my disposal rendered it absolutely impracticable to station troops along the border of Sonora. I could only send in pursuit, after receiving information of expeditions, and this information was late and vague.

To effectually put a stop to such operations the force must be greatly increased, or we must abandon the protection of our people from the Indians and we must also be provided with detectives and scouts to give early and accurate information, and locate camps, &c., of filibusters. Soldiers are not competent or available for such work.[56]

On September 9, 1880, Chihuahua's governor reported to Díaz that a campaign composed of seven or eight hundred men would be launched against the hostiles. About one week later, Colonel George P. Buell, Fifteenth Infantry, commanding Fort Stanton, New Mexico, received permission from Colonel Joaquín Terrazas and Chihuahua authorities to cross into Mexico after Victorio. Approximately 3,000 United States and Mexican troops were in pursuit of Victorio, who had no more than 150 men. When American troops did cross the border after Victorio, they were ordered to withdraw by Terrazas, who did not wish to share the glory of a hoped for victory with the United States. Buell states his reply to Terrazas in his official report as follows:

> Much as I regretted to give up the chase, I felt that I was in Mexico by the invitation of the Chihuahua or state authorities more than by any legal or proper right. I felt satisfied that Terrazas had received an intimation or order to forbid my advancing farther toward Chihuahua . . . I therefore commenced the withdrawal of my advance the 10th day of October.[57]

According to the October 20, 1880, *Periódico Oficial*, colonels Joaquín Terrazas and Lorenzo García, with 400 men, defeated Victorio at Tres Castillos on October 15. Victorio and 86 warriors had been killed and 89 women and children captured. The great Warm Springs chief Nana and 50 warriors had escaped to join Geromino.[58]

Mexico's victory in Chihuahua against Victorio deceived both nations into thinking the Apache menace had ended. In his annual message to Congress on December 6, 1880, President Hayes proclaimed the end of hostilities with Victorio's death, saying, "By the combined and harmonious action of the military forces of both countries, his band has been broken up and substantially destroyed."[59] Apache depredations did not end with Victorio's death; the following month Mescaleros fled their New Mexico reservation to join the remnants of Victorio's band in Chihuahua. Apache troubles were far from over. During the next six years, they would, in fact, increase.

THREE

A Reciprocal Crossing Agreement, 1881–1882

✢

Victorio's death in Mexico in October 1880, did not end hostilities; Indian and outlaw depredations escalated. Crook maintained that at least fifty people were killed by Indians in Arizona and New Mexico between the time of Victorio's death and September 2, 1882. Crook also admitted these same Indians committed constant depredations in Mexico.[1]

Mexico complained on January 13, 1881, of raids by United States outlaws and reservation Indians. The Secretary of Foreign Relations informed the Secretary of War that Mexico would have to prove that raiders came from the United States in order to make a formal protest, and added that the governors of Coahuila and Chihuahua had been asked to provide information on raids during the previous year. Mexico's Secretary of War announced to the Foreign Relations Ministry on January 25 that he finally had proof that Indians from U.S. reservations were carrying out raids in Mexico.[2]

That same month, the governor of Arizona territory was instructed to investigate Mexican allegations that Robert E. Martin, the Texas outlaw raiding Chihuahua, was hiding in Arizona. General John Pope, commanding the Department of the Missouri, concluded "that should the citizens of Mexico make the proper effort, the band could readily be broken up, as [it occupies] that country at pleasure." Secretary of State William M. Evarts ordered P. H. Morgan, the American ambassador to Mexico, to inform Mexico that it should take equal responsibility for Martin's capture.[3]

Arizona newspapers published articles in February complaining of depredations in Sonora caused by outlaws organized in the United States. The governor of Arizona petitioned Congress for a force of one hundred men to be stationed at once on the frontier to fight outlaws. On February 24 the *Arizona Daily Star* protested that "these bands of desperados steal cattle from the American side of the boundary line, and sell them in Sonora and Chihuahua; they then steal other animals in those states, which they sell in Arizona and New Mexico." The *Arizona Daily Journal* published an article on January 31 describing American outlaws raiding Sonora "as being worse than the Apaches."[4]

The United States could not stop the rustlers. In June, Mexico again complained to Secretary of State James G. Blaine of Texan cattle thieves operating in Chihuahua, referring not only to "robberies committed in Mexico by outlaws having their residence in the United States, but to the dangers to which the owners of stolen property are exposed" when they cross into the United States. Governor of Chihuahua Luis Terrazas reported to Mexico's secretary of foreign affairs Ignacio Mariscal that the *El Paso Progresista* had published an account of two Mexicans murdered by Americans while endeavoring to recover stolen cattle. Terrazas added that "when any cattle are sold by their owners, and driven out of the State, customhouse officers are there in abundance for the purpose of collecting the duties; but when large numbers are driven off by thieves, this goes unnoticed."[5]

To put an end to Indian raids, the United States agreed to cooperate with Mexican authorities. On April 28, 1881, Secretary of State Blaine instructed Morgan at the United States Legation in Mexico City to mention in conversation with Mariscal the fact that New Mexico's commanding officer ordered scouts and cavalry to the border in order to show United States friendliness and desire to pursue hostiles. Blaine cautioned Morgan that his "representations, however, should be carefully guarded in order not to leave the impression on the mind of Mr. Mariscal that they implied an international agreement between the two governments to that end."[6]

In spite of United States declarations of willingness to cooperate with Mexican authorities to prevent raids, Mexico continued to complain about not only United States outlaws but also reservation Indians. Both the *El Paso Times* and *El Progresista* blamed U.S. reservation Indians for incursions. One raid, resulting in four deaths, occurred in Mezquite, Chihuahua, on February 14, 1881. In April, Mariscal referred to an article in El Paso's *Progresista*, dated April 25, which asked that Chihuahua's governor supply proof that Indians raiding Mezquite were from U.S. reservations. Chihuahua's Governor Terrazas responded in May 1881, saying he believed that Indians attacking Mezquite were from Juh's band. Adding that these were Indians who had been expelled from Mexico and now lived at San Carlos,

Terrazas declared that there was no doubt of the Indians being from the United States.[7]

Although Mexico vowed to end Indian attacks, raids continued, while Mexico blamed the United States. The secretary of war reported raids on Chihuahua haciendas by U.S. reservation Indians in April and June 1881. Two hundred head of stock were taken by sixteen Indians during the June attack, and the secretary of war declared the stock would probably be found in United States communities or on reservations. Mariscal informed the Mexican Legation in Washington that owners of stolen stock should try to determine if the animals had been taken to United States reservations. He also reminded the secretary of war that he could not make a formal protest unless there was proof of the raiders' United States origins.[8]

In April, M. de Zamacona at the Mexican Legation informed Secretary of State Blaine that Mexico believed that:

> the depredations committed by the savages on the frontier are due, and particularly referring to the location of some Indian reservations, to the permits granted to the Indians to make extended raids beyond the limits of said reservations, and to the reception which they usually meet with on their return from committing ruinous depredations.[9]

Zamacona warned that Indians who were permitted to leave reservations near Chihuahua were preparing to depredate that state.

In May, Captain George W. Baylor, Headquarters Company A, Texas Rangers, informed Mexican authorities that six Mescaleros had received permission to be absent from their Fort Stanton reservation for sixty days, "and as the scope of the country they are authorized to travel over is nearly five hundred miles, they will very likely cross into Chihuahua and depredate on the people there." Baylor added, "They left on foot; but no one acquainted with Apaches will doubt their riding back, and likely with a drove of horses." He concluded by saying that if General Terrazas should get their trail, "I hope the general will follow them into Texas, as I am quite sure the government of Texas would not object."[10]

Zamacona sent Blaine a July 8, 1881, article from the *El Paso Times* confirming fears that Indians permitted to leave their United States reservation would commit outrages in Chihuahua. The *El Paso Times* article mentioned that Apaches had already killed five engineers of the Mexican Central Railroad and attacked a Chihuahua stagecoach. Thomas Key Pugh, son of the former senator from Ohio and son-in-law of the former governor of Indiana, was among those killed. Chihuahua's governor confirmed that Pugh had been killed by Indians, adding that Pugh did not own Mexican property. Nevertheless, the *New York World* suggested in July that Pugh may not have been killed by Indians, but by whites disguised as Indians who wanted his Mexican mineral claim.[11]

In August, the *New York Times* called for an investigation of Pugh's murder to determine why the murderers destroyed Mexican paper money at the scene but carried off U.S. notes. Reservation Apaches would only have had use for the United States currency. In September, Chihuahua's governor again wrote to the Foreign Relations Ministry, affirming that Pugh undoubtedly was killed by Apaches. An American claiming to have survived the attack alleged that the murders were committed by Victorio's band. Chihuahua's governor, however, attributed Pugh's death to U.S. reservation Indians. Mexico claimed that some reservation Indians had been pushed across the border by United States troops.[12]

Mexico continued to ask the United States to prevent incursions of reservation Indians, complaining of the alarming increase in depredations by Mescalero and Navajo Indians in frontier districts. The *New York Herald* concurred, and on August 6, 1881, reported murders in New Mexico by a part of Victorio's old band, now led by Nana. The article warned that Mescaleros were raiding Mexico, and that General Hatch believed some Navajos to have joined them. The *New York Herald* reported on August 13 that Indians fed by the government during the winter were now on their "regular summer tour" of murder and devastation in New Mexico and headed toward Mexico. The *New York Herald* blamed the government's peace policy and the Indians' "passion for blood" for the raids, complaining that the Indian received a sixty-day pass to go off on a pleasure trip, with no questions asked when he returned.[13]

To substantiate Mexico's claims, Zamacona sent Blaine an article from the *Chicago National Republican*, dated August 8, 1881, which stated: "The Mescalero Indian Agency is to blame for all of this, as it is favorably situated as a starting point for raids and a secure haven of refuge when the Indians are too closely pressed." The article encouraged an increase in available troops so that the Indians could be disarmed and dismounted, and peace achieved. The *New York Herald* published the same date agreed with Mexico's claims, saying that as soon as the military was withdrawn from the Mescalero reservation, Indians slipped off by twos and threes to raid, reappearing at the reservation as "good Indians."[14]

Zamacona again complained to Blaine about the practice of granting leave permits to reservation Indians. He included in his letter a report from Mescalero agent Llewellyn, published in the *Chicago National Republican* on

August 16, 1881, in which the agent stated that Indians at the agency were given a permit "to go to Old Mexico." Llewellyn added that Indians had been driven south by United States troops, where they formed a war party of about seventy, proceeding to commit the usual depredations. Mexico's consul in El Paso asked for removal of Fort Stanton Mescaleros, blaming them for Chihuahua hostilities. The consul asserted that these Indians were the ones responsible for the murder of Pugh and the Central Railroad engineers. As an afterthought, he added that Navajos were thought to be uniting with them.[15]

In September 1881, not only Mexico, but also Arizona pressured the federal government to remove Apaches. General Orlando B. Willcox suggested moving them to either Indian Territory or the Dry Tortugas. Governor of Arizona John C. Frémont offered another solution to the secretary of the interior, a suggestion that was proposed to the Mexican government.

Frémont maintained: "Arizona, New Mexico, Sonora, and Chihuahua, all of which are infested by Indians," are "singularly adapted to Indian warfare." He advocated removing all Apache tribes from their natural strongholds, and suggested that "some arrangement" might be made by the two governments to use the peninsula of Baja California for this purpose. Because the peninsula measures only 150 miles wide at the boundary line, "a few alternating posts on either side of the line would effectually bar all egress by the Indians."[16] Mexico was not receptive to Frémont's suggestion, wanting the Indians removed away from its border, not placed within its own territory.

Zamacona also complained to Blaine of abuses committed by Texas police officers crossing the border to exercise jurisdiction in Mexico. On February 25, 1881, the Mexican consul in Tucson sent the Foreign Relations Ministry an article published two days earlier in the *Daily Arizona Citizen*, which declared that United States troops and some Indian scouts had chased Apaches into Mexico. Governor Luis Terrazas said that he had received no word of such a crossing.[17]

In May, Mexico protested a border crossing by Lieutenant John L. Bullis and Seminole scouts from Fort Duncan, Texas. Bullis followed a trail into Mexico for two days, surprised a Lipan camp, and killed five warriors.[18]

Governor of Sonora Carlos Ortiz warned the Foreign Relations Ministry in September that United States troops might invade his state. In October, the secretary of war sent General Bernardo Reyes to the Sonora frontier, ordering him to work with the United States commander. That same month, General Gerónimo Treviño telegraphed the Foreign Relations Ministry to report that the governor of Arizona had requested permission for his troops to cross the border. On October 31, 1881, the *New York Sun* claimed that Mexico was willing to make a crossing treaty, but President Hayes refused to negotiate.[19]

Blaine did not believe a formal crossing pact was necessary. In June 1881, in an attempt to assuage Mexico's fears, Blaine wrote two letters describing United States plans for economic investments in Mexico, while reaffirming the country's lack of desire for territorial expansion in Mexico. Reyes warned, however, of a dangerous buildup of United States influence in Sonora.[20]

In September, Sonora braced for another Indian invasion from the San Carlos Reservation. On September 30, 1881, White Mountain and Chiricahua Apaches led by Juh, Geronimo, and Naiche fled San Carlos, believing that United States soldiers planned to kill them. The *New York Herald* described the hostiles as well-armed and headed for the mountains, where, because of their ability to use the terrain to their advantage, one of them was equal to ten soldiers. The *Herald* reported that the Indians had left their women and children at the reservation for the government to care for them. Just a week earlier, settlers in Arizona had urged that San Carlos be placed under military control and the Indians either be removed to Indian Territory or exterminated. Settlers warned that they would treat all Indians off the reservation as hostiles.[21]

The San Carlos renegades, numbering approximately 75 warriors, joined forces with Nana and the remnants of Victorio's band and soon began causing trouble in the Sahuaripa District of Sonora, according to the November 5, 1881, edition of the *New York Herald*. The next month, the *New York Times* reported San Carlos Indians raiding Sonora. Mexico's Secretary of Foreign Relations Ignacio Mariscal asked M. de Zamacona, head of the Mexican Legation in the United States, to use these newspaper articles as proof that reservation Indians were depredating Sonora even while he negotiated with the State Department.[22]

United States newspapers did not just report reservation Indians' raids in Mexico; they also praised Mexico for the capture of forty-six hostiles. The *New York Sun* said the capture showed that Mexican troops were more successful against renegades than were United States forces. The *Sun* added that if the policy of allowing United States troops to cross the border was again resorted to, it would not be because Mexico was not doing its part to end raids.[23]

In January and February of 1882, Mexico again complained of raids in Sonora and Chihuahua by United States cowboys and Apaches from the San Carlos, Arizona, and Fort Stanton, New Mexico, reservations. Mexico apprehended five United States citizens and twenty Apaches with arms and munitions in Chihuahua in February. Although the Americans claimed they were campaigning against the Apaches, the Mexicans believed that they were Apache allies. The Bureau of Indian Affairs blamed Lipans and other Mexican bands for the raids, while admitting that some of these renegades had formerly belonged to United States reservations. Commissioner H. Price said that Congress had appropriated funds and appointed special agents to facilitate the return of Indians to the reservations, but that such efforts were unsuccessful because of the opposition of local Mexican authorities and traders who purchased plunder.[24]

Although the United States denied that San Carlos Indians were responsible for raids, Mexican accusations were substantiated. The United States was forced to admit Juh's return to San Carlos, Arizona, from Mexico on April 17, along with some sixty Chiricahuas. The following day, Juh compelled the remaining forty Chiricahua and Warm Springs men, along with three hundred women and children, to leave the reservation under Loco's leadership.[25]

Tucson's *El Fronterizo* warned Arizona to prepare to save itself from the Chiricahuas. Mexico's consuls in Tucson, El Paso, and Brownsville warned that Apaches would soon cross from Arizona into Chihuahua and Sonora. One hundred warriors under Juh had been reported in Janos, Chihuahua.[26]

On April 27, the *New York Herald* reported that United States miners had been killed in Sonora by Chiricahuas; Lieutenant Colonel George A. Forsyth was in pursuit. The article added that General Carlos Fuero was going north from Janos with two hundred men. Forsyth encountered Colonel Lorenzo García's troops in Sonora, Mexico, on April 30. García refused to allow Forsyth to continue his pursuit, explaining that his own troops had just defeated the San Carlos renegades Forsyth was chasing. Forsyth accompanied García to the battle scene where seventy-five Indians had been killed and twenty-eight women and children captured. Forsyth loaned García his surgeon and praised "the splendid work done by the Mexican troops and the good discipline of the command." Although García handed Forsyth a written protest against the United States border crossing, Forsyth reported "the officers and troops of both republics parted with cordial goodwill."[27]

The following month, Forsyth returned with his troops to Sepor, New Mexico, but he was already planning another border crossing. By May the United States determined to end new Indian uprisings in Arizona and New Mexico by mounting a campaign with 2,500 soldiers. This was a substantial commitment of the total United States army numbering 25,639 troops in June 1882. On May 3, General Sheridan asked Mexico to permit Forsyth's forces to cross the border. Mexico's Matías Romero spoke with the United States president and secretary of state and became convinced the United States was determined to end uprisings in Arizona. Therefore, Romero recommended that Mexico grant the border crossing request, saying that if the United States used such a large force in Arizona, the Indians would surely invade Mexico.[28]

Mexico replied on May 4 that the Senate had to give permission for border crossings, but the president would not ask Congress to consent unless the crossing was reciprocal. That same day, however, Arizona Indians crossed into Chihuahua, and Mexico's president agreed to cooperate. The United States again requested permission to cross the border on May 6, with the understanding that any agreement would be reciprocal. That day, Mexico informed the United States, in a ciphered telegram, that its president would recommend that the Senate approve a reciprocal agreement. Mexico's Senate approved an agreement for one year on May 11, 1882, under the conditions previously approved May 28, 1878, and October 14, 1880. The agreement was not approved a moment too soon; there followed another Chiricahua uprising. General Bernardo Reyes followed the hostiles toward Arizona, believing they were trying to reach San Carlos.[29]

An international incident occurred when Reyes met Tucson volunteers under Captain William J. Ross on Mexican soil. Ross kept forty Mexican and United States volunteers in the field for two months without encountering hostiles, until on June 2 they killed thirty-seven Apaches in Mexico, mostly women and children. The following day, Ross ran across seventy Mexicans under Captain Ramírez. On June 5, Ross met General Reyes and Colonel García and their 650 men. The troops camped together for four days, Captain Ross and the Mexican commanders alternately eating in each other's quarters.

Then, without warning, Reyes disarmed Ross and his men, informing them that they must return to the United States immediately. Reyes gave a receipt for arms confiscated, and Ross said the United States would probably try to recover them. Ross had ordered his men to cut a long branch and place it across the saddle to give the appearance from a distance that they carried arms. Tucson's citizens complained that the Mexicans should have escorted the United States troops to the border, allowing them to keep their arms. Luckily, Ross and his troops traveled the 250 miles home, unarmed, without incident. Reyes admitted disarming a company of Tucson volunteers thirty-seven leagues within Mexico on June 20. Reyes said he had not left Ross and his troops for Apaches to eat, however, because he was certain there were no Apaches around when he disarmed the Americans.[30]

United States officials were quick to criticize Mexico for incidents like the Ross affair; but they were slow to praise Mexican successes against renegades, especially since United States troops were not doing as well. In May the *Washington Evening Star* published a telegram from Tombstone, Arizona, describing the San Carlos Indian campaign waged by Reyes. The article observed that Mexican troops seriously pursued the Indians, obtaining better results in a few days than United States forces managed to after quite some time.[31]

The *Tucson Sun* praised Mexican troops for defeating Victorio, Nana, and Loco, while criticizing General P. H. Sheridan for failing to acknowledge Mexican victories in his dispatch to Major General John Pope. Sheridan told General R. C. Drum that the successful pursuit of Apaches "is due to the careful management of Col. Mackenzie and Lt. Col. Forsyth, in keeping scouts in Mexico to watch the Indians," and their cooperation with Mexican commanders.[32]

Although not eager to praise Mexican forces, Sheridan was forced to acknowledge Mexican victories. On June 3, Sheridan relayed a dispatch from General Carlos Fuero in Chihuahua to General Pope, informing him that Juh's band was defeated by Mexican troops on May 25, with thirty-seven Indians killed. The following month, the United States secretary of state relayed the gratitude of the secretary of war and the commander-in-chief of the army for Mexico's successful Indian campaign. In July, Sherman praised the Mexican army at a state dinner, confiding to Minister Romero that the Indians know they had more to fear from Mexico than from the United States. Along these lines, Sherman then referred to a new uprising of Arizona Indians; the hostiles had decided to stay in the United States, instead of going to Mexico as they had done in the past.[33]

While the United States praised Mexican troops, Mexico declared that the United States was incapable of containing the Indians and made preparations to fight off additional Chiricahua invasions of Sonora. Mexico continued to blame the United States reservation system for hostilities, terming reservation Indians *niños mimados*, or "spoiled children." Mexico urged the United States to disarm and educate reservation Indians, and to move reservations inland.[34]

The Mexican consul in El Paso recommended separating all children under fourteen from their families to educate them. He also proposed temporary segregation of the sexes in order to prevent reproduction and suggested isolation of reservation Indians on an island. Chihuahua's governor supported the consul's suggestions, with the exception of separation of the sexes.[35]

In September, Minister Matías Romero complained to the Foreign Relations Ministry that the United States was powerless to contain the Chiricahuas. He blamed the reservation system and agents, who enriched themselves by selling Indians liquor, guns, and ammunition, while cutting back on rations until Indians often had no choice but revolt.[36]

The *New York Tribune* claimed that Indians left the reservation because of bad treatment by agents and lack of food. The *New York Herald* published an editorial urging the United States to abandon policies of extermination or maintenance of reservation Indians in misery and instead to use the money for their education. The secretary of the interior concurred with Mexican suggestions that reservation Indians be disarmed and educated. He agreed that Indians should be removed from the border, but added that such a move would be difficult both because the Indians would cause problems in another place and because special interests involved in the system would oppose removal.[37]

Pope complained in May that Mescaleros were starving and not receiving necessary rations from the Department of the Interior. Maintaining that the War Department should be in charge of the Indians, he said the army should either feed or guard the Indians with enough troops so that they would starve peacefully. Pope added that money appropriated by Congress for rations was gone, and the agent was refusing to feed them for the rest of the year. Pope concluded that this was the reason Indians committed crimes.[38]

Not only Pope but others in the War Department blamed civilian management of the reservations for hostilities. In 1882 General George Crook was again placed in control of Arizona's reservations, reinstituting disciplinary measures, such as roll calls. Hostilities still did not end, however.[39]

Not only the United States experienced conflicts between civilian and military authorities with respect to Indian policy. Mexico's rivalries between officials at the state level often required presidential mediation. Sonora's Governor Carlos Ortiz verbally attacked General José Guillermo Carbó, commander of federal forces in his state, in a July 25, 1881, editorial in the official state organ *La Constitución*. Ortiz blamed Carbó for Indian attacks in Sonora, claiming that Carbó had no humanitarian feelings, and accusing him of giving false reports on Apaches to the president.[40]

On January 25, 1882, Ortiz complained to Minister of Development Carlos Pacheco about Carbó's conduct. Pacheco acted as an intermediary

between governor of Oaxaca Porfirio Díaz and President Manuel González. Díaz had stepped down from the presidency in 1880 in accordance with
Mexico's no reelection law. He supported González's election for a four-
year term. Ortiz and others wrote directly either to Díaz or to Pacheco,
who claimed that González had authorized his role as a go-between with
the governors of Sinaloa, Sonora, and Chihuahua.

Believing that Carbó disliked him and wanted to destroy his government,
Ortiz asked Pacheco either to give Carbó a different command or to make
Sonora directly responsible to the secretary of war. Ortiz claimed that
Carbó's arrival in Sonora was causing more alarm among the populace than
had Juh's invasion. According to Ortiz, one of Carbó's first acts was to
summon General José Otero, who was busy beginning the Apache campaign. Ortiz alleged that Carbó ordered Otero away from the Apache front
only because he wanted Otero to shine his boots for him. Ortiz continued
his criticism, saying that Carbó had ordered Colonel Lorenzo García to
relocate the Sixth Battalion currently guarding Hermosillo to Guaymas,
a move that would leave the state capital unprotected. Ortiz added that
Carbó had also come into conflict with Bernardo Reyes.[41]

Unsigned letters, suggesting that Reyes exchange his Sinaloa command
for Otero's in Sonora, and probably written by Carbó, were sent to Pacheco
and Minister of War Francisco Naranjo in February. The president agreed
to the transfer.[42]

Meanwhile, Governor Ortiz was accused of using Otero's forces so that
Otero was unable to provide protection against Indians. Lorenzo García
reported that Ortiz had ordered him to return part of the Guaymas force to
the capital in Hermosillo, allegedly to fight Apaches. Rafael Izábal, one of
the largest hacendados in Sonora, advised Carbó on February 1 not to
believe Otero's reports of Apaches, because he was unreliable. Izábal added
that Apaches were hiding in the sierras and that all was peaceful.[43]

One week later, García advised Carbó that the Apaches had left Chihuahua. In mid-February, García complained to Carbó that Ortiz and Otero
were both exaggerating the Apache threat. Several days later, García again
wrote Carbó, alleging that the governor had confiscated arms allotted to
Reyes for the Indian campaign, thereby demonstrating his hostility. Reyes
did write to Carbó in late February, however, saying that the governor
had offered his small forces when Apaches attacked Nacori and Arizpe,
Sonora.[44]

Contradictory reports of Ortiz's dispute with Carbó continued to reach
Porfirio Díaz and Manuel González through Secretary of Development

Carlos Pacheco. In March, Pacheco reported to Díaz that he had received a great deal of correspondence from Ortiz, Otero, Reyes, Carbó, and Corral regarding the dispute, and added that he hoped Carbó would be moved to another zone. Pacheco eventually sided with Ortiz in the quarrel, telling Díaz that it was Carbó who had broken relations with Ortiz in order to destroy the Sonora governor's administration.[45]

The Carbó-Ortiz conflict worsened, and on March 15 Pacheco informed Díaz that a mediator was being sent to Sonora. Pacheco saw no hope for a reconciliation between Carbó and Ortiz and suggested that Díaz advise Ortiz to use moderation. Díaz wrote to Ortiz asking him to be conciliatory while offering to pressure Carbó to change his conduct. Díaz's efforts were to little avail. In April, Carbó wrote President González complaining of Ortiz and, in turn, Ortiz denounced Carbó in the official state newspaper. An editorial in Sonora's *La Constitución* attacked Carbó for removing Otero from the Apache campaign.[46]

While Ortiz and Carbó quarreled, the Apache campaign continued in Sonora. At the beginning of March, Reyes arrived to take charge of it. García again complained to Carbó that Ortiz was exaggerating the Indian threat, and Sonoran Ramón Corral concurred, saying there was no news of Apaches — only fear. President González told Reyes that the reports from Ortiz, Otero, and García about the Sonora situation were contradictory, and asked Reyes to tell him exactly what was happening.[47]

Although Sonora and Chihuahua were peaceful during March, the following month, because of Apache raiding, the secretary of war ordered Carbó to organize an expedition under General Fuero. On May 8, Reyes and Fuero defeated Indians at Casas Grandes, Chihuahua, earning congratulations from the minister of war. In spite of this victory, Reyes complained to Carbó of the difficulties of the campaign and called Colonel García inept. In April, Reyes protested García's actions again, this time when Apaches sued for peace in Janos. Reyes reported that the "stupid and malicious" García did not make peace, but left with his entire force, leaving towns within twenty leagues of Apaches unprotected. Describing García as an "animal," Reyes added that he believed García thought that he could disobey orders, as he had done with Otero. García wrote Carbó during the summer, saying he really did not know why Reyes disliked him.[48]

Reyes's problems continued. He received a force of two hundred men on July 3, but he complained to Carbó that the force was useless because more than 150 of the troops were convicts. On July 7, Reyes reported Apache depredations in Chihuahua and asked that Sonora's forces be increased.

Reyes complained that Guaymas was without a garrison, and that Hermosillo had only a small guard — and that was needed to serve as custodian to the convict troops.[49]

Reyes still had to contend with the unsettled conflict between Ortiz and Carbó. Reyes called Carbó his "only friend," and he cautioned Carbó not to seek vengeance against Ortiz, because it would only make him look bad. Carbó must have followed this advice, because in July President González thanked Carbó for trying to maintain good relations with Sonora's Governor Ortiz and Sinaloa's governor Martínez de Castro. González was keeping a close watch on Ortiz, even asking Carbó to determine why Ortiz constantly wanted arms, since he had already requested permission to buy five hundred Remington rifles.[50]

While Ortiz and Carbó did not get along, Reyes was still able to tell González in September that he was happy under Carbó's command. When Carbó's letters to Reyes showed coldness, Reyes was quick to assure Carbó of his loyalty, though admitting his independence. Reyes carefully tried to maintain good relations with Carbó, his superior, but he did not hesitate to complain of the inadequate forces under his command.

On August 3, Reyes protested to Carbó that he had repeatedly asked for extra forces. Reyes said he feared he would lose his reputation; that those who criticized him failed to understand that this was not a regular war. He complained that he had too few troops and he was unable to supervise those because they were too scattered.[51]

Reyes reportedly considered resigning, believing he had lost the president's support. In September, Reyes complained to Carbó about the poor condition of the colonias militares. He said that commanders were constantly changed, the colonias poorly administered, that there were not enough troops, the horses were very skinny, and discipline was lacking. Reyes concluded that the colonias militares would not improve, because they were led by the "totally inept" First Captain Angel Elías. He added that he thought it sad that the government spent money on such worthless people.[52]

In spite of reports from Reyes and García of the worsening situation in Sonora, González informed Carbó that there were few federal troops available for the Apache wars. González said he would try to increase forces, but suggested that Carbó use auxiliary troops.[53] One reason troops were unavailable for the Sonora Apache campaign was the renewal of the Yaqui and Mayo war.

By this time, Ortiz had come to distrust Reyes and his use of federal forces. Ortiz accused Reyes of wanting not only federal but also all state troops under his personal command for the Apache campaign. He agreed to place troops under Reyes if Reyes would stop using his "hostile" federal troops to threaten the state government. The governor even went so far as to suggest that federal forces arriving in Hermosillo were not destined for Apache wars, but were instead to subdue the local populace. Ortiz added that he needed the National Guard to protect himself and Sonora's citizens, at least until unfriendly Reyes moved his forces elsewhere.[54]

While Mexico's officials squabbled, the Apache threat continued unabated. Public opinion on both sides of the border advocated doing something to end the Apache threat. Both Mexico and the United States now agreed to negotiate a formal agreement for reciprocal crossing of troops in pursuit of hostiles as the only way to end depredations. The United States–Mexico agreement was signed during the new presidential regimes of Mexico's Manuel González and Chester A. Arthur of the United States. The constitutionally based González government did not have the problem of diplomatic recognition from the United States that had plagued Díaz's relations with Rutherford B. Hayes.[55] Mexico no longer feared a United States invasion of its territory, and in May 1882 the United States began negotiations for a pact. The reciprocal agreement was signed on July 29, 1882, by Mexican minister Matías Romero and United States secretary of state Frederick T. Frelinghuysen.

Neither a treaty nor a law, the accord did not require confirmation by the Senate of either country. The agreement, to be in effect for two years, could be terminated by either country with four months' notice. The accord was amended in September to be in force for one year, because Mexico's Senate granted approval for one year only. It became obvious that Mexico no longer viewed passage of United States forces as a pretext for control or conquest of Mexico, since it was willing to extend the 1882 agreement each year, until the pact was allowed to lapse from 1886 to 1890.

The pact was not intended to be applicable to the Texas border, where Indian raids were no longer significant. Crossings would be allowed only in unpopulated or desert areas, at least two leagues from an encampment or town in either country. No crossing would be permitted between Capitán Leal, a town on the Mexican side of the Rio Grande twenty leagues above Piedras Negras, to the mouth of the Rio Grande.

The commander crossing the border was, at the time of crossing or before, if possible, to inform the nearest military or civil authority of the country entered. The force in pursuit was to retire to its own territory as soon as it either encountered hostiles or lost the trail. Foreign forces were not to establish themselves or remain in the other country longer than necessary. Abuses committed by foreign forces would be punished by their own government, as if the offense had been committed in their own country.[56]

With the signing of the 1882 agreement, there was optimism that the United States Indian "problem" would soon be solved. In 1882 Lieutenant General P. H. Sheridan wrote:

> The majority of the wasteful and hostile occupants of millions of acres of valuable agricultural pasture and mineral land has been forced upon reservations under the supervision of the government.

Sheridan predicted that settlements would "absorb the remnants of the once powerful Indian nations who fifteen years ago vainly attempted to forbid the destined progress of the age."[57] His optimism was premature; the 1882 pact would permit the fighting of hostile Indians for the next four years. It would then lapse, only to be renewed.

FOUR

The Tiger of the Human Species, 1883–1885

✠

The crossing agreement, used primarily when United States troops crossed into Sonora, made possible Brigadier General George Crook's 1883 Sierra Madre campaign. Trouble began in 1881 when Chiricahuas fled their reservation to raid in Mexico. Although Apaches now threatened Mexico instead of the United States, Crook "became fully convinced that their return was merely a question of time."[1]

Mexico received a report from Tombstone that Apaches invading Sonora fled their reservation when forced to engage in subsistence farming. A public meeting in Tucson blamed Apache trouble on San Carlos, "where the Indians supplied raiders with arms, men, and a safe base," and suggested a ranger attack on the reservation. Crook criticized border newspapers, like the *Tombstone Daily Epitaph*, for disseminating "all sorts of exaggerations and falsehoods about the Indians, which are copied in papers of high character and wide circulation, in other parts of the country, while the Indians' side of the case is rarely ever heard."[2]

In spite of allegations in the *Tombstone Daily Epitaph* that Apaches received 4,000 acres of the best land in Arizona, each "filthy beast" being supplied two pounds of beef daily, in addition to flour, sugar, and tobacco, conditions were apparently not good enough to keep the Chiricahuas on the reservation. Geronimo recounted in his autobiography that he left San Carlos for Mexico because of a rumor that officers planned to imprison Indian leaders. "We thought it more manly to die on the warpath than to be killed in prison."[3] Apaches resisted the reservation because of conflicts between the Bureau of Indian Affairs and the army, corruption, the concentration policy, and demoralizing rationing.

White settlers encroaching on the reservation contributed to the discontent. Arizona's population doubled from 40,000 to 80,000 between 1880 and 1882. Mining and agricultural settlements intruded on Indian lands. Mormon farmers diverted Gila River water from reservation crops. According to one historian, "Conditions at San Carlos would have severely tried the most docile and obedient Indians. The Apaches were neither docile nor obedient."[4]

Crook explained Indians' unhappiness with reservation life, saying "Indians are often robbed of their rations and of the goods provided by Government for their subsistence and support." He added:

> In almost every Indian war which I have known anything about, the prime cause therefor has been, either the failure of our Government to make good its pledges or the wrongs perpetrated upon them by unscrupulous whites.[5]

Crook concluded that Indians must either be treated fairly or exterminated. Mexico also blamed United States policy for the Apache wars, suspecting the hostiles came from the San Carlos Reservation. In 1883 Chihuahua's deputies and senators asked the national Congress to persuade Washington to do something about the reservations.[6]

Meanwhile, Indians continued to raid Mexico. Early in 1883, Apaches raided the Arizpe, Moctezuma, Sahuaripa, and Ures districts of Sonora. In March, four American prospectors were killed by Apaches in Sonora. These deaths were attributed largely to the negligence of local authorities not abiding by government recommendations that travelers be escorted. On March 25 Sonoran politician and writer Ramón Corral lamented in a letter to General José Guillermo Carbó that hostile Apaches were invading everywhere but Sahuaripa. He also reported that Apaches were being pursued everywhere, but without success, adding that chasing them was like chasing shadows. Two days later, however, Carbó told President González he believed the Indians had left Sonora without committing the usual depredations.[7]

Corral concurred, reporting to Carbó two days later that Apaches had left Sonora in relative calm. But, that same day, García reported to Carbó that Apaches were raiding the Ures District of Sonora. Also in March, González cautioned Carbó that diversion of troops to the Apache campaign must not allow Yaquis to renew their war.[8]

While Yaquis caused as much fear as Apaches in Sonora, in United States frontier states Chiricahuas inspired the greatest dread. The able Chiricahua fighters dominated all of northern Mexico as well as much of Arizona and New Mexico. In January 1883, the *Tombstone Daily Epitaph* declared the Apache as untamable as the hyena, adding that he was classed as human only because of his erect position and articulation approaching language. Crook called the Chiricahuas "bad Indians, probably the very worst on the continent."[9] Comparing Apaches to coyotes, Crook explained why it was so difficult to defeat them:

> Where man raises no harvest, dries no fish, preserves no meat, lives simply from hand to mouth, the trouble in effecting his capture becomes immeasurably greater, and after he has been provided with improved breech-loaders he is transformed into a foe of the most dangerous character within human knowledge.[10]

The Chiricahua Apaches lived habitually in seclusion in Mexico's rugged Sierra Madre, safe from both United States and Mexican troops. In early March 1883, a number of Chiricahuas left their Sierra Madre hideout, dividing into two raiding parties. About fifty, under Geronimo, raided Sonora for stock, while another twenty-six, under Chato, raided Arizona for ammunition, "with a side mission of persuading old chief Loco and his Warm Spring Apaches to leave their reservation and join the hostiles."[11]

Chato's party crossed the border on March 21, and on March 28 killed Judge H. C. McComas and his wife. Their six-year-old son Charlie was taken captive. He was never found and was alleged to have been killed. Chato's raiders traveled four hundred miles through Arizona in no more than six days, killing at least eleven people. Crook maintained that Chato's band traveled so fast that effective pursuit was impossible. Crook said "every conceivable effort was made and artifice employed which an experience of a generation of Indian wars could suggest," but, "although the party was so closely followed that twice they were compelled to abandon their horses and plunder and take to the rocks on foot," they "left no more trail than so many birds." Crook reported that, in spite of

> the most vigilant action on the part of officers and men, such are the difficulties to be met in pursuit of a raiding party, through such a region as southeastern Arizona, that not an Indian was seen by any of the various parties at different times on their trail.[12]

Chato and his band escaped back into Mexico, with only one of their men killed, "without any of the United States troops, or in fact anyone at all except their victims, having laid eyes for certainty on a single one of the hostiles."[13]

While United States forces failed in attempts to punish hostile Apaches, Mexican troops met with more success than their American counterparts. In early April, President González boasted to Carbó that peace reigned since General Bonifacio Topete had been fighting the Indians. Auxiliary forces led by Emilio Kosterlitzky were pursuing Apaches in the Ures District of Sonora, hoping to capture them before they divided into small groups to hide in the Sierra Madres on Chihuahua's border.[14]

Sonoran statesman Corral reported that he had 60 armed Pima Indians protecting towns in Ures, 120 soldiers in Arizpe, and was organizing 25 cavalry. Corral added that local prefects would organize additional forces if necessary. Because President González was unable to send additional cavalry, Carbó organized auxiliary troops to fight the Indians, a difficult task because of expected high salaries and sparse population. By mid May, Corral was able to report to Carbó that Apaches had left Sonora in peace, having returned to the United States after their defeat in Mexico on April 25.[15]

While Mexico experienced success in Indian wars, the United States met defeat. Because of failures to catch Chato and other raiders' parties, Crook became convinced that the only way to defeat what he termed the "tiger of the Human species" would be by a surprise attack in their Sierra Madre hideout. Crook admitted his task would be difficult, because "a dozen Indians in the rocks can withstand the onset of a battalion of soldiers." Apaches could allegedly travel seventy miles a day on foot in rugged country, outdistancing men on horses. They could endure long periods without water and were indifferent to physical pain. Only Apache scouts were able to follow the hostiles, often through mountainous terrain where horses were useless and supplies had to be carried by pack-trains.[16]

Crook believed: "In operating against them the only hope of success lies in using their own methods," by employing Indian scouts against the Apaches. Defending his use of scouts, Crook said he "selected, preferably, the wildest that I could get," maintaining "the Apache scouts, for this class of warfare, are as worthy of trust as any soldiers in the world, and in all the experience I have had with them they have proved themselves energetic, reliable, truthful and honest."[17]

In his Apache campaign, Crook experimented with scouts to a greater degree than anyone ever had before, with about two hundred out of three hundred men being Apache scouts. "Never before did a commander start on such an expedition, relying so largely on Indian warriors and trusting so implicitly to Indian fidelity."[18] Crook first needed an Indian who could lead him to the Sierra Madre Apache stronghold. He got his scout during Chato's raid. Although Crook's men failed to catch Chato's band, a deserter called "Peaches" would later act as Crook's guide to the Sierra Madre hideout.

Peaches and the 1882 reciprocal crossing agreement made possible what historian Dan Thrapp termed "the most important and dangerous United States army operation against hostile Indians in the history of the American frontier."[19] He was referring to Crook's expedition into the Sierra Madres between May 1 and June 10, 1883. Crook could cross into Mexico under provisions of the 1882 pact, but he knew that a literal interpretation of the agreement would not give the desired result. In order to defeat the Chiricahuas, Crook could not be limited to hot pursuit. Instead, Crook would need to establish his forces in Mexico. Crook also planned to rely primarily on Apache scouts for his campaign, another violation of the agreement.

After trying unsuccessfully to get the State Department to obtain a liberal interpretation of the pact, Crook traveled to Sonora and Chihuahua to ask Mexican officials for their cooperation. Tucson's *El Fronterizo* unjustly accused Crook of taking advantage of the crossing treaty by acting in Mexico "as if he were in his own home."[20] On the contrary, Crook was sensitive to the feelings of his Mexican counterparts, establishing friendly relations with Sonora and Chihuahua officials. Crook praised Generals Carbó and Topete and Sonora's new governor Luis E. Torres in Sonora for his warm reception. He thanked Governor Mariano Samaniego and General Ramón Reguera of Chihuahua for agreeing informally to a liberal interpretation of the crossing agreement. The only stipulation made by the Mexican officials was a request that Apache scouts wear a distinguishing red headband.[21]

Although Crook had arrived at an understanding with Carbó, in April Mexico's minister in Washington protested that Mexico's Senate still needed to approve Crook's expedition. In spite of this protest, on May 3 Corral reported to Carbó that, according to an article in *El Fronterizo*, Crook was going ahead with his preparations for a large campaign in Sonora. On May 24 Corral again wrote Carbó, saying he knew nothing definite about Crook. Corral reported all that was known was that Crook had passed through Bavispe, a frontier town in Moctezuma District, on May 5 on his way into the Sierra Madre. An officer of the National Guard gave Crook some guides he had requested in Bavispe. After that, there was no news. Corral added that a rumor circulating in Fronteras, a town six leagues from the border, said that Apaches defeated Crook.[22]

Mexico soon learned that Crook had encountered the Apaches in their mountain hideout. On May 15 Crook met the renegades, persuading Geronimo, Chato, Mangus, Loco, and Cochise's son Naiche to return to the reservation. Crook actually returned to the United States with women and children only, however, starting back with nearly 250 of them on May 23. Mexico's Tucson consul complained that the Indians returning to the United States were primarily women and children, leaving warriors and chieftains in Sonora. When Geronimo did return to the United States in 1884, bringing some 350 head of stolen Mexican stock, Mexico was outraged.[23]

Mexico complained about Crook's lack of captive chieftains in 1883, and indeed, his campaign did not end raiding. Still, Crook's expedition to force Chiricahuas back onto the San Carlos Reservation can be considered "the climactic event in the Apache wars."[24] In spite of disagreement over the impact of Crook's campaign, he deserves credit for being the first to reach the Apaches' hideout. Never before had Spaniards, Mexicans, or Americans been able to follow Apaches in that hostile country. The result "was tremendous, for it showed the Apaches that Americans could follow them anywhere."[25]

After Crook returned from the Sierra Madres with some of the Chiricahuas, he was chagrined to learn that the San Carlos agent was protesting their return to the reservation. After a trip to Washington for consultation, Crook obtained an agreement in July 1883, signed by the secretaries of war and interior, giving him police control of the entire reservation. Crook claimed, as a result, "for more than two years there was not a single depredation committed by the Apaches" in Arizona and New Mexico.[26] In spite of Crook's claims, Mexico continued to protest raids.

Sonoran Corral complained to Carbó in July that Apaches were still depredating in Moctezuma, in spite of General Crook's "overrated triumph." Corral said that Crook only went to the Sierra to escort Apache families back to San Carlos, leaving warriors free to continue raiding Mexico. Corral added that General Topete, meanwhile, was doing everything possible to defeat the Indians, even though with families back on the reservation, the war was more difficult because the Apaches no longer gathered where they might be vulnerable. He said with hostiles dispersed in the mountains, it was almost impossible to catch them.[27]

In October, Carbó, commander of the First Military Zone, wrote to Sonora's governor Torres, complaining of Crook's Indian policy. He said that the Apaches returning to San Carlos remained at liberty, and that they allegedly had 43,000 cartridges, provided by Crook. Carbó said frontier military commanders should determine whether Crook actually gave ammunition to Indians for Mexican raids. In addition, Carbó maintained that

Apaches returning with Crook took a large number of stolen Mexican stock, for which there had been no reimbursement. Finally, Carbó stated that United States conduct with respect to Indians was inexplicable and either a punishment from God inflicted on frontier towns or an injustice committed against Mexico by this powerful nation claiming to be Mexico's best friend.[28]

Although Mexico doubted the nature of United States intentions, on June 11, 1883, Mexico's Senate agreed to a one-year extension of the reciprocal crossing agreement. The commander of federal forces in Sonora expressed satisfaction at the pact renewal, saying that with additional troops it would be possible to exterminate the Apaches. He suggested the agreement not be limited to unpopulated areas, so that troops could pursue Apaches anywhere. United States President Chester A. Arthur praised this renewed cooperation in his annual message to Congress. Although a new Apache uprising was being fought by Colonel Torres in Moctezuma and Sahuaripa, Sonora, in December 1883, Arthur told Congress: "The operations of the forces of both governments against these savages have been successful."[29]

The reciprocal crossing agreement was renewed before Geronimo's return to San Carlos in 1884, when his possession of stolen stock enraged Mexico and created renewed suspicions of United States motives. Mexico's previous criticism of Crook now became distrust of the United States government.

Geronimo and the other bands promised Crook in 1883 to return to the reservation as soon as they could round up their people, who were scattered over an area 100 by 50 miles. The chiefs delayed, however, in order to raid Mexican ranches. According to Lieutenant Britton Davis, Third Cavalry, "the Chiricahuas knew that there was a premium on horses among the Indians of the Reservation and they wished to be well equipped for barter on their arrival."[30]

Davis and his Chiricahua scouts had orders from General Crook to escort the surrendering bands to the reservation, but the stolen stock complicated the task. An escort was needed because citizens of Arizona and New Mexico, protesting the return of the Indians to the reservation, threatened to organize posses to attack Apache bands. Davis had previously avoided attack from Arizona citizens by traveling forty or fifty miles daily and staying away from frequented routes and ranches. However, whereas Chato and other chiefs each returned with about 100 animals, Geronimo and his band brought about 350 head of stolen stock. Davis could have made the 175-mile trip to the reservation in four or five days, but with Geronimo's slow cattle, the trip would take two weeks. They could travel only twenty miles a day, and it was now necessary to stop at ranches for water. Geronimo, complaining that his cattle "had been driven hard for fear of pursuit by the Mexican owners," and would not be fat enough for trading at the reservation, now demanded a three-day rest.[31]

On March 8, while Davis and his charges rested at a ranch 30 miles from Fort Bowie, the United States marshal for Southern Arizona and the Nogales, Arizona, customs collector arrived to declare Geronimo's stock in contraband. Adding that Geronimo was wanted for murder in Arizona, the marshal ordered Davis to escort the Indians and their smuggled stock to Tucson to stand trial. Knowing his men would be outnumbered if he attempted to arrest Geronimo, Davis determined to defy the marshal, in spite of the fact that he feared the marshal would organize a posse. He recalled: "I wondered who would kill me, the posse or the Indians," and "if by any chance I escaped both, and the citizens of Arizona didn't lynch me, there was the Federal court and jail in the background." Davis talked Geronimo and his followers into leaving with their stolen stock at midnight. The marshal and the collector, sleeping soundly after being plied with a bottle of scotch, awoke to find the Indians and their stock had disappeared under the supervision of Davis's old friend, Second Lieutenant John Y. F. "Bo" Blake.[32]

Mexico soon learned of Davis's scheme to get Geronimo and his stock back on the reservation without incident. Crook quickly telegraphed Mexico's legation in Washington, declaring Geronimo's stolen stock subject to War Department orders. Tucson's *El Fronterizo* called for justice for Mexico, saying Crook would never have dared to allow Indians to return to the United States with stolen Mexican property if it were not for Mexico's weak position vis-à-vis the United States. *El Fronterizo* declared that Mexico must demand return of the stolen stock in order to retain national dignity.[33]

In response to Mexico's demands, Secretary of State Frederick T. Frelinghuysen told Mexico's minister in Washington Matías Romero that, by the time Geronimo and his band reached San Carlos, they had only 88 animals, about one-fourth of the original number. Frelinghuysen added that Crook doubted the animals would reach their owners if they were returned and, that, if the stock were delivered, a new Apache uprising might occur. The *Diario Oficial* reported in June that to avoid such difficulties, the Mexican stock would be auctioned off, the proceeds to be given to Romero to distribute to the owners. Mexico's Tucson consul protested that an auction would not yield even one-fourth the stock's value and asked the government to refuse to accept the sale's proceeds as compensation.[34]

Failing to obtain more satisfactory compensation from the United States,

Mexico began trying to determine the owners and value of the stolen animals. Owners were requested to supply proof that Geronimo had stolen their stock. Mexico's citizens responded to the inquiry, writing to the Ministry of Foreign Relations describing brands and requesting payment for stolen stock. Mexico realized that citizens from Sonora and Chihuahua would need to travel to San Carlos to identify animals with Mexican brands. Mexico's consul in Tucson complained to the ministry that owners of the stock should not have to pay travel expenses to San Carlos, requesting instead that special Mexican agents be sent to the reservation to identify brands.[35]

Sonora and Chihuahua authorities were informed in November 1884 that the United States government would pay $1,772.50, the proceeds from the auction of Geronimo's stock. Mexican owners valued their cattle at $25 a head and considered United States compensation inadequate. Claiming that Geronimo stole 155 of his cattle during March 1884, Pedro Ortiz of Janos, Chihuahua, hired a New Mexican law firm in January 1885 to collect compensation from the United States government. Appraising his cattle at $25 a head, Ortiz asked for $3,875. He named four other Chihuahua citizens who had lost an additional 62 head of cattle. Ortiz gave power of attorney to Henry Holgate, who went to San Carlos to search for the cattle. Holgate found only 97 cattle belonging to Ortiz and surmised that this number were all that were sold under War Department orders. Complaining that the auction would not compensate him for the remainder of his cattle, in January Ortiz sought a special act of Congress to pay for the balance.[36]

A week later, Mexico's minister Matías Romero responded to Ortiz's request that he collect the money from the United States government. Romero said that on October 19 the secretary of state had sent his legation a check for $1,762.50, the proceeds from the sale of the remaining 91 cattle stolen by Geronimo, along with an inventory of the brands, descriptions of the cattle, and the prices of each. Romero advised Ortiz's attorneys to apply to the Ministry of Foreign Relations for compensation. That ministry announced in January 1886 that governors of Chihuahua and Sonora would distribute funds from the San Carlos auction. Ortiz and other Mexican owners were reimbursed, but only in the amount raised by the sale. Mexico, bitter over this incident, continued to criticize Crook and United States Indian policy.[37]

Not only Mexico criticized Crook's policy; so did Arizonans. On March 12, the *Arizona Daily Star* claimed Crook's acquiescence to Geronimo's demands (he had threatened to put two thousand Apaches on the warpath if his stock was taken) showed that Crook had lost control of the Indians. Calling for an investigation of Crook by the people of Arizona, the *Daily Star* announced: "Crook is a flat failure."[38]

The following day, the *Arizona Daily Citizen* also criticized generals Crook and Pope for requesting honors for those who served in the Indian campaigns, saying the people of Arizona considered this a joke since the military was usually to the rear of the Indians. The *Daily Citizen* said Crook should have killed the Chiricahuas in their hideout, instead of returning them to the reservation as honored guests. In an opposite stance, the *Daily Star* defended Crook, saying that all Apaches would have returned to the reservation if Crook had possessed sufficient supplies to remain longer in the Sierra Madres.[39]

While the *Citizen* criticized Crook's reservation policy, the *Star* defended military control of the reservation, but only until the Indians could be moved to Indian Territory. The *Citizen* said Crook should now recommend removal. The *Star*, agreeing with the *Citizen* that Arizona wanted the Chiricahuas to be sent far away from the territory, also requested that Crook recommend removal. Crook, however, did not believe it would be practical to move the Chiricahuas for the reasons stated in his 1883 annual report:

> Since the return of the Chiricahuas, there has been a clamor from a portion of the press for the removal of the Apaches from this Territory. The glibness with which people generally speak of moving them from their camps, as you would chickens from a roost, without reflecting that to attempt their removal would bring on the bloodiest Indian war this country has ever experienced, besides this, where shall they be located? No other state or territory wants these Indians. The mere mention of it to the Apache Indians would create a feeling of insecurity among them which would tax to the utmost every means in our power to quiet.[40]

In spite of Crook's protest that removal was impossible, the *Star* warned that if the government failed to remove Apaches to Indian Territory, the people of Arizona would exterminate them, the San Carlos Reservation included. Declaring the country tired of an expensive reservation policy that did nothing to defend the territory's citizens, the *Star* said it was time to act while the Indians were in Arizona's control. The *Star* added that removal was the only way to guarantee Mexico protection from raids. Rejecting Baja California as too large, in March the *Citizen* suggested isolating the San Carlos Indians on the Santa Cruz and Santa Rosa Islands near Santa Barbara and then opening the reservation to settlement.[41]

Calling San Carlos a "loafing ground" for Indians, the *Citizen* declared that an outbreak was certain. The *Star* disagreed, saying that the Chiricahuas were content on the reservation, adding that they were not dangerous if properly treated. The *Star* said that if another outbreak was going to happen, it would have occurred when Geronimo was forced to surrender his stock. Accusing the *Citizen* of abusing Crook, in March the *Star* called its rival alarmist for predicting another San Carlos outbreak. The following month, the *Citizen* reported that eighteen warriors had fled San Carlos.[42]

Alarmed by the prospect of more raids, Mexico concurred with Arizona that Apaches should be removed from the frontier. Mexico's consul in Tombstone suggested to the Ministry of Foreign Relations that the governors of Chihuahua and Sonora urge the United States to relocate the San Carlos Indians in Indian Territory.[43]

The economic benefit of the military's presence in Arizona was recognized by both countries. Mexico's Tucson consul called the United States military the main obstacle to removal because, if Indians were moved, troops would not be needed. Tucson's consul said Arizona lived off government reservation contracts and money from soldiers. The consul added that, because the entire Arizona territory lived off the fort income, the military and Indian agents encouraged raids. The Mexican consul in Tombstone agreed with his Tucson colleague's assessment.[44]

Mexico now distrusted the United States' desire to end raids. In February 1884, in response to raids by well-armed escapees from San Carlos, Mexico's Foreign Relations Ministry asked consuls in Tucson, El Paso, and Tombstone to find out if United States authorities or agents were encouraging incursions. If true, the ministry asked the consuls to discover the motive, and called for suggestions to end United States complicity with Indians.[45]

Mexico's consul in Tombstone responded to the inquiry in March, saying he could prove that United States agents and officials encouraged incursions into Mexico by giving Indians arms and munitions, presumably for hunting. The consul cited as proof the fact that Indian returnees to San Carlos were not imprisoned, disarmed, or forced to work. Another example given by the consul to illustrate United States' intent involved Lieutenant Davis's refusal to turn over stolen Mexican stock to United States customs officials. Mexico's consul declared that the United States' motive was greed. According to the Tombstone consul, a second aim was to depopulate the frontier to prepare for another seizure of Mexican territory. As proof, he cited United States purchase of Mexican land and mines.[46]

Mexico's consul in Tucson agreed with the Tombstone consul that the United States probably had a plan to absorb Mexico's frontier territory, citing as proof the ominous situation in Sonora, where many Mexicans had allied themselves with the United States. The consul said the desire to take part of Mexico was the only reason the United States did nothing about corrupt agents.[47]

The Tucson consul advised the Foreign Relations Ministry that spies would be needed to prove corruption at the reservation. The spies must be intelligent, fluent in English, and willing to do menial work, since that was all Mexicans were hired to do. The consul suggested a Mexican living at Bavispe, Sonora, as the San Carlos agent. Because José M. Montoya had been with Crook in the Sierra Madre, he could return to San Carlos to work without causing suspicion. The Mexican government heeded the consul's advice, hiring a secret agent stationed at San Carlos for $150 per month. Governor of Sonora Luis Torres and General José G. Carbó arranged payment for Montoya without informing the consul, fearing an indiscretion on his part could compromise his life or effectiveness. Fearing that the United States would not inform him of Apache movements, and distrustful of American officials, Torres continued retaining Montoya at the San Carlos Reservation. In July 1885, Torres asked Carbó to renew the spy's monthly salary of $150 in view of the valuable information he supplied regarding Apaches. Mexico continued to pay Montoya until January 4, 1886.[48]

While Mexico criticized United States reservations and questioned United States motives, Crook defended his Indian policy as the only viable method to solve the "Indian question." Crook ruled out extermination, because, he said, the United States shared guilt for past atrocities and, more important, the Chiricahuas would be difficult to defeat. Crook concluded: "It follows that we must satisfy them that hereafter they shall be treated with justice, and protected from the inroads of white men. The reservation system offers the easiest way to this end." Crook said that "the Chiricahuas, whom we could not kill, should be brought on the reservation, where we could control them." Crook believed that "Indians must be segregated until they learn the way of whites."[49]

Crook's first step in solving the Indian problem was not disarmament, since he considered it impossible. He pointed out that Indians could not be prevented from buying arms and ammunition, because "in this country money will buy anything." Crook warned: "Deprive the Apache Indians of their arms, and in a short time there would not be a hoof of stock on the reservation" since a main reason Indians raided was to obtain munitions or the means to purchase them.[50]

Instead of disarming Indians, Crook believed the solution to the Apache threat was to transform them into self-sustaining farmers to "raise the Indians beyond the state of vagabondage." In order to put his plan for the Apaches into effect, Crook assigned Captain Emmet Crawford and Lieutenant Britton Davis to supervise the farming. In July 1883, Crook obtained an agreement between the Interior and War departments to divide administration of the White Mountain Reservation, giving the War Department military responsibility. Crook entrusted this responsibility to Crawford, Third Cavalry, who considered "no phase of administration at San Carlos beyond military control."[51]

In his annual report for 1884, Crook termed his reservation policy a success. Claiming all Chiricahuas were now at peace on the reservation "for the first time in the history of that fierce people," Crook added they were being taught farming. While sheep and cattle ranching might seem more practical in Arizona than irrigation farming, Crook was enthusiastic. He reported "the two Chiefs — Geronimo and Chato — who last year were our worst enemies — have this year made the greatest progress and possess the best tilled farms." Crook boasted that, in spite of inadequate seeds and farming implements, the following crops had been raised during the previous season on four thousand acres of land:

3,850,000 pounds of corn; 550,000 pounds of barley; 54,000 pounds of beans; 20,000 pounds of potatoes; 50,000 pounds of wheat; 200,000 pumpkins; 50,000 watermelons; 40,000 muskmelons; and small quantities of onions, cabbage and peppers.[52]

After demonstrating through farming that the Chiricahua "will drop from the list of worthless idlers and relieve the Government from the responsibility of caring for him," Crook recommended sending White Mountain Reservation Indians needed seeds and equipment. Crook also asked for the erection of one or two mills for wheat grinding and reiterated his request for additional trading stores, so that competition would beat down the current exorbitant prices. Crook's annual report for the following year expressed hope that the Chiricahuas would continue to farm peacefully on the reservation.[53]

Crook's 1884 report listed only one troublesome incident during the past year — young leader Kayatennae's speech at a dance referring to past victories over whites and expressing hope for more such victories. Kayatennae was arrested by Indian soldiers, tried by an Apache jury, and sent by Crook in irons to serve three years in prison at Alcatraz, but was pardoned after eighteen months. Reiterating that the Chiricahuas were content, Crook said his main concern was to secure return of Apache women and children held captive in Mexico. Crook said the Chiricahuas released thirteen captives to show their good faith, and he now expected the Mexicans to do likewise. If the Mexicans did not release their captives, Crook warned that the Apaches would likely be tempted to raid Mexico in reprisal.[54]

The United States requested return of Apache prisoners in July 1884, and Mexico agreed to cooperate. In December 1884, Lorenzo García, fearing Mexico would send prisoners to the United States to be reunited with their families, requested Carbó to omit the name of his adopted Indian daughter on any list of prisoners. In February 1885, the Mexican government asked the United States for names and ages of Chiricahuas allegedly held captive. The United States replied with a list of 93 Chiricahua and Warm Springs captives in Mexico. Mexico's border officials were instructed to report any Chiricahua prisoners remaining in their states to the Foreign Relations Ministry.[55]

In June, governor of Sonora Luis Torres told the Foreign Relations Ministry that his state had neither Chiricahua nor other Indian prisoners. He added that federal troops had taken twenty-eight prisoners when they defeated Apaches on April 29, 1882, and that General Bernardo Reyes had distributed sixteen captive children under ten years of age to families. In July, Torres said he had located five Apache children given out by Reyes, but three were very sick and could not be returned to the United States.[56]

Chihuahua's governor, Carlos Fuero, responded in February 1885, saying he had found only one seventy-year-old woman from the San Carlos Reservation still imprisoned. In June Chihuahua's governor admitted that his state had other captives, but he said they were all small children. After Geronimo's escape from San Carlos, he detained others heading in that direction and informed the secretary of war.[57]

As late as October 1886, Matías Romero asked Chihuahua's governor to find Chato's wife and two children, who had been captured in 1882. When Chato's wife was located, she agreed to visit her husband only if she would not be forced to remain in the United States. Two Mexican families had adopted Chato's children and did not want to give them up. The governor concluded that Chato's family did not want to return because they preferred a civilized life in Mexico.[58]

Although Mexico was not forthcoming with Chiricahua captives, Apaches remained quiet on their reservation in 1884, one exception being a small invasion of Chihuahua by Apaches during June.[59] With the Apache menace ended, Carbó asked President González to renew the Yaqui campaign. González said he wanted to allocate enough funds to the Yaqui and Mayo campaign to defeat the Indians, but had none. In addition, Secretary of War Francisco Naranjo informed Carbó of a possible revolution in the interior, adding that he did not want to move his troops. As a result, the campaign was suspended.[60] The Yaquis would not be defeated for years.

Yaqui revolts during the Porfiriato, resulting in deportation of unknown numbers of Indians to Yucatán and other parts of the nation, were caused primarily by the Yaquis' determination to keep their lands. Fiercely independent, Yaquis refused to submit to government laws, thus frustrating the Mexican government's attempts to end all regional hegemony. The federal government wanted to incorporate the Indians, or at least their lands, into the nation.

Rich Yaqui river bottomlands possessed a soil and climate capable of growing almost any crop. Therefore it was considered in the best national interest to open these lands to commercial development and foreign investors. Yaquis reacted to the plan to take their land with total warfare. Therefore Díaz, who returned to the presidency in September 1884, resorted to the use of force with his policy of *pan* or *palo*, "bread or the club." The regime responded harshly to revolts, which increased with rapid economic development of Sonora in the 1880s when the first railroad reached Sonora and when Governor Luis Torres encouraged development of mining and foreign investment.[61]

The call for a Yaqui and Mayo campaign was renewed during 1885. General Bernardo Reyes accused Sonora's government of unjust treatment of the Yaquis; others insisted that only a massive infusion of arms and men would end the uprising. Secretary of War Pedro Hinojosa called for Yaqui submission through just treatment only when it was apparent that Mexico's treasury lacked the funds necessary to defeat the Yaquis.[62]

In spite of Mexico City's refusal, Sonora and Chihuahua expected the federal government to end the Yaqui war, because their meager resources were insufficient to end this large-scale uprising. In February, a Sonora citizen requested federal help, calling it disgraceful that in twelve years the state had been unable to defeat the small Yaqui tribe. That same day, Sonora's Governor Luis Torres complained to Carbó that Yaquis were raiding, but that he lacked *federales* for a formal campaign. On February 24, Chihuahua's governor Carlos Fuero advised Díaz that Yaquis had invaded Guaymas.[63]

To the fear of Yaquis was added fear of Yankee encroachment in Sonora and Chihuahua. In February, Torres advised Díaz that Mormons wanted to

live in Sonora and were even going so far as to talk with Yaqui chief Cajeme
about an agreement. Díaz responded that he was certain Cajeme and the
Mormons had signed an agreement, and he predicted trouble and perhaps
an international incident. In April Chihuahua's Governor Fuero told Díaz
he wanted the Mormons in his state expelled after their harvest, calling it
bad policy to allow foreigners to live on Mexico's frontier with the United
States; Díaz agreed.[64]

Not only Mormons wanted to move to Mexico. Osage Indians in Indian
Territory expressed an interest. Without revealing why the inquiry was
made, Mexico asked the United States Department of the Interior for
information on the number and status of Osage Indians. A United States
Indian agent tried to discredit the Indians' letter, ostensibly signed by
Osage chiefs, saying it had been written by a disreputable half-breed.[65]

While Mexico did not view the Osage as a threat, it remained fearful of
United States hegemony. Citing the example of Texas, Secretary of War
Hinojosa warned that if Mormons were allowed into the frontier, little by
little Mexico would lose these rich states. Hinojosa added that he did not
favor extermination of Yaquis, because it would be a mistake to bring in
Yankees to replace these valuable Indian laborers. When Torres wrote Díaz
in August, however, saying that Mormons wanted to colonize Sonora and
Chihuahua, Díaz reversed his earlier decision and gave his approval.[66]

While worried about the Mormon threat to the border states, Mexico's
officials were of necessity preoccupied with ending the fierce Yaqui fighting. In February 1885 Sonora's governor Torres reported to Díaz that
General Bonifacio Topete was in charge of protecting towns on the Yaqui
River from the Cajeme uprising. Later that month, Topete advised Carbó
that a formal campaign would be necessary to defeat Cajeme, a chief commanding some two thousand Indians. Torres wrote Díaz during the same
month, asking for a big federal campaign against the Yaquis and saying that
Sonora lacked the necessary resources to defeat the Indians.[67]

A week later, Díaz responded, giving orders for Carbó to wage an offensive battle with his troops, augmented by five or six hundred National
Guardsmen. As soon as Carbó was placed in command of the Sonora Yaqui
campaign, his old enemy Carlos R. Ortiz began complaining to Díaz. Defending Carbó's handling of the Yaqui campaign, Díaz told Ortiz that
Sonora could not be divided against a common enemy. Díaz also praised
General José Otero for putting the Indian campaign above local Sonora
politics.[68]

While Díaz tried to end the political jealously undermining Carbó's
efforts, Carbó was notified that funds were not available for the Yaqui war.

Díaz assured Sonora's governor Torres in February that Carbó would begin an offensive fight; still, Hinojosa advised Carbó that the government lacked funds for a formal Yaqui campaign. During March, Carbó and Torres employed all their resources against hostiles on the Yaqui and Mayo rivers, but Carbó complained to Díaz that Sonora was unable to finance the war.[69]

That month, Hinojosa and Díaz informed Carbó that because of conflicts with Guatemala, it would not be possible to send funds for the Yaqui campaign. In a confidential letter, Hinojosa explained that Justo Rufino Barrios of Guatemala wanted to take Chiapas to form a republic of Central America. Realizing that troops could not be spared for the Yaqui and Mayo war, Carbó nonetheless asked for more auxiliary forces and requested that Díaz order the Treasury to distribute funds to pay his troops.[70]

The Guatemala conflict was so serious that Mexico asked the United States to allow Mexican troops destined for the war to pass through United States territory. Mexico made this request only after Lieutenant General Sheridan's April 1885 request to move the Tenth Cavalry Regiment from Texas to Arizona via Mexican territory. Sheridan made his extraordinary request because the Rio Grande flow was so high troops could only cross via the bridge joining the two El Paso populations. The only other alternative was to cross one hundred miles farther north, or to wait for the river to subside. Stressing that United States troops would only cross ten or twelve miles into Mexican territory to avoid Rio Grande floodwaters, Sheridan said his request was entirely peaceful. In contrast, the United States considered Mexico's request a violation of American neutrality, because the Mexican forces were destined for the Guatemala war.[71]

Mexico's request was denied, in spite of assurances that some of the troops Mexico wanted to pass through United States territory were destined for the Yaqui campaign, an internal war in Sonora. Ignoring the United States' refusal to reciprocate, the Mexican Senate agreed to allow American troops to cross the border at El Paso del Norte, returning to the United States fifteen miles to the north. Chihuahua's governor was told to be on the alert, in case of violence.[72]

Although Mexico was denied permission to transfer troops for the Guatemala conflict, the crisis was soon over. On April 27, Hinojosa informed Carbó of the overthrow and death of Barrios. Carbó once again allowed himself to hope he would get federal support for the Yaqui campaign. A new Apache threat, however, diverted funds.[73]

A *tizwin* drunk led to the 1885 Apache outbreak. Crook strictly forbade the brewing and drinking of *tizwin*, a strong beer made of corn, on the San Carlos Reservation. The Chiricahuas considered the jailing of their people for making *tizwin* an unfair punishment. Assigned to police the reservation, Lieutenant Britton Davis recalled: "With the coming of the cold weather, even the little pretence at farming ceased. The Indians drew their rations, gambled, loafed, and quarreled."[74]

Now, in open defiance of Crook's orders, Chihuahua and other chiefs confronted Davis to say they

> had been drinking Tiswin the night before and now they wanted to know what I was going to do about it — whether or not I was going to put them all in jail. He added in his opinion that I did not have a jail large enough to hold them all.
>
> Things had evidently come to a show down. I told Chihuahua that the matter was serious and that I would not act upon it myself but would telegraph the circumstances to General Crook and await his orders which I would make known to the Chiefs as soon as I received them.[75]

Davis's telegram never reached Crook, however, because it was first shown to Al Sieber, who was in charge of scouts on the reservation. Sieber termed the matter "just an ordinary Tiswin drunk," and the telegram was not sent. Davis said that "had it reached General Crook I am convinced that the outbreak would have been nipped in the bud."[76]

Instead, after waiting three days for an answer to their ultimatum, the Indians grew suspicious of Davis's excuses. Fearing punishment, about forty men and one hundred women and children fled the reservation on May 17. Geronimo, Mangus, Chihuahua, Naiche, and Nana led them south toward Mexico. They made up only one-fourth of the 550 who had surrendered to Crook. The majority stayed on the reservation, "notwithstanding the threats of the fugitives to return and kill them all."[77] This outbreak began the famous Geronimo campaign of 1885–86. Before the campaign ended in 1886, Captain Emmet Crawford had been killed, Crook's policy of using Apache scouts and negotiation had been discredited, and Crook had been replaced by Brigadier General Nelson A. Miles.

Emmet Crawford, 3rd Cavalry.
(Courtesy Arizona Historical Society/Tucson, Photo # 19581.)

Crawford's Apache scouts.
(Courtesy Arizona Historical Society/Tucson, Photo # 63674.)

Geronimo and warriors. Chief Natchez [Naiche] center and
Geronimo next to horse.
(Courtesy Arizona Historical Society/Tucson, Photo # 78168.)

Scene in Geronimo's camp with sentinel.
(Courtesty Arizona Historical Society/Tucson, Photo # 78160.)

Apache men, women, and children prior to their surrender to General Crook.
(Courtesy Arizona Historical Society/Tucson, Photo # 78152.)

Apache Kid.
(Courtesy Arizona Historical Society/Tucson, Photo # 15755.)

Nana.
(Courtesy Arizona Historical Society/Tucson, Photo # 19720.)

Illustration of a Yaqui and a Samurai. The newspaper caption reads:
"Will the bloodthirsty Yaqui Be Wiped Out by the Samurai?"
(San Francisco Chronicle, *November 5, 1905.*)

Company of enlisted Apache scouts at San Carlos Reservation, Arizona.
(Courtesy Arizona Historical Society/Tucson.)

Troop A, 6th Cavalry in camp on Mexican border during Geronimo campaign.
(Courtesy Arizona Historical Society/Tucson, Photo # 19521.)

Victorio.
(Courtesy Arizona Historical Society/Tucson, Photo # 19748.)

FIVE

The Crawford Affair, 1885–1886

✝

Mexico learned of the May 17 Apache outbreak the following day. San Carlos's agent telegraphed Sonora's governor Luis Torres on May 18 to advise him that Geronimo had left the day before with fifty men, and was heading south. Chihuahua's governor Carlos Fuero took precautions, informing Díaz on May 19 that it was true that Indians had escaped from San Carlos. Only the week before, Fuero had complained to Díaz that he had only about two hundred soldiers on the frontier. Fuero asked for, and received, two squadrons of the Mexican Eleventh Cavalry to protect border towns.[1]

Torres received another telegraph from Tucson advising him that one hundred Indians were headed for Sonora. Torres immediately alerted the frontier districts and Mexico City. That same night, he asked for help from the federal government, General Fuero in Chihuahua, and General Hipólito Charles, commander of the Gendarmería Fiscal. In addition, Torres requested that Mexico's Tucson consul ask Arizona's governor to send troops in pursuit. Torres also asked the Indian agent at San Carlos to relay any information on the flight of the Apaches and their pursuit by the United States.

Torres advised Carbó on May 22 that he had received word that a large number of United States troops and scouts were pursuing the Apaches, hoping to catch them before they reached Sonora. Torres was disappointed, though, when he received a report that the United States troops had lost the trail and were hoping to intercept the renegades on their return from Mexico. Although Sonora's officials had hoped United States forces would capture the Apaches before they entered Mexico, the Mexicans remained vigilant after receiving the first news of the outbreak. Cooperative in the face of danger, Torres relayed information to General Carbó, even sending a Sonora map so that Carbó could better comprehend telegrams published in *La Constitución* regarding hostile Apaches.[2]

Although Torres and Carbó aided one another during the Apache campaign, Carbó lacked cooperation from his quarreling generals. On May 20, 1885, Carbó complained to President Díaz, on his rebound as president after the González interim. Carbó alleged that generals Topete and García hated each other and were unable to work together. Torres asked Díaz to separate them; because they spent so much time complaining about each other's conduct, the Indians defeated them. In addition to having problems with officers' jealousies, Torres and Carbó lacked troops. General Fuero offered his Chihuahua forces, but as late as May 22, Torres still had received no reply from Mexico City to his request for aid. Sonora requested that arms and munitions destined for the Apache war be admitted duty free.[3]

Instead of sending arms, Díaz told Carbó he would order several dynamite cannons from New York. President Díaz claimed that the cannon supposedly killed without causing wounds, which would arouse fear among the Indians. Díaz promised to send Carbó one if it worked.[4] The cannon was an intriguing idea; however, Sonora's officials wanted men and ammunition.

On July 21, instead of receiving additional troops from Mexico City, Torres learned that the secretary of war had ordered Sonora to continue loaning forces to the federal government. Torres informed Carbó that National Guard forces would be sent to the frontier to serve in the Apache war in lieu of federal troops. The prefects of Sonora's Sahuaripa, Arizpe, and Moctezuma districts were ordered to organize National Guards, with Arizpe's prefect leading a force of two hundred men that he had personally organized. Carbó told Díaz he hoped the National Guard would at least be able to end robberies and murders while he awaited the arrival of the Mexican Eleventh Regiment.[5]

As late as June 25, Torres complained to Carbó that the Eleventh Regiment still had not left Parral for the Indian campaign. Meanwhile, Apaches passed through Arizpe and Moctezuma districts on their way to the Sierra Madre. The renegades did not kill anyone or steal anything during their passage, prompting Torres to call this conduct remarkable. While admitting that the incident was notable, Torres said he had no great hopes that the Apaches wanted to be friends, and he feared their inevitable return after they had left their families in a secure mountain hideout.[6]

Carbó's fears were aggravated by the continuing Yaqui-Mayo uprising. The Apache campaign was more urgent than the Yaqui war, however, and both auxiliary forces and the Eleventh Regiment were sent to the frontier. Secretary of War Pedro Hinojosa told Carbó he was confident that, if this measure did not lead to extermination of the Apaches, at least they would be forced to retreat to the United States. Hinojosa hoped to exterminate the Apaches, confiding to Carbó, "I hope, as you do, that soon these savage hordes will be entirely destroyed."[7]

Extermination of Apaches was hoped for during this era because, according to Sonoran politician Ramón Corral and others, they lacked the desirable qualities of other Indians. Corral said they had always been nomadic, existing primarily by raiding, forming no permanent settlements, and having no occupations. Corral concluded, however, that the Chiricahuas, although responsible for much of the raiding, were far from savage. Many spoke both Spanish and English, wore clothing manufactured in the United States, and used Remington and Winchester firearms.[8]

In order to fight their formidable enemy, the Eleventh Regiment, with 366 men, reached the frontier in August. When Díaz suggested moving the regiment to Sonora's Yaqui war that same month, Carbó requested that additional infantry be sent first so that frontier towns would not be left unprotected. Secretary of War Hinojosa wanted to send Carbó state auxiliary infantry and cavalry then in federal service, while moving the Eleventh Regiment to the Yaqui campaign. Díaz assured Carbó that he would consult him before moving troops and promised not to move the Eleventh Regiment until the infantry arrived. When Torres disagreed with Carbó's use of troops, Díaz sided with Carbó. Torres complained to Díaz that Carbó retired troops from the Yaqui River because of rain, thereby losing the advantage. Díaz replied, however, that he agreed forces should not be moved during the rainy season because of poor roads and the threat of yellow fever.[9]

The Yaqui war continued to make Sonora's fight against Apaches difficult. In June, however, Torres optimistically advised Díaz that the Yaquis wanted peace, adding that he was confident it would not be difficult to defeat Yaqui chieftain Cajeme. Meanwhile, troops needed for the Apache campaign continued to be diverted to the Yaqui war. In July, Díaz offered to send Carbó forces that had been destined for the Yaqui campaign, but never sent because fighting had been suspended due to rain and the threat of yellow fever. Carbó thanked Díaz, but reported that the Yaquis were in such a disadvantageous position that they might surrender without the necessity of a formal campaign.[10]

Both Torres and Carbó underestimated Yaqui resistance, and Sonora continued to fight both Apaches and Yaquis, making distribution of troops difficult. Sonora's *La Constitución* reported that the entire frontier was being invaded by many parties of Indians. Because Apaches traveled so fast, precise news of their movement was difficult to obtain. In June, however, they left a sick Apache woman in Moctezuma, and two American miners in Sonora were reported killed by Indians. As additional proof of Apache presence, on July 4 Torres sent Carbó a report from the Ures prefect stating that three Americans had died at the hands of about nine Indians near Moctezuma. In August, *La Constitución* listed three Americans and one Mexican killed in a battle with Apaches in Arizpe District. In October, four more Americans were attacked by Indians in Sonora, and Chihuahua's governor reported the murder of additional United States citizens.[11]

Although both countries suffered from raids, Mexico continued to blame the United States for the Apache menace, even suggesting that the Indians were armed by United States authorities. Lieutenant General Philip H. Sheridan denied these insinuations and the idea that Geronimo had fled San Carlos with Crook's acquiescence. Believing the hostile Apaches to be escapees from the reservation, Sonora's governor inquired whether Mexico could ask the United States for reparation. The Foreign Relations Ministry responded that restitution was a delicate matter because the United States abrogated responsibility for preventing raids into Mexico with the Gadsden Treaty, and a mixed commission had previously rejected all such damage claims.[12]

Although Mexico hoped the United States would defeat the renegades, it was exasperated by the Americans' failure to kill or capture the Chiricahuas. Fearing the United States would not inform him of Apache movements, and distrustful of American officials, Torres continued retaining José M. Montoya, Mexico's secret agent at the San Carlos reservation.

In August 1885, Montoya wrote Torres from San Carlos, reporting that General Crook had created border observation points to prevent renegades from crossing back into Arizona undetected. In spite of these precautions, hostiles crossed back into Arizona, committing murders. Montoya said Crook had troops from the Fourth and Tenth Cavalry, aided by Indian scouts, stationed at various points with orders to look for hostiles. Approximately three thousand soldiers, three-fourths of them cavalry, patrolled the border. In addition, Crook established his headquarters at Fort Bowie, located in strategic Apache Pass in the northern Chiricahua Mountains.[13]

Such efforts proved unsuccessful, however, prompting Matías Romero, head of Mexico's legation in the United States, to ask Sheridan why Ameri-

can troops could not capture Geronimo's band of fewer than thirty warriors. Sheridan emphasized difficulties of the campaign, such as each Indian's possession of three horses, which enabled him to cover more than
seventy-five miles a day. After Sheridan detailed measures the United States
was taking against Geronimo and his band, Romero advised the Foreign
Relations Ministry that, in the end, the United States would defeat the
Chiricahuas.[14]

Defending America's considerable efforts in the 1885 Geronimo campaign, Sheridan reported that Captain Emmet Crawford crossed the border on June 11 and was operating in Sonora with 150 men, consisting of a
Sixth Cavalry troop and 92 Indian scouts. Meanwhile, Captain Wirt Davis,
Fourth Cavalry, operated in Chihuahua with two companies of scouts,
numbering about one hundred men, and a Fourth Cavalry unit.[15]

Mexico's El Paso consul complained that Chato, who was responsible for
crimes in Mexico and might fight again, was leading Davis's scouts. He sent
the Foreign Relations Ministry a clipping from the *El Paso Daily Times*
dated September 8, 1885, in which Davis said he had stopped pursuit because he overtook a Mexican force, had no more food, and some of his men
were sick. El Paso's consul asked the Foreign Relations Ministry for a copy
of the reciprocal agreement or *convenio*, because he was uncertain whether
troops crossing borders were allowed under its terms to take prisoners back
with them. The Foreign Relations Ministry replied that the consul should
read the agreement.[16]

In spite of complaints about United States scout and reservation policy,
Díaz told Carbó in October 1885 that he was optimistic about the outcome
of the Apache campaign, having been kept constantly briefed by Secretary
of War Hinojosa. Later that month, Díaz was grieved to learn that Carbó
had died unexpectedly of a cerebral hemorrhage. Díaz assured Torres he
would appoint one of the governor's friends to replace Carbó as commander of the First Military Zone, adding the situation was not urgent
because General Marcos Carrillo was to be in charge of federal forces
during the interim.[17]

Mexico and the United States remained optimistic that they would eventually defeat the hostiles by working together. The 1882 reciprocal crossing
agreement was renewed for another year at America's request. While both
nations agreed to cooperate in the Indian campaign, distrust persisted on
both sides. Romero advised the Foreign Relations Ministry in December
that Sheridan believed Apaches were protected in Casas Grandes, Chihuahua, and in Sonora, even alleging that Mexico had established a type of
reservation for the renegades. Mexico denied this allegation, saying hostiles

were imprisoned in Casas Grandes pending transfer to Mexico City, and Sheridan admitted that his belief was probably based on a rumor.[18]

Mexico also heard rumors, one declaring Geronimo had been killed. Geronimo, however, was very much alive, having returned to his United States reservation in October for two women and weapons before crossing back into Mexico. According to the son of Lieutenant Charles B. Gatewood, "there were weeks and months when none of the troops anywhere at any place had the slightest idea as to the location or approximate location of the hostiles." In fact, Gatewood's son maintained, Geronimo and the other hostiles were not "madly running around searching for cover."[19]

With limited success, both the United States and Mexico continued the Apache campaign. Late in November 1885, Captain Crawford reentered Mexico to continue the chase. Crawford's troops differed from previous forces, consisting of four officers, an interpreter, and nearly one hundred Indian scouts. Mexico's secret San Carlos agent Montoya told Torres that most United States forces in Sonora were scouts, with the officers, a few white soldiers, and the remaining troops stationed on the border. Torres had no faith in United States scouts, alleging that Indian scouts turned United States troops away each time they neared the enemy.[20] An international incident involving Crawford's scouts would soon make Crook's policy of using Indian scouts unpopular in the United States, also.

Crawford's force pursued the Chiricahuas some two hundred miles into Mexico and, after an eighteen-hour march, located the hostile camp at Teópar, some forty miles southeast of Nácori Chico, Sonora, on January 10, 1886. Shipp, commander of one of the scout companies, recalled a successful attack "seemed almost assured" until mules alerted the hostiles to the danger. The scouts scattered and "allowed themselves to be held in check by the fire of the hostiles." Shipp remembered, "It was impossible for us to tell friends from foes." He called the scouts' behavior disappointing, saying "soldiers in the place of scouts would have behaved much better."[21]

From what I saw of the Chiricahua scouts on this occasion, and subsequently when we had talks with the Indians, I am satisfied that, though they fired a good many shots, yet they had little desire to kill, in spite of their wish to see the war ended by the surrender of the renegades. These men worked too hard and were too faithful under temptation to give any reason to suspect them of treachery. But it does not seem unreasonable to believe that they did not strongly desire the death of people belonging to their own tribe. They had not only been their friends, but some were relatives. Moreover, in their eyes the hostiles had committed no crime, for they themselves had likewise been on the warpath. They wanted peace, but not at the expense of much bloodshed.[22]

Although the hostiles escaped, Crawford's men captured the camp, and the Apaches agreed to meet for a talk the next day. First Lieutenant Marion P. Maus said later that because the Chiricahuas had no supplies, "had this talk taken place, I believe most of the band would have surrendered." Crook concurred, saying Crawford was the only man besides himself who could have obtained the surrender of the bands of Geronimo and Naiche.[23]

The meeting never took place. The following morning at dawn Chihuahua irregulars, a group of citizens who were not regular troops, attacked the American camp, mistaking the United States forces for the enemy, and a fight ensued. Crawford was fatally shot.

After Crawford fell, the scouts returned fire, the volley continuing for several minutes. The Mexicans lost their commander, Mauricio Corredor, and three others in the fight. Spanish interpreter Tom Horn received a wound, as did three scouts. Shipp recalled "that the hostiles were spectators during our fight with the Mexicans. How they must have enjoyed it!"[24]

This unfortunate incident, resulting in deaths on both sides, led to a thorough investigation in both countries. Shipp lamented the "strange mischance that caused these two commands to meet at this particular time. . . . Either might have done good work but for the presence of the other." This lamentable affair not only caused the deaths of valuable officers; it prolonged the campaign for eight more months. Shipp commented that given the number of people killed and the property losses after January, "We can realize that the importance of that little fight is not to be measured by the number of slain."[25]

Shipp and Maus agreed that the first firing was probably a mistake because of a heavy fog. Both claimed, however, that the second firing, which killed Crawford, could not have been in error. They recalled that at the battle onset Horn, Maus, and Shipp declared in Spanish that the forces were American. Crawford fully exposed himself in broad daylight, waving a white handkerchief. They estimated that the Mexican firing the single fatal shot was only twenty-eight paces from Crawford, adding "the Captain had a brown beard and wore his uniform, so that he looked altogether unlike an Indian." Maus agreed with Shipp's assessment, saying that when Crawford advanced after the initial firing, "I am sure that they knew who we were perfectly well at this time. Lieutenant Shipp and Mr. Horn were

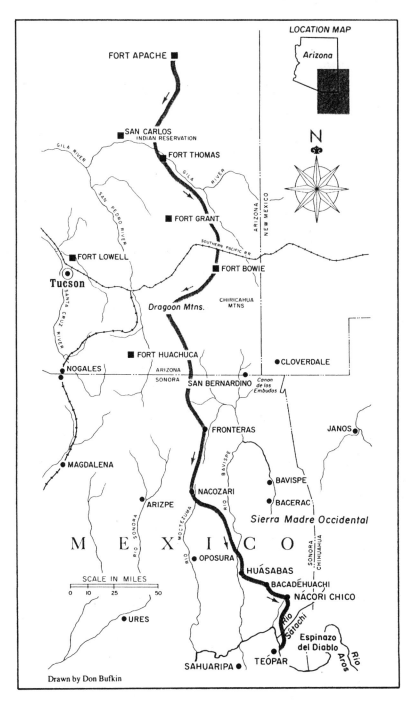

Map 2. The Death of Emmet Crawford
(Courtesy Arizona Historical Society/Tucson, Don Bufkin map.)

also shouting at another point, telling whom we were — that all was right. Mr. Horn speaks Spanish very well."[26]

The Mexicans also yelled, "no tiras, no tiras," or "do not fire," but all were powerless to stop the shooting. Matías Romero attempted to explain the tragedy:

> As the volunteers of Chihuahua were not regular troops, they were, therefore, not under strictest discipline, and accordingly the orders of their officers to stop firing when Captain Crawford proposed its cessation were not obeyed, as neither were those of Lieutenant Maus obeyed by the Indian scouts of the United States Army in regard to the cessation of their firing, as stated by him in his said report.[27]

After an initial denial, Mexico later admitted to the second firing, which killed Crawford and Corredor. Despite the Americans' protests, Romero believed the Chihuahua forces were not persuaded that Crawford's men were United States troops until after the second volley, and perhaps not until the following day.[28]

Although Mexico called the attack a mistake, Shipp suspected that the Mexicans hoped to overpower and plunder the Americans. As proof he cited the fact that Maus and the Apache interpreter Concepción Aguirre, a Mexican, were detained on the twelfth and forced to ransom themselves with six mules, "all marked U.S."[29] Mexico accused the scouts of possessing stolen Mexican stock and claimed the Chihuahua volunteers needed animals to transport their wounded. Romero discounted robbery as a motive for the attack, saying that the Chihuahua troops organized to defeat the hostiles, having no reason to fight United States troops, "unless on the hypothesis that the Mexicans had wholly lost their reason."[30]

A San Francisco dispatch dated January 28 said that Major General Pope believed the Chihuahua volunteers mistook — perhaps wishfully — the United States force for hostiles, hoping to gain Sonora's scalp bounty.[31] Extermination was rejected in the United States, but it was official policy in some Mexican border states, though never a federal policy.

An official Chihuahua newspaper suggested in 1881 that dispersement or extermination continued to be the only viable Apache solution because reservations were counterproductive. An American visitor to Chihuahua in 1883 reported that bounties were still being paid, both for scalps and prisoners.[32]

Romero discounts the theory that the Chihuahua volunteers planned to turn the Indian scouts over to the state government for a reward, saying compensation was paid for hostiles only, "and the Indian scouts are not in the category of wild Indians, as they form part of the troops of the United States." The desire to collect a scalp bounty does seem to have been a viable motive for the attack, however, because the reward was paid for any scalp, adult or child, male or female. Also, this was the only compensation the Chihuahua volunteers could receive, "since they were paid no allowance as soldiers, nor rations, or any other compensation."[33]

Not only did the Chihuahua force lack compensation; Maus says they claimed to be without food and transportation as well. Unable to spare rations for the Mexicans, Maus consented to loan them some captured horses. The United States War Department said the charge that Americans possessed livestock recently "stolen in the district is explained by the fact that the hostile Indians had just fled, leaving behind them their animals and camp equipage." Maus admitted that "the scouts had selected the worst [horses to give the Mexicans], and they were not serviceable." The scouts considered the captured horses their property, refusing to give the Mexicans better animals. Maus concluded, "It was considered best not to insist on their being sent."[34] Maus's decision prompted Secretary of Foreign Relations Ignacio Mariscal to ask the United States: "Does not this seem like connivance on the part of Lieutenant Maus with the Apache Indians — his permitting them to retain in their possession property stolen on Mexican territory?"[35]

When Maus did not force the scouts to relinquish the Mexican horses, the Chihuahua volunteers demanded mules to transport their wounded. Maus requested and obtained a receipt for the six mules given under duress, and the American camp was moved on January 13. Maus recalled: "I took all precautions to prevent any trouble from the Mexicans when leaving, as I believed they would attack us if they were sure of success." Describing the Mexicans as "a hard-looking crowd," Maus called "their manner . . . threatening," and his "position . . . indeed helpless," all the more so since he had no identification papers with him, having left them with his pack train. Maus did produce a letter from Sahuaripa's prefect addressed to Crawford, but to little effect.[36]

Although Maus feared another incident, the Mexicans wanted no more trouble. The Chihuahua volunteers were weary, without food, and their wounded needed medical attention. At the Mexicans' request, Maus ordered his doctor to treat the four wounded Mexicans. Both sides then exchanged papers claiming the attack was a mistake.[37]

Shipp argued with critics, both military and civilian, "who seem to think all we had to do was to attack the Mexicans in their position and avenge Crawford's death."[38] Maus agreed that the United States force had no alternative, saying:

> Our position at this time, confronted as we were by a hostile Mexican force, while behind us was the entire hostile band of Indians evidently enjoying the situation, is probably unparalleled. We had scarcely any ammunition, no food and our supplies were with the pack-train almost unprotected.[39]

Parting from the Mexicans without further incident, Maus resumed negotiations with Geronimo, resulting in the surrender of nine of his band as hostages. Nana and one other warrior agreed to return to the reservation, along with the wife and child of both Naiche and Geronimo and Geronimo's sister. Maus reported that the remaining warriors included twenty-two hostiles, comprising chiefs Naiche, Geronimo, and Chihuahua. The chiefs told Maus they would meet Crook in "two moons" near the border at San Bernardino. Observing "they had scarcely anything, and are poor and miserable," Maus told Crook he thought they would surrender. After the Chiricahuas promised to meet Crook, Maus headed home, burying Crawford at Nácori Chico on the way. On February 1, the United States forces reached the border.[40]

Crawford was considered a martyr by the United States and his death initially created a great deal of animosity in the United States toward Mexico, causing "some talk of war upon that country." In April, Tucson's *Arizona Star* called Crawford's killing premeditated, intentional murder, and in May the *Los Angeles Times* said the United States consul in El Paso del Norte was convinced the attack was "maliciously and knowingly made."[41]

Correspondent Charles Lummis reported in the May 9, 1886, *Los Angeles Times* that the United States contingent "was attacked by a Mexican force for the apparent purpose of robbery. . . . When they were whipped and driven back, they suddenly discovered that it was a 'mistake.'" Lummis concluded that the "damning facts," indicated that Crawford "was shot down in absolute wantonness" by "those Mexican semi-military banditti." The Los Angeles correspondent mentioned as precedents of Mexican misconduct the brief jailing in Mexico of Lieutenant Elliott during the summer of 1885 and Lieutenant McDonald's four-day incarceration with eighteen scouts in Casas Grandes during 1882.[42]

The Eastern press was slower to blame Mexico. On January 29, the *New*

York Times speculated that "the Mexican soldiers' terrible mistake may have been due to the employment of Indians by Crawford and their presence among the forces commanded by him." The *Times* blamed the United States reservation policy and lack of cooperation between troops of both nations for the "accidental and deplorable encounter" in Sonora. After declaring the Mexican government blameless in the affair, the New York paper demanded that Mexico either disprove the statements made by Maus, Shipp, and Horn, or else punish those responsible for Crawford's death.[43]

Faced with public outcry, on February 15, 1886, the United States demanded a full inquiry into the Crawford affair. Henry Jackson, United States consul in Mexico City, wrote Secretary of Foreign Relations Mariscal the following accusation:

> From the report of Lieutenant Maus, it would seem that the second volley fired by the Mexicans in broad daylight, after the conference had been held in the open field, when the nationality and friendly mission of Captain Crawford's party had been plainly announced, and the white signal of the parley had been displayed, was not simply inexcusable, but was an act of grievous wrong.

Several days later, Mariscal informed the United States legation that Mexico already knew of the incident and that the Mexican Foreign Relations Ministry was collecting all data necessary for an investigation.[44]

As late as April 10, however, Chihuahua's governor Félix Francisco Maceyra wrote Díaz, asking for information on Crawford's death in order to refute Maus's report. Three days later, the United States legation sent Mariscal Maus's report, saying "the treatment of Lieutenant Maus and the interpreter by the Mexicans was a gross violation of treaty stipulations," adding that it was Mexico's "duty to inflict punishment on such offenders and make proper reparation." In spite of United States admonishment, more than a week later Mexico still had not made an official statement regarding the Crawford affair.[45]

Mexico's only official statement continued to be Díaz's April 1 message to Congress. Accusing United States papers of distorting the encounter, Díaz said the matter was still under investigation. Díaz added, however, that he believed the Mexican troops mistook the American force for hostiles, because they were following the renegades and their stolen cattle. He concluded that the Mexicans always thought the American scouts were hostiles, because they knew that only regular troops could cross the border under the reciprocal agreement.[46]

Though denying responsibility for the incident, in February Mexico City ordered Chihuahua's district attorney to conduct an in-depth investigation. On May 19, 1886, Mexico furnished the United States with the results, based on eyewitness accounts by Second Lieutenant Santana Pérez and others. Pérez maintained that his 128 men were on the hostiles' trail when they encountered Crawford's camp, mistaking his scouts for renegade Apaches. He admitted that he "is not certain whether his companions fired before the enemy did so, because the volleys were simultaneous."[47]

According to Mariscal, the encounter took place on the very spot "where Nana had fixed his ranchería, where Chief Geronimo also was and whence he fled — a place well known as a point of assembly for Indians upon the warpath." He alleged that Crawford's scouts had been raiding, "another reason why anyone might have mistaken Crawford's force for a band of hostile Apaches." In addition, the Mexicans stated "that the Americans had with them no military insignia whatever," and the Apache scouts "were nearly naked." They added "that the Americans also wore moccasins." It was true that the United States officers wore moccasins, but Crawford had been wearing his full uniform when shot, although Maus only wore an officers's overcoat.[48]

Pérez claimed that "in the American camp were found animals stolen by the Indians upon national [Mexican] territory" and alleged that scouts had stolen stock at three places in Sonora, killing an American at Las Varas and three people at Dolores. Mariscal complained: "Maus promised to return to the Mexicans the mules stolen by the Apaches at the mining town of Dolores; that he failed to do so, and said mules were found killed, the brands having been cut out." Because the animals were Mexican, Mariscal reasoned that Pérez was justified in demanding other mules to transport their wounded. However, both Maus and Shipp stated that the mules requisitioned by the Mexicans were clearly marked United States property. Probably concurring on this point, Mexico later agreed to either return the mules and other property taken, or to fully compensate the United States.[49]

Although willing to compensate the United States for the mules, Mexico refused to accept blame for Crawford's death, Mariscal even suggesting he might have been intentionally or unintentionally shot by his own scouts. Víctor Mendoza postulates that Geronimo's band infiltrated the scout camp the night before the shooting. There is also a *corrido*, or ballad, from Chihuahua claiming these hostiles shot Mexico's commander Mauricio Corredor in revenge for his killing Apache warrior Victorio at Tres Castillos.[50]

Accused by the Mexicans of shooting Corredor, interpreter Tom Horn emphatically denied the charge, saying their accusation only proved that the Mexicans recognized him when they shot him. The assailant remained unknown, prompting Mariscal to ask who could have foreseen that "through an accidental and unforeseen circumstance, which in all respects is lamentable, the heroic Mauricio Corredor would be killed by a force of Indians under the command of American officers?" Mariscal added that the United States must deplore the death of Corredor just as Mexico deplored Crawford's.[51]

While calling the incident an unfortunate mistake, Mexico asserted that the United States was at fault for employing Indian scouts in clear violation of the reciprocal crossing agreement, which specified that only regular federal troops could cross the border in pursuit of hostiles. The United States replied that Indian scouts were a "regularly enlisted, paid, armed, and commanded" part of the United States Army. Mariscal argued that in international law regular federal troops refers to troops of the permanent, standing army, and not to troops organized for temporary service.[52]

The United States defended the use of scouts because "the broken country and uninhabited regions along the boundaries of the two countries made the movement of regular troops practically futile against such hostile fugitive Indians." The United States then asked if Mexico objected to Indian scouts, why this objection had not been brought up when the agreement was twice renewed, "notwithstanding the fact that the employment of Indian scouts in the frontier service of the United States Army would, at least, seem to have been notorious."[53] Mariscal replied, saying:

Had it been suspected that the selfsame savages who, after escaping from their reservations, or in any other manner, came to Mexico there to commit their crimes, should be considered as soldiers of the Regular Army of the United States, without their even changing their habits or dress — they would clearly have been in most positive terms excluded from such permission, which does exclude even the State militia or United States Volunteers solely on account of their being less disciplined.

He said the Chihuahua force had reason to believe it was in pursuit of the enemy because it could not possibly have imagined that "two or three hundred armed Indians in the guise of American soldiers would cross our frontier."[54] Mexico may have decided to complain about the American scouts in order to absolve the Chihuahua volunteers of responsibility for Crawford's death.

However, not only Mexico complained about United States scouts. Tucson's *El Fronterizo* claimed Apache scouts caused more trouble in Sonora than did openly hostile Indians. Accusing scouts of numerous depredations in Sonora's Moctezuma District, Mexico warned the United States that an indemnity for damages would be requested. In March, Secretary of War Hinojosa appointed General Crispín de S. Palomares to investigate the charges; in May he filed a seventy-eight page report listing crimes committed by Crawford's scouts in Sonora.[55]

Moctezuma's prefect reported disorders committed by scouts "in a state of drunkenness" in late December 1885. According to one citizen, the scouts committed disturbances such as "forcing their way into houses, especially into those where women were alone, and taking from them what they wanted." Second Lieutenant Britton Davis confirmed that drunkenness was a problem, complaining that Mexicans sold mescal to the scouts.[56]

Scouts were allegedly so disorderly in Huásabas on December 23 that local authorities requested protection from Rurales Captain Emilio Kosterlitzky, who happened to be in town. After being attacked, Kosterlitzky wounded one Indian and imprisoned another. Maus promised to pay a five-dollar fine for the scout's release. As proof that scouts committed the depredations, Sonora's *La Constitución* cited the fact that they occurred on the day Crawford's force passed through town, a day when there had been no notice of hostile Apaches.[57]

Chihuahua's governor claimed that scouts conducted themselves well only when supervised by officers, committing depredations when out of sight on the pretext of scouting or discovering a trail. Others reported that the "so-called 'tame' Indians" shot cattle without being restrained by their commanding officers. There is evidence that officers were afraid to chastise the scouts for misdeeds.[58]

Davis admitted one incident that occurred when scouts, believing one of their number to have been killed by a Mexican, were caught "'taking it out' on the Mexican cattle. They must have killed a score or two, but we thought it best not to interfere. A hundred dollars would cover the damage." One American residing in Sonora accused scouts of shooting cattle not to eat, "but from a natural inclination to destroy." Another Sonora citizen claimed only two of the cattle "were cut up for beef, the rest being left untouched" to spoil on the ground. Sonora reported that Crawford's scouts had killed seventeen head of cattle worth more than twenty dollars a head.[59]

Before killing cattle, Crawford's scouts allegedly camped for four days on the cornfield without permission. During that time, they allowed their cattle to eat the entire corn crop, and they destroyed the farmer's fences for firewood. In addition, another farmer accused them of stealing about one thousand sugarcane plants from a neighboring field. When asked to reimburse the owners, Crawford promised to pay, but as of March no payment had been received.[60]

Stating that the commission of the "aforesaid depredations" made it natural for the authorities "to confound said force with hostile Apaches," General de S. Palomares concluded that Pérez's forces "did not thereby commit any imprudent or punishable act; that the death of Captain Crawford was the result of a simple error."[61]

While Mexico and the United States continued to blame each other for the Crawford incident, Maus resumed negotiations with the hostiles, obtaining Geronimo's promise to meet with Crook in "two moons'" time. Geronimo kept his word, meeting Crook on March 25 and 27 at El Cañon de los Embudos, Sonora, near the Chihuahua border and twenty miles south of the United States. Crook told Geronimo and the others "they must decide at once upon unconditional surrender or fight it out." The renegades replied they wanted either to return to their old reservation status or be sent east with their families for not more than two years. Because he had to act immediately, Crook accepted this latter proposition, a proposal quickly rejected by the president, who would agree to nothing but unconditional surrender.[62]

SIX

The Beginning of the End, 1886

We were reckless of our lives, because we felt that every man's hand was against us. If we returned to the reservation we would be put in prison and killed; if we stayed in Mexico they would continue to send soldiers to fight us.

GERONIMO RECALLING HIS DESPERATE WAR

Geronimo and Naiche headed back into Mexico with twenty men and thirteen women followers on March 29. Britton Davis blamed Geronimo's flight on Tribolet, an American living nearby who sold mescal to both scouts and hostiles, saying the Apaches had fled because they were drunk. Chief Packer H. W. Daly blamed Crook for Geronimo's departure, claiming the band would not have left if the general had escorted them back to the United States. Instead, Crook had returned alone to Ft. Bowie immediately after meeting Geronimo and his followers in Sonora on March 25 and 27. Daly also accused Crook of favoring Chihuahua in the conferences, causing Geronimo and Naiche to become jealous. Chihuahua and twelve men remained in the camp, while Maus and his scouts gave chase.[1]

Geronimo's final flight prompted historian Hubert Howe Bancroft to write that "this misfortune, or blunder, brought upon Crook a storm of abuse." Lieutenant General Sheridan, greatly disappointed at Geronimo's escape, expressed surprise that the hostiles had fled without the scouts' knowledge. On April 1, Sheridan suggested that, since the offensive campaign with scouts had failed, it would be better to give defensive protection to Arizona and New Mexico. Sheridan made it clear to Crook that he "would not permit that the service of the troops should be made secondary to that of scouts."[2]

Crook replied that another offensive could only be undertaken with the help of Indian scouts. Defending his scouts, Crook asked to be relieved of his command. Although Crawford's death had created a storm of criticism over Crook's use of scouts, it was probably Geronimo's betrayal that prompted Sheridan to accept Crook's resignation. On April 2, Sheridan replaced Crook with Brigadier General Nelson A. Miles, who opted for a policy midway between those of Crook and Sheridan.

According to Matías Romero, head of Mexico's United States legation, Miles's appointment caused jealousy within the War Department because Miles was not a West Point graduate. Romero claimed that the president's influence was decisive in giving Miles command of the entire frontier.[3] While Miles might have had enemies in the United States, Mexico was relieved to have Crook ousted, and hoped for a new policy no longer based on extensive use of scouts.

Miles initiated a defensive policy as Sheridan suggested, protecting vulnerable water holes and ranches. At the same time, however, he planned an offensive war using regular troops. Although Davis reported Miles's dismissal of the majority of the scouts except for a few guides, Mexican sources claimed that significant numbers of scouts continued to operate in Mexico in conjunction with regular troops.[4] Miles also devised a system of heliostatic signaling using mirrors to reflect sun rays, "the Army counterpart of Apache smoke signals," enabling troops to communicate rapidly over much of Arizona and New Mexico.[5]

In spite of these measures, however, governor of Sonora Luis Torres complained to Sonoran Ramón Corral that, although United States forces were everywhere, the Apaches continued raiding undisturbed. Geronimo, whose family was murdered in Mexico, recalled his war in Mexico as follows: "On our return through Old Mexico we attacked every Mexican found, even if for no other reason than to kill. We believed they had asked the U.S. troops to come down to Mexico to fight us."[6] During April, while "pursued constantly by various commands in futile efforts to destroy or capture them" the hostiles returned to Arizona to raid before escaping back into Sonora. Sonora feared that the Apaches would continue raiding the state, especially with the vigorous American campaign driving them south.[7]

Although Díaz received a rumor that American border troops gave arms to Apaches for Mexican raids, he realized that the United States wanted to end hostilities on both sides of the border, especially since American citizens continued to be killed by Apaches in both countries. American miners in Sonora were especially vulnerable to Indian raids.[8]

Determined to end these crimes, Miles agreed with Crook that an aggressive campaign must continue. Saying his plan was to wear the Chiricahuas out eventually, on May 5 Miles ordered Captain Henry W. Lawton, Fourth Cavalry, to Mexico to take up the chase. The expedition, formed at Fort Huachuca, consisted of the thirty-five men in Lawton's Fourth Cavalry troop, twenty infantrymen from the Eighth Regiment, twenty Indian scouts, and one hundred pack mules with thirty packers. This was a small force when compared with the total United States army numbering 26,254 men in 1886, but troop skills not numbers were the most important factor in Lawton's campaign. "Five days in the mountains of northern Sonora finished the mounted cavalry," forcing Lawton to rely on the infantry.[9]

Lawton described the caliber of infantrymen needed to defeat the Apaches:

> Believe we can yet come up with hostiles and meet them successfully, but I *must* have *good strong* men who believe in [the] possibility of success and officers willing to sustain a few hardships and set [a] cheerful example. [I] want officers who can *walk*. Inds. have respect only for absolute authority, endurance and strength. I must have an officer who can climb a mountain or run on a trail with them, who is not dependent upon a *mule* to carry him over rough ground. With the Infty the example of the officer in command *riding* while his men are marching is absolutely damaging, and I would prefer no officer at all. In writing [the] above I do *not in any way* mean to reflect on any officer now with me — they have all done their duty cheerfully and well. If the hostile Inds. are overcome it must be by *hard* and *continued* labor content with much hardship and self denial, and only men of character and physical strength are fit for such work — and to send any others is only to assure failure.[10]

Lawton's plea went unheeded, however, and two months later he complained that although he had requested good men, he received the "worst ones," some being sent to him for punishment. He finally sent word to Miles that he wanted no more infantrymen because "he might as well try to hunt Indians with a brass band."[11]

Lawton also requested that no more guides and scouts be sent, saying "they make trouble and I don't want them." Confirming Mexican complaints about scouts, Lawton admitted that he had problems with scouts "getting drunk, selling ammunition and being insubordinate," adding that he would "send to Huachuca any so bad I can't get along with." In spite of such difficulties, Lawton said, "generally speaking, we are in first rate condition, and I hope soon in shape to start work in earnest."[12]

Having received previous communication from Miles, Torres was relieved to know that the United States would soon begin an aggressive campaign. On May 4 Torres wrote Miles:

Our state troops have orders to act in perfect accord with yours in pursuit of savage hostiles who seem now boldest and most decided to fight than ever. Please inform me what I can do to help you as I think that this time not a moment respite can be given to them or fatal results will come.

That same day, Miles telegraphed Torres: "Our mutual efforts may bring peace and protection to the people of both countries."[13]

The following day, Mexico's secretary of interior warned Sonora's governor to advise United States commanders that they were required to inform Mexican officials of their plans. Responding to the governor's cordial manner, Miles continued to advise Torres by telegram of movements of Apaches and United States troops, reporting on May 7 that "at last reports our troops were following [the] hostiles together."[14]

On July 5 Lawton reported to Miles that "Torres has been unusually polite," even offering to go on the campaign with Lawton were it not for his poor health. Instead, Torres offered to place twenty-five or thirty "picked" men under Lawton's command. Lawton liked the idea and asked Miles to authorize rations and transportation for the Mexicans. Unfortunately, several weeks later, Lawton reported that the plan to send Mexican troops with his command could not be carried out because Moctezuma prefect José María Torres, brother of Governor Torres, who was to select the men, had been assassinated by revolutionaries. Lawton's surgeon, Dr. Leonard Wood, reciprocated the Mexicans' goodwill by visiting some of the very ill in Oposura, Sonora, at the prefect's request.[15]

Mexico attempted to aid United States forces, even considering the possibility of transporting American troops in Sonora via Mexican railroad. When Lawton's supplies were delayed in reaching his troops in Sonora, Miles did not hesitate to telegraph Torres requesting assistance. In addition, Lawton described an incident in June when he encountered Major Ruiz and his troops on the trail, recalling: "Maj. Ruiz continued with us and gave us great assistance by his advice and knowledge of the country."[16]

Although willing to cooperate fully with the United States, Mexico was still unable to commit her resources to the Apache war because of the simultaneous campaign against Sonora's Yaquis. When Angel Martínez, commander of the First Military Zone, took the Yaqui fortress of Buatachive in May, Torres informed Díaz that the campaign could be considered closed. But Yaqui chief Cajeme escaped, and the Yaqui war was far from over.[17]

While Mexico was preoccupied with the Yaqui campaign, American troops pursued Chiricahuas in Sonora with little success. Captains Thomas

C. Lebo and Charles A. P. Hatfield did manage to engage the enemy in Sonora during May, but they failed to kill or capture any warriors, while suffering several killed and wounded in their respective commands. After fighting Hatfield's troops, the Chiricahuas separated into two parties and headed north. In early June, the Tucson volunteers chased the Apaches south into Mexico's Patagonia Mountains, where Second Lieutenant R. D. Walsh, Fourth Cavalry, captured their horses and supplies.[18]

On July 14 Lieutenant Brown and his Indian scouts captured more ponies and equipment. Davis cautioned that this meant little to the hostiles, however, because "within a week or ten days they re-equipped themselves through raids on Mexican settlements or American ranches." It was suggested that Apaches "frequently allowed easy 'captures' rather than precipitate a fight which they were not ready for, or considered unnecessary."[19]

After Brown's encounter with the hostiles, Lawton's forces lost the Chiricahuas for a week. Scarcity of water and temperatures over one hundred degrees prompted Dr. Leonard Wood to report on July 14 that these conditions "have broken down a good many men of the command, mostly the older and heavier ones." Wood, who marched on foot with the infantry as their volunteer commander, said poor shoes created another hardship. He added that men should not be over thirty-five and should be in top condition to carry on this kind of campaign.[20]

Lawton complained on July 14 that he had only ten men fit for duty, saying, "I will send in the dead-beats, *sick, lame* and lazy by the wagons." Lawton could not use his cavalry because there was "*absolutely* no grass," and he also lacked meat rations for an extended scout in the mountains. In spite of these difficulties, on July 21, Lawton discovered Geronimo's camp on the Yaqui River, nearly three hundred miles from the border. Capturing only the band's supplies and horses, he lost Geronimo's trail.[21]

Lawton surmised that the Indians, no longer being pursued, may have gone north, "in which case they may be looked for on the reservation." On August 8 Lawton admitted that he had heard nothing of the renegades since July 21 and complained that Sonora's rains were so bad that no trail could be tracked after twelve hours. Lawton suggested using bloodhounds to trail Indians. He did not get discouraged, however, and specifically asked not to be relieved of his command, saying: "I shall do my *best* as I always have done — and *fully believe* I will *kill, capture* or compel Geronimo to surrender."[22]

Lawton's mission was hampered by conflicts with Sonora's citizens. When he was accused of letting his scouts go out alone and of failing to contact a prefect upon his arrival in a district, he denied the charges, saying, "I *always* try to show the Mexican officials *all possible* attention and *cour-*

tesy."[23] Such declarations notwithstanding, Lawton infuriated the Mexicans when he refused to return Mexican horses captured by his scouts in a hostiles' camp.

The scouts had been told they could keep any horses captured in a camp of renegades. After Mexicans claimed the horses, however, Lawton informed the scouts that they would probably have to relinquish them. The scouts protested, saying "they had *always* been given the horses — and referred to Gen'l Crook as having promised them the horses." Faced with this dilemma, on July 31 Lawton requested immediate instructions from Miles, fearing trouble from the Mexicans if he did not acquiesce.[24]

Trouble, in the form of a Mexican complaint, began on August 20. Sonora's Governor Torres and Ramón Corral wrote the Foreign Relations Ministry, forwarding the complaint from Sahuaripa's prefect against Captain Lawton's force, said to consist of 110 Americans and 30 Apache scouts. The prefect claimed he had given Lawton four guides as requested, but then, when he asked Lawton to return five or six stolen animals, Lawton refused. The prefect alleged that Lawton did not return the animals because the scouts refused to relinquish them unless paid ten dollars a head, even threatening to kill the animals next time. Critical of the Americans for taking his district's property, the prefect asked the governor how he should treat United States troops in the future. Torres told the Sahuaripa prefect not to place obstacles in the way of United States troops, but he added that if Americans or scouts committed abuses, to get proof and inform the governor, who would in turn inform the Foreign Relations Ministry.[25]

A month later, that ministry told the War Department that the United States refused to return the Mexican stock taken from the hostiles.[26] The United States Department of State sent confirmation of this refusal on January 4, 1887. The report admitted that three animals did have Mexican brands, but stated that the Mexicans considered the ten dollars a head requested by the scouts as compensation for their trouble justified. Eventually, Lawton claimed, the Mexicans said the animals were not theirs, and he did not hear again from either the Sahuaripa or Moctezuma prefects about the matter.[27]

Not only Mexicans had complaints; United States forces also criticized the Mexicans. Lieutenant James Parker, Fourth Cavalry, alleged that one United States contingent had been kept under surveillance by a Mexican detachment. However, this encounter between forces of the two nations ended cordially, with Mexican troops saluting the American flag as they departed. Parker said he supplied the Mexicans with rations before they left. Still, Parker pointed out that there was an "evident inclination of the

Mexican officials we have hitherto met to interfere with the movements of any small bodies of American troops." Americans remained suspicious, reporting that Mexican troops were following Parker's command for the "purpose of ordering it out of Mexico."[28]

Though Geronimo's surrender appeared to be near, in April 1886 Crook warned Sheridan that "unless this war is ended by the surrender of the hostiles, it is likely to last for years."[29] Unable to defeat the Chiricahuas, by July the United States was convinced that the Apaches might be encouraged to surrender if suitable emissaries could be selected to begin talks. Therefore, Miles chose Lieutenant Charles B. Gatewood and two trusted Chiricahuas to convey United States terms. Geronimo was well acquainted with Gatewood, known to Apaches as the Long Nosed Captain. With Britton Davis having resigned, Crawford dead, and Crook reassigned, Gatewood was the only officer left that Geronimo might trust. The two Apaches accompanying Gatewood, Kayihtah and his cousin Martine, were related to members of Geronimo's band.[30]

By August 1 Gatewood's party, with an escort of about thirty men and twenty-seven days' rations, began its search for renegades. Charged with supplying Gatewood's escort, Lieutenant Parker said, "I shall take great pains to conceal from the Mexicans our present object."[31] Both nations distrusted the other's motives while continuing to express willingness to effect Geronimo's surrender.

Each country hoped to obtain a Chiricahua surrender for itself. Each hoped to be victorious against this seemingly invincible foe. Each side feared the other would make peace with Geronimo, while secretly permitting him to continue raiding across the border. Acting on that fear, Lieutenant Colonel George Forsyth asked a Mexican official if his nation's "terms would include a prohibition against Geronimo raiding into our territories."[32]

Mexico expressed the same concern, based on Matías Romero's 1886 accusation that Brigadier General Oliver O. Howard made an informal agreement, which amounted to a truce, with the Apaches in 1872. This "treaty" allegedly contained an understanding that Cochise and Chiricahua Apaches would be allowed to live at San Carlos as long as they did not raid in the United States. In his 1883 annual report, Crook affirmed that this "so-called treaty was made," which assured Apaches "that in consideration of sparing this Territory their raids into Mexico would not be interfered with by our Government." Though unable to prove his allegation, Romero accused Crook of offering Howard's earlier proposition to the Apaches during his 1883 campaign: allowing the Indians to raid in Mexico for six months before returning to the San Carlos Reservation.[33]

Expressing similar fears, on August 24, 1886, Miles warned Lawton that, rather than surrender, the Apaches might want to make peace with the Mexicans and war against the United States. Miles conceded that it was "possible some Mexicans are concerned in the conspiracy to encourage and excite hostile Indians against our settlements in case of war." He added, "There will probably be no war and every effort shall be made to discover and destroy this conspiracy."[34]

Geronimo and his small band reportedly numbering twenty-five men, sixteen women, and two boys, still had two countries jealous over which could negotiate his surrender. On August 13 the band appeared about fifteen miles south of Fronteras, on the road to Narcosari, Sonora. A "reliable Mexican scout" encountered the hostiles and reported that they had told him "that they did not wish to harm the Mexicans any longer but wished to secure a peaceful home with them so that they might raid in New Mexico and Arizona."[35]

On August 15 Geronimo and his party began to make peace overtures to the Fronteras authorities. Army Packer Daly recalled: "I did not think that Geronimo was seriously considering this, as it would mean their extermination, but that he was secretly endeavoring to procure supplies as well as mescal."[36] On the seventeenth, however, United States forces in Mexico learned that the hostiles were making known a plan to surrender to Mexico's Arizpe District prefect. They informed Miles immediately so that he could take action.[37]

On the eighteenth, Torres informed Miles that he had ordered his forces to obtain the Chiricahuas' unconditional surrender or to attack them, adding that if they did surrender, the band was to be sent to Mexico City. If no terms could be agreed to, Arizpe's prefect was to organize Mexican volunteers to prevent the Indians from heading south. Meanwhile, Torres said it would be a good idea for the United States to send more troops.[38]

The United States responded quickly, sending Forsyth on August 18 to Fronteras with ninety men and ten days of rations. Lawton's command remained nearby. Because of his good relations with Torres, Miles was willing to wait and see if the Apaches surrendered to the Mexicans.[39]

While waiting to see what transpired, First Lieutenant Wilber E. Wilder accidentally noticed two women from Geronimo's band who were purchasing goods in a Fronteras store. Although they tried to avoid him, he managed to talk with them. They admitted that:

the entire party are [*sic*] pretty well broken down; Geronimo is in bad health, nearly blind and badly wounded in [the] right arm, and is nearly helpless. The entire band [is] so harassed by U.S. forces that they see it is only a question of time till they are exterminated unless they make terms.

Wilder told the women Miles's surrender terms, and they seemed pleased. Saying "there was no doubt that [the] band would accept [the] terms," the women offered to guide Wilder and one interpreter to the hostile camp.[40]

Instead, Wilder asked the women to obtain safe conduct for him and two others to visit Geronimo's camp. Wilder then returned to his troops, camped with Forsyth's men, and sent Lawton a message asking whether Lawton or Gatewood should also meet with the hostiles. Meanwhile, the two Indian women remained in town, where they became intoxicated. Two warriors came into Fronteras to look after them, and Lieutenant McDonald wanted to capture all four. The local *jefe político* protested, however, and Forsyth forbid their capture.

The Mexican official then asked the United States officers to remove their troops and keep out of sight, saying that the hostiles would not come so long as the Americans were in sight. Wilder asked to be present at the interview if United States troops agreed to withdraw, but the Mexican "seemed desirous to make terms alone." Meanwhile, Forsyth advised Lawton to wait two days for Geronimo to consider Miles's peace offer, adding "there is no doubt but Geronimo will accept [the] terms offered, possibly to the chagrin of the Mex. official who is a clever, shrewd man." Forsyth added in a letter to Captain W. A. Thompson: "I think we are at the beginning of the end, and if Geronimo does not surrender, Capt. Lawton will capture Geronimo, unless Lt. Parker anticipates him."[41]

Although Forsyth was confident of success, he complained when the Arizpe "official firmly maintained that Geronimo would not treat with the U.S. Gov't on any terms whatever." Miles reported that Mexico's terms were harsher than those the United States was prepared to offer, adding that "Geronimo's Indians were refused all terms by [the] Mexicans except unconditional surrender and punishment for their crimes, and very vigorous measures will now be taken by [the] Mexican authorities against them."[42]

Although these were indeed Torres's initial terms, Mexico offered more liberal terms during actual bargaining with Geronimo. The Arizpe prefect received instructions to tell the band that if they surrendered their lives would be spared, and they would be sent to Sonora's interior where they would be well treated and given food, clothing, and homes. If they refused, they would be attacked and completely exterminated.[43]

In spite of the new terms, Geronimo distrusted the Mexicans and, in fact, probably never had any intention of surrendering to them. Many years later, Geronimo declared: "I have no love for the Mexicans. With me they were always treacherous and malicious. I am old now and shall never go on the warpath again, but if I were young, and followed the warpath, it would lead into Old Mexico."[44]

Torres also doubted that Geronimo would surrender to Arizpe's authorities. On August 24 he advised Miles "not [to] expect this surrender to take place," adding that he hoped Miles's "troops acting in accordance with Sonora troops on the field now can go close after [the] Apache hostiles and perhaps get them after overtures are broken." Torres mentioned that he had Pima Indians ready to enter the fray if the Sonora and American troops failed.[45] That same day, Miles informed Lawton that he was sending an auxiliary force of forty-eight Pimas after the Chiricahuas, who "want a chance to hunt them in their own way," claiming "they got 135 Apache scalps in a campaign twenty years ago." He added that he thought they would be successful.[46]

Not wanting to be outdone, the next day Torres offered his soldiers the following reward: if Geronimo came to terms, and was brought safely to Ures, Torres would give 4,000 pesos to those who had effected the surrender. If hostilities resumed, however, Torres was ready to offer 500 pesos for each Indian killed or taken prisoner and 500 pesos to the family of anyone who died fighting hostiles.[47]

Although Torres and Miles hoped the Pimas would defeat the Chiricahuas if hostilities resumed, both also still hoped for a surrender. Gatewood bolstered United States hopes when he established communication with Geronimo's band on August 23 through the Apache emissaries Martine and Kayihtah.

The following day, Gatewood met with Geronimo and Naiche and their followers in their camp along the Bavispe River near Sonora's northern border. Gatewood offered these terms: "Surrender, and you will be sent with your families to Florida, there to await the decision of the President as to your final deposition. Accept these terms or fight it out to the bitter end."[48]

Geronimo responded that they would surrender only if allowed to return to their reservation. Gatewood advised the band that the Chiricahua and Warm Springs Indians at Fort Apache were already being sent to Florida. Naiche, eager to be reunited with his mother and daughter, was leaning toward surrender.

When Gatewood met with the hostiles the next morning, Geronimo inquired about Miles since he did not know him. Gatewood advised Geronimo to trust Miles at his word. Geronimo finally made peace overtures to Gatewood on August 25 under the conditions that his warriors would be sent with their families to Florida. Three days later, Gatewood was on his way to the border at San Bernardino with thirty-eight hostiles, including Geronimo and Naiche.[49]

Later, Lawton also started for the border, but without informing the Mexican authorities. The furious Arizpe prefect overtook Lawton's troops with a force of Mexicans. The prefect wanted to keep Geronimo in Sonora but was told by Lawton that the Chiricahuas had already surrendered to the United States forces. Leonard Wood reported that the American troops were "on the whole rather hoping that there would be a fight and thereby have a chance to even up with the Mexicans for poor Crawford's death."[50]

An interview with Geronimo, arranged with "some difficulty" by Lawton, persuaded the Mexicans not to pursue the Chiricahuas. In the subsequent interview Geronimo told the Mexicans not to follow him and they agreed. Nevertheless, Lawton reported, "the Indians are alarmed and will move out of their camp to-night and cross the line before morning. They do not trust the Mexicans and are afraid they will try and play them false some way." Lawton said he hoped General Miles would send instructions without delay because he was certain of Geronimo's surrender.[51]

Fearing the Indians would not surrender to anyone but Brigadier General Miles, on August 30 Lawton contacted him to arrange a meeting with the hostiles. The following day, Miles admitted to Torres that the Apaches were talking with the Americans about surrendering. He added, however, "I do not think they intend to surrender, and [I] believe it would be well to take every precaution against their raiding or returning to the Sierra Madre country."[52]

Torres was well aware of what was transpiring. However, that same day he wrote Miles saying he had just received news from Arizpe that Geronimo had surrendered to the Americans and wanted to know if it were true. Undoubtedly disappointed that Geronimo did not surrender to Mexico, Torres was still relieved to hear that the band had made terms, telling Miles: "I anxiously expect to have the certainty of such good news."[53]

Miles did not tell Torres on the thirtieth that a surrender was close at hand, probably because he feared Mexican interference. The very next day Miles agreed to head for the border immediately if Lawton was sure the Indians would surrender to him. Meanwhile, Torres was still waiting for a confirmation from Miles. On September 3 he wrote: "I am without news about Apaches. My troops or your troops. Can you give me any?"[54] Torres did not receive an answer because Miles was already with the hostiles.

On September 4, 1886, the Apaches surrendered to Miles at Skeleton Canyon, approximately twenty miles north of the border, on the old raiding route between Mexico and Arizona. Miles discovered that the Chiricahuas would only accept two years imprisonment in Florida, terms rejected by President Grover Cleveland. Miles nevertheless reassured the Indians that these terms would be kept. At the same time, the War Department had the impression that the surrender was unconditional.[55]

The Chiricahuas still refused to surrender their weapons at Skeleton Canyon. Miles drove Geronimo, Naiche, and other armed warriors to Fort Bowie in a buckboard. Miles reached Ft. Bowie on September 5 with Geronimo and Naiche; Lawton arrived several days later with the rest of the band. Only Mangus and a few followers remained out, and they were soon captured.[56]

On September 3, while Miles began his final effort to bring about the Apache surrender, the *New York World* had reported that United States and Mexican troops fought over which side would take Geronimo. The paper claimed five Mexicans had died, two Americans had received wounds, and Geronimo had escaped during the fight. On the same day, the *Washington Star* declared that war had begun with Mexico over what was to be done with Geronimo. Both countries denied these reports, and on the fourth the *Washington Post* quashed the rumors.[57]

Miles thanked Torres on September 6 for his help during the campaign, assuring him that the Apaches would be sent two thousand miles east in order to bring lasting peace to the frontier. Mexico, Arizona, and New Mexico had long sought removal of Apaches. Mexico, however, had always feared that Apache removal would not take place due to War Department fears of a general Chiricahua uprising. Mexico was dismayed to learn in July that Miles authorized the Chiricahuas to send a commission to Washington to lobby against their removal. Chato, accused of murdering the McComas family in 1883, led the Washington delegation, prompting complaints in the *New York World* that a "murderer" was being entertained in Washington.[58]

In addition to the public outcry favoring removal of the Chiricahuas, Miles recalled that "there was quite a demand at the time for the immediate trial and execution of the principal Indians." Tucson's *Daily Citizen* called for a civil trial in order to give the Indians "peace — that lasting peace that passeth all understanding." Miles pointed out the impossibility of a fair trial and the difficulty in proving the guilt of individual Indians having committed atrocities. He said: "So intense was the feeling against the Indians in that Territory [Arizona] that it was even suggested that the braces of the railroad bridges be destroyed in order to wreck the train conveying them to Florida." On September 17 the *New York Times* reported that some citizens took comfort from the thought that the Apaches would surely die of yellow fever in Florida.[59]

It was rumored that Miles disappointed not only the public in the frontier states but also his military superiors and the president when he agreed to Geronimo's conditional surrender accepting temporary imprisonment with families in Florida. The *New York Daily Tribune* said Miles had disobeyed orders when he spared Geronimo's life. *The New York World* accused the War Department of treating Miles badly, hypothesizing that Miles incurred General Drum's displeasure by complaining of the poor quality of the Leavenworth-produced shoes issued to his men. President Cleveland finally ended the controversy in his December 6 annual message to Congress, commenting that "it was considered best to imprison them in such manner as to prevent their ever engaging in such outrages again, instead of trying them for murder."[60]

Instead of sending the Indians with their families as promised, warriors were imprisoned at Fort Pickens in Pensacola while their families were sent to Fort Marion in St. Augustine. About 75 men and 325 women and children living peacefully at Fort Apache, including loyal scouts, were also imprisoned in Florida. Even Kayihtah and Martine received this punishment in spite of their part in obtaining Geronimo's surrender.[61]

In 1894 the Chiricahuas were moved to Fort Sill, Oklahoma, where they remained prisoners nineteen more years. Only in 1913 were the remaining 261 Chiricahuas allowed to choose between remaining in Oklahoma or moving to the New Mexico Mescalero reservation. Many of the older generation died at Fort Sill. Old Nana died there in 1896, and Chihuahua and Mangus followed in 1901. Loco died in 1905. Geronimo lived until 1909, selling souvenirs in Oklahoma.[62]

Matías Romero suggested that Miles granted conditions to Geronimo that were never honored in order to persuade him to surrender to the United States instead of to the Mexicans. Although disappointed that Geronimo had surrendered to the Americans, Mexico nevertheless rejoiced over the termination of Apache hostilities, and Díaz congratulated Torres for having concluded the campaign.[63]

Although relieved by Geronimo's defeat, Mexico was disturbed by a *Washington Post* editorial published October 2 entitled "Mexico's Bad Faith: Why the Indian Campaign Was So Prolonged." The editorial blamed Geronimo's final outbreak from the reservation on Mexico, where Chato's women and children had been held captive. Claiming that the United States Army had to fight Mexicans as well as Indians, the paper accused Mexico of purchasing stolen United States stock and selling arms and ammunition to the hostiles.[64]

Saying he thought these represented Crook's ideas, Romero called the *Post* a political organ of the Democratic party and suggested that the editorial may have emanated from the War Department. Cincinnati's *Commercial Gazette*, dated October 4, agreed with Romero, saying that the eastern Democratic press only reflected the administration's hostile attitude toward Mexico. Meanwhile, Romero asked the Foreign Relations Ministry for facts to refute these latest accusations against Mexico.[65]

On October 15 Sheridan allayed Romero's fears, denying that the *Post* editorial of October 2 had come from the War Department. On the contrary, Sheridan expressed approval of Mexico's conduct during the Apache campaign, saying that Mexico's cooperation had been manifest.[66]

The *Washington Post* published a subsequent favorable report of Mexico's behavior during the war. Tucson's *El Fronterizo* praised not only Cleveland, but also Torres and Díaz, for concluding Geronimo's surrender. The *New York Herald* reported Miles's thanking of Sonora's governor for his help in Geronimo's capture. Finally, declaring that Torres deserved praise, the *New York Times* added that Mexico also aided in the defeat of Victorio, Juh, and Nana.[67]

As further expression of American goodwill, in December a company of United States soldiers returned to Chihuahua mules stolen by Mangus. This spirit of cooperation, exemplified by the reciprocal crossing agreement, facilitated Geronimo's surrender. With the Chiricahuas no longer a threat, the agreement was allowed to terminate on November 1, 1886. Mexico now turned its attention to fighting revolutionaries, bandits, and the indomitable Yaquis.[68]

SEVEN

Apaches, Yaquis, and Bandits, 1887–1911

✠

Geronimo's 1886 surrender did not bring the expected peace with Apaches. Mexico's secretary of war prematurely declared in January 1887 that, because the Chiricahua threat was eliminated and the reciprocal crossing agreement was no longer in force, United States forces would no longer be permitted to cross the border, even if only to return stolen mules, as a United States company had in December.[1] However, additional Apache threats would lead to renewals of the reciprocal crossing agreement in 1890, 1892, and 1896. Unauthorized border crossings continued prior to the renewed agreements.

In addition, the Mexican government still feared that the Chiricahua Apaches might be allowed to return to the Southwest. In May 1887, Mexico's minister in Washington Matías Romero reported to the Foreign Relations Ministry that a rumor in American newspapers that Geronimo was to be returned to San Carlos was false. Romero went on to assert, however, that while five hundred Apaches had gone to Florida, the threat continued with five thousand remaining on the reservation.[2]

In early June, Sonora's Governor Torres received word that seventeen Indians had fled San Carlos, and the *Washington Post* reported that Sonora again was offering five hundred pesos for each enemy scalp. By the end of the month, however, the escapees were back on the reservation.[3] In October 1887, Mexico received another report that Indians had fled San Carlos and joined with Mescaleros to raid, prompting the prefect of Sonora's Moctezuma District to organize a force of fifteen men to combat them.[4]

Although still alarmed at isolated Apache threats, Mexico's fears of Indian depredations had diminished with Yaqui defeats, the Battle of Buatachive in

May 1886 being the most decisive. Yaqui chief Cajeme was captured and executed in 1887.[5]

After Cajeme's death, Mexico's attention was temporarily diverted to combating unauthorized border crossings. For example, a March 1887 border incident did not involve Indians at all, but rather a Mexican colonel who sent his soldiers to Nogales, Arizona, to kidnap his Mexican lover. Arizona's governor sent two companies from Fort Huachuca to repel the Sonora soldiers, resulting in one Mexican being killed and one American suffering wounds.[6] Immediately after the incident, Governor Torres went to Nogales to apologize to the Americans. This caused Sonora's opposition candidate for governor to charge that Torres had humbled himself before the United States.[7] When a Mexican military court condemned the colonel and his two associates to death for the so-called Nogales Affair, Torres asked Díaz to commute the sentence, and the president complied.[8]

Another example occurred in 1888 when a Mexican sergeant and a soldier again crossed the border, allegedly to apprehend a deserter. The fatal shooting of the sergeant by a bullet fired from the American side resulted. This "Eagle Pass Tragedy" prompted Díaz to lament these two cases of military officers crossing the border illegally in less than a year.[9]

On February 29, at about the same time as the "Eagle Pass Tragedy" occurred, United States officials also crossed the border without permission. Three United States sheriffs and two Papagos entered Mexico in pursuit of robbers who had held up a Southern Pacific Railroad train. The sheriffs declared themselves covered under the reciprocal crossing agreement, but were informed, first, that the convenio allowed only regular troops to cross and, second, that the pact had expired more than a year before.[10]

The sheriffs and Papagos were disarmed and arrested in Janos, Chihuahua. On March 10, 1888, Díaz ordered their release, while confiscating their arms, which were to be given to a designated United States representative. The *Washington Post* protested the incident the following day, saying: "Janos is the place where a plot was put up which massacred Capt. Crawford while in pursuit of Apaches and where Lt. McDonald was arrested with a whole U.S. troop."[11]

The *Post* complained that not only arms but also the Americans' horses had been confiscated, compelling the men to make their way home as best they could. One of the horses died, and Mexico, while investigating whether it had been treated properly, offered recompense to its owner. The two Papagos accompanying the United States sheriffs were released from custody in Janos without further incident.[12]

Although the United States considered asking for damages in this affair, Arizona's *Daily Citizen* suggested that the United States did not have a valid claim against Mexico, reminding its readers of the similar "Nogales Affair" and the "Eagle Pass Tragedy."[13]

Papagos, who traditionally lived on both sides of the border, added to the border crossing disputes in April 1888. When six Arizona Papagos living near the border, under the supervision of Los Pinos Indian Agency, went to Sonora to attend a festival, they were fired upon by Mexicans, and they narrowly escaped injury. When the United States protested the shooting, Mexico replied that the United States had heard only the Papagos' side of the incident. Sonora's acting governor Ramón Corral claimed that the Papagos had taken stolen Mexican stock to the United States, and added that he would seek their extradition from Arizona's governor.[14]

An Apache escape from San Carlos in June 1888 forced both Mexico and the United States to put such conflicts aside. The prefects of Sonora's Moctezuma and Arizpe districts gave chase to the Apaches, led by José María Elías, who had fought with Geronimo but then had remained out after the band's surrender. Mexico's El Paso consul reported one Mexican killed. Miles was in pursuit, and Romero predicted that the United States would probably want to renew the reciprocal crossing agreement.[15]

Although there was talk of renewing the pact, the 1888 Apache outbreak did not pose sufficient threat to warrant renewal of the convenio; and mutual distrust continued to be more important than cooperation. Believing that Americans unfairly blamed Mexico for the raids, Mexico paid a United States citizen, William M. Edwardy, to publish an account of the Apache campaign from the Mexican point of view.

Claiming he was present at Geronimo's surrender as a "white scout," Edwardy published an article in the August 18, 1888, issue of *Harper's Weekly*, entitled "Border Troubles." Edwardy's article asserted that scouts were allowed to keep stolen Mexican stock, and "in no instance is it ever returned to the rightful Mexican owners." He added: "There are even instances of Mexicans being killed in Sonora by Indian scouts while in the service of the United States and wearing the army uniform." Claiming that "the Apache scouts were always treacherous," Edwardy wrote that Mexicans had been unable to distinguish the scouts from the hostiles during the 1886 Crawford tragedy. He maintained: "From the evidence of the two or three white men who were in the fight it is almost certain that Geronimo's band joined in the battle and helped the scouts to drive off the Mexicans."[16]

As a rebuttal to Edwardy's accusations, Second Lieutenant W. E. Shipp, Tenth Cavalry, published an article in the October 27, 1888, issue of

Harper's. Saying he also had been present when Crawford was shot, Shipp denied that Geronimo's band helped the scouts drive off the Mexicans. The article cited the Maus report as proof that "the killing of Crawford was deliberate, and with [the] knowledge that he was an American officer." Refuting Edwardy's charges against the scouts, Shipp declared: "The Mexican stories of misdeeds of the Apache scouts in their country were told to balance the account for the murder of Crawford."[17]

Undaunted by the army officer's attack on his article, Edwardy wrote Romero on March 8, 1889, proposing to publish a full account of Apache troubles, claiming "in the killing of Capt. Crawford the Mexicans were entirely in the right, and the same is true in a thousand other instances." Edwardy told Romero he wanted to put the facts before the American people. Admitting that because of army opposition he could no longer publish in *Harper's*, Edwardy said he would have no trouble finding a publisher.[18]

Determined to write a book expressing his belief that scouts were to blame for Crawford's death, Edwardy asked Romero to finance his research trip to Arizona, New Mexico, Chihuahua, and Sonora. Romero told the Foreign Relations Ministry that he really did not want to subsidize Edwardy before the book was written. Nonetheless, at the request of the Foreign Relations Ministry, on April 1, Romero paid for Edwardy to travel to Washington for an interview. After conversing with Romero, Edwardy wrote a deposition, at the Mexicans' request, in which he declared that he had been a scout with Lawton's troops and had been present at all talks between Geronimo and Lawton.

In addition to his deposition, Edwardy brought to Romero a letter of support from Brigadier General Miles and word that Lawton would also recommend him. Edwardy showed Romero his *Harper's* piece and, the following day, Romero suggested the Foreign Relations Ministry accept his request for money. Mexico agreed, and in late April Romero advanced Edwardy three hundred dollars to travel throughout the Southwest, in order to take pictures for his book. Romero cautioned that the money would appear to be a loan.[19] Mexico's advance to Edwardy, however, did not result in a published book affecting United States opinion toward Mexico's contribution to the Geronimo campaign. Considering the Apache wars all but finished, Mexico hired Edwardy in hopes of setting the record straight on its role in the Geronimo campaign.

The next month, however, Mexico again had to turn its attention to renewed Apache threats when Sonora's Arizpe prefect reported residents asking for increased protection from Apaches. In November one of Elías's band was killed by the Mexicans. On the Indians's body, Mexican commander Kosterlitzky found a gold watch that had belonged to one of the two United States sheriffs recently murdered by hostiles in Arizona's Whetstone Mountains. The next day, Fort Huachuca's commander telegraphed Sonora's acting governor Ramón Corral, advising him that Indians who had killed the two Arizona sheriffs were trying to reach his state.[20]

As late as 1889 the governors of Sonora and Chihuahua feared that Geronimo's band might be returned to the Southwest. Romero warned the United States secretary of war in October that Geronimo's band would raid Mexico if returned to Arizona. In December, the Foreign Relations Ministry ordered Romero to do everything possible to assure that the Indians were not returned to the frontier. In January 1890, in a letter to Mexico's Foreign Relations Ministry, Romero again referred to the pact Crook and Howard allegedly had made with Apaches, allowing them to raid Mexico and bring their plunder into the United States on the condition they did not steal or kill in the United States.[21]

These concerns and the depredations of Apache Kid, a former Aravaipa Apache Indian scout turned outlaw, and his companion Chiquito led Mexico to approve a new reciprocal crossing agreement, which was signed June 25, 1890. Crawford's death was the impetus for a new requirement that only two Indian scouts could accompany each company as unarmed guides. Before signing the new pact, Secretary of State James G. Blaine asked for assurance that it would not be necessary to ask Mexican officials in frontier states for permission *each* time it was necessary to cross the border, since this would cause delays and trails would be lost.[22]

Due to rains in August, Miles lost the trail of Kid and Chiquito. Subsequently, the United States asked Mexico to interpret the "hot pursuit" provision of the agreement liberally by allowing pursuit to continue even if a trail were lost. Mexico agreed on the condition that this privilege would be reciprocal, while rejecting Miles's request for permission to continuously chase renegades. Under the Miles plan, there would have been one force from each country, and the United States would have paid all expenses.[23]

Kid's raids continued on both sides of the border, leading to renewal of the expired reciprocal crossing agreement on November 25, 1892. Meanwhile, in January 1891, Tombstone reported two Americans killed by Apaches near the border at San Bernardino; Fort Huachuca troops were in pursuit.[24]

Although Sonora and Chihuahua reported peace in February 1891, it was a momentary respite. Late that year Sonora was warned of another San Carlos escape, forcing Sonora's National Guard again to prepare to fight

Apaches in 1892. In October 1892, a month before renewal of the crossing agreement, Sonora learned that Apache Kid and five other raiders were heading for the state.[25]

In addition, Navajo threats were added to this very real threat from Kid's band. The next month, Mexico's acting minister in Washington Cayetano Romero reported a *Washington Evening Star* claim that Navajos had fled their New Mexico reservation. Romero feared United States forces would chase them into Mexico. The Navajo threat did not materialize, however, and outlaws caused as much concern as hostile Indians during the period from 1891 to 1893.[26]

Mexico was especially concerned in 1892 about the movements of the notorious border bandit Catarino Garza. Chihuahua's Governor Lauro Carrillo claimed to have two agents in Texas looking for Garza. Carrillo warned that it would be difficult to capture Garza and his men so long as Mexican troops could not cross the border to give chase.[27]

On January 11, 1892, the *New York Herald* reported that Mexican minister Romero's proposal for a reciprocal crossing agreement that would allow troops to capture outlaws like Garza had not been well received by the War Department. The *Herald* quoted an officer who had been with Crook to the effect that:

> He asserts that the soldiers of that country [Mexico] would be glad of an opportunity to shoot down and plunder U.S. troops, and that even the officers would encourage and assist in committing the outrages. The hatred of the Mexicans for the Americans is intense, and while this feeling is held in abeyance by the higher authorities of that Republic, yet among the common people and the criminal classes of the army it finds vent whenever opportunity occurs.[28]

San Francisco's *Morning Call* asserted that Mexico had not called out troops because it considered lawbreakers like Garza to be bandits and not revolutionaries. The San Francisco newspaper gratuitously added that most outlaws were half-breeds, the product of the worst elements in both countries.

Troubled by these allegations, Mexico's consul general defended the professional standards of his country's army. The consul declared that would-be revolutionaries had no chance of success in Mexico because "the old idea that the army is recruited from the prisons and criminal classes is not now true." He added that Mexico's soldiers could travel more easily than other armies because:

The wives of the soldiers run along ahead of the army, and, when the soldiers come up to their camping places, they find the fires lighting and meals cooking. As they can get along with less food than the soldiers of any other nation, it is possible for Mexican soldiers to make forced marches with far greater ease than the armies of this country [United States] or Europe.[29]

By early 1892, the bandit trouble appeared to be over, only to be replaced by the recurring Yaqui menace. Torres admitted to Díaz that extermination of the last Yaqui warriors would take some time, describing them as the last remnants of an indomitable and brave race making their final stand against civilization.[30]

In March 1892 Díaz directed Torres to prevent arms sales to Yaquis. Torres replied that Sonora's prefects were watching for arms sales and that he was even attempting to stop arms sales in Nogales and Tucson. This was an old problem; as early as 1885, Torres and Corral had taken measures to prevent Yaquis and Mayos from buying arms through a third person.[31]

In December 1892 Mexico denied a *New York Evening Post* dispatch claiming Yaqui and Mayo hostilities in Sonora. Yaquis, continuing to lose both land and battles, sought peace in 1896 under their new leader Juan Maldonado, alias Tetabiate. As late as 1897, Mexico continued to deny reports of Yaquis on the warpath. It is probable that Mexico denied Yaqui warfare in order not to jeopardize valuable American mining interests in Sonora. Mexico furnished armed escorts to Americans, but conditions deteriorated to the point that Sonora temporarily forbade foreigners from filing mining claims.[32]

Mexico attempted to downplay the Yaqui threat, but in 1896 incidents allegedly involving Yaquis resulted in unwelcome publicity in America's press. On August 12, 1896, some forty Yaquis attacked Sonora's Nogales customhouse, killing three guards. Seven Yaquis died and two were captured before the rest escaped into Arizona. United States troops from forts Huachuca and Grant gave chase but failed to catch the culprits. Sonora belatedly organized a force to pursue the Yaquis, but to no avail.[33]

During the customhouse attack a battle cry of "Viva Dios" rang out, and one of the dead Indians had a picture of the Chihuahua religious cult leader Teresa Urrea, the Santa de Cabora, on his person.[34] Also found on him was an article from *El Independiente*, an anti-Díaz paper published in El Paso by D. Lauro Aguirre. This suggested that the attack might have been organized in the United States. Aguirre criticized Mexico's handling of the affair in the August issue of *El Independiente*.[35]

The paper criticized Mexico's consul in Nogales, Arizona, for asking Arizona's National Guard to help put down the attack, saying the new 1896 crossing agreement did not allow United States troops to cross the border to defend Mexican offices or towns. The article suggested that Mexican officials had invited this violation of Sonora's territory, but that Díaz would not reprimand them.[36]

The *Oasis*, published in Nogales, Arizona, agreed, saying that Americans had done most of the killing, but had no right to do so. Calling it absurd to blame the attack on the peaceful Santa de Cabora, the paper declared the incident the work of revolutionaries. The paper concluded that the Mexican government was attempting to blame the attack on the Santa so that the trouble would appear to be a local incident instead of a well-organized revolution. San Francisco's *Examiner* blamed the attack on rebellious Yaquis, saying they bought arms with paychecks earned from work on Arizona's Southern Pacific Railroad. Mexican authorities suspected the raid was the work of revolutionaries, but when Lieutenant Colonel John M. Bacon, commander of Fort Huachuca, personally inspected the destruction, they took pains to convince him the raid was a simple robbery, without political motivation.[37]

Additional evidence that Yaquis organized their rebellion on United States soil came to light the following month. The Nogales Mexican consul learned from a Papago informant that well-armed Yaquis were using a Papago village within United States territory, less than fifty miles from Tucson, as their base of operations against Mexico. Reports of the number of Yaqui warriors at the village ranged from twenty to three hundred. Although the Yaquis had warned the Papagos not to reveal their presence to American authorities, Mexico's Nogales consul had noted that Papagos were purchasing more rifles and taking more arms to Tucson for repair than usual. Soon Sonora's governor and the secretaries of foreign relations and war learned of the consul's report, leading Mexico's minister in Washington to ask the United States State Department to put an end to this Yaqui base and punish the guilty.[38]

While the Yaqui rebellion created friction between the United States and Mexico, the continuing Apache threat fostered cooperation between the two nations in 1896. In February, Arizona's governor Louis C. Hughes reminded Sonora's governor Corral that a few years back they had discussed jointly sending scouts to the Sierra Madres in pursuit of Apaches. The governor then asked Corral for permission for eight men and fourteen animals to cross the border and enter the mountains in pursuit of Apache Kid, adding that a five-thousand-dollar reward existed for Kid, dead or alive.[39]

The Foreign Relations Ministry reminded Corral that the reciprocal crossing pact was no longer in force. Secretary of Foreign Relations Ignacio Mariscal suggested that Corral make an agreement with Arizona to the effect that Mexican troops would pursue Indians after they crossed the border, turning any captives over to the United States. Obeying Mariscal's instructions, Corral offered to place Mexican troops at a designated location on Sonora's border, asking Arizona's governor to advise the Mexican force when the Indians crossed the border. Believing that Kid could be captured only in his Sierra Madres hideout, Arizona's governor was disappointed with Mexico's terms.[40]

Disagreements between leading United States officers plagued attempts to reach an agreement. In May, Brigadier General Frank Wheaton arranged with Mexico's Sonora commander Emilio Kosterlitzky for a combined United States and Mexican movement against the hostiles, who were described as thirty "remnants" of Geronimo's band. On the other hand, Brigadier General Miles maintained that the renegades were not from Geronimo's band and numbered no more than ten or twelve persons. He added that he saw no reason for American troops to cross into Mexico on June 1 as Wheaton was requesting. Instead, Miles suggested that United States troops following in close pursuit not cross the border until they communicated with Mexican forces.[41]

Mexico no longer doubted American wishes in May, when the United States requested a new reciprocal crossing agreement. Mexico quickly approved another pact and the convenio was signed on June 4, 1896. Although essentially a copy of the 1892 pact, the new agreement did contain several additional provisions. Specifically designed to defeat Kid, the new convenio was to remain in force until Kid's band was either exterminated or defeated. The pact also specified that the temporary loss of the trail was no reason to end the chase. The agreement came not a moment too soon; Colonel Edwin V. Sumner, Seventh Cavalry, reported that Kid's band was just across the border, saying United States troops could catch its members if allowed into Sonora.[42]

As soon as the pact was signed, however, both Mexico and the United States resumed accusations based on mutual distrust. On June 14, the *Washington Post* declared the new agreement a reminder of Crawford's "deliberate murder." The *Post* article said only two scouts would be allowed with each company because Mexico believed hostiles entered its territory disguised as American scouts. Finally, the article said blacks were not to be sent across the border because Mexican peasants allegedly feared them almost as much as Apaches.[43]

A few days later, the *Washington Post* caused Mexico additional concern by reporting that two United States cavalry companies with sixty scouts were pursuing Kid in Sonora. The United States secretary of war called the *Post* article "false from beginning to end." Sumner also denied the *Post* report, saying that the United States had strictly complied with the 1896 agreement. In July, Mexico received reports of American companies with as many as twenty-four scouts, a clear violation of the pact. In early August, Mexico's secretary of war reported that the United States had suspended its controversial Mexican campaign.[44]

In September, the United States proposed a new plan to capture Kid, and this plan was clearly outside recent pact stipulations. The scheme had been devised in July, when former scout Archie McIntosh wrote Miles saying he could capture Kid with the aid of six Apaches, who requested immunity for themselves in return.[45]

Archibald McIntosh was born in Canada to a Scottish father employed by the Hudson Bay Company and a Chippewa Indian mother. Educated by the company after his father's murder, at age twelve Archie went to school in Edinburgh, Scotland, for two years. His knowledge of Indians and his wilderness skills made him one of General Crook's most valued scouts. After marrying an Apache woman, Archie was in charge of rations at San Carlos. Discharged in 1884 for taking illegal profits, Archie must have yearned to return to army life when he proposed his plan to capture Kid.[46]

Previous attempts to capture Kid with regular troops having proved unsuccessful, Miles endorsed McIntosh's plan, suggesting that both the United States and Mexico provide an officer to command in their respective countries and three enlisted men each to accompany McIntosh and his Apaches. Miles added that the United States would pay all expenses, except the Mexican soldiers' salaries. He said the pursuit would continue until Kid was captured, and that the outlaw would be turned over to the country where the capture was made.

The United States War Department approved the plan, and Díaz agreed to the scheme in October 1896. Although Mexico and the United States ignored provisions of the crossing agreement in this last desperate attempt to end Apache hostilities, McIntosh was fired for drunkenness before his expedition began. The reward for Kid was never claimed.[47]

Nevertheless, Apache raids diminished after 1896, and cattle and horse rustling eclipsed Indian hostilities in importance. The Maya and Yaqui campaigns would be officially closed in 1904 and 1909, respectively. In the meantime, Mexico became concerned with peaceful United States Indians hoping to emigrate.

The General Allotment Act of 1887 replacing Indian reservations with citizenship and land in severalty was a powerful incentive for emigration. In the 1890s, the allotment of Oklahoma tribes proceeded rapidly, followed by repeated land rushes after the 1889 opening. The Five Civilized Tribes held out longest against the onslaught of white settlers in Indian Territory. The Seminoles were allowed to remain in Florida. On April 1, 1899, however, allotment began with the rest of the great Southern tribes: first the Creeks and the Cherokees; Choctaws and Chickasaws soon followed. White settlers poured into Indian lands. Indian groups sought permission to sell their allotments and purchase Mexican land for colonies where they could preserve the integrity of their tribes.[48]

In 1893 Romero had advised the Foreign Relations Ministry that Cherokees were planning to purchase land in Mexico, but this report was not confirmed. Four years later, Romero again said the Cherokees were interested in moving to Mexico, where they wanted an independent nation with their own laws.[49] That same year the *Brooklyn Citizen* claimed that three thousand Oklahoma Indians were considering relocating in Mexico. Romero also reported that the Five Civilized Tribes wanted to buy Mexican land because they were unhappy with recent government treaties. In 1898, however, Mexico's secretary of development stated that no official action had been taken in the matter.[50]

The San Antonio consul advised Mexico's secretary of foreign relations in 1897 that Chickasaws wanted to relocate in Mexico. The following year Cherokees again inquired about the possibility of moving the Five Civilized Tribes to Mexico, asking what education would be provided and whether they could retain their independent tribal government. Informing the Cherokees that they would not be allowed to maintain an independent government if they emigrated, Mexico offered to admit their household goods duty free. A member of the Cherokee delegation visited Sonora and was not favorably impressed, however, according to an article in the *St. Louis Globe-Democrat*. Nevertheless, reports of Cherokees relocating in Mexico continued as late as 1908.[51]

In 1899 an Indian from Oklahoma requested permission to emigrate, but Mexico's secretary of development discouraged the move, saying the Indian did not have money for resettlement and would lose his United States benefits if he moved.[52] That year United States newspapers reported that ten thousand Indians wanted to move to Mexico from Indian Territory. The papers declared Creeks, Cherokees, and Delawares would pay their own expenses, giving cash for Mexican land. The *Boston Transcript* claimed that the Indians wanted to live in independent settlements, with no whites allowed. In February 1899, the Foreign Relations Ministry assured the secretary of development that Mexico had made no concessions to the Indians.[53]

American Indians did purchase Mexican land, however. In 1905 the United States Interior Department requested Mexico's help in an investigation of land fraud involving seven Kickapoos. Mexico agreed to cooperate with a special investigator from the Interior Department, and two years later three United States senators were appointed to investigate the Mexican Kickapoos. In 1908 these investigators accused an American attorney named Martin J. Bentley of defrauding Oklahoma Kickapoos of their land, giving them poor Coahuila land in exchange. Claiming that Bentley was unable to pay taxes on the Coahuila land, the United States asked Mexico not to sell the Kickapoos' land for nonpayment of those taxes until their investigation had been completed.[54]

A Douglas, Arizona, newspaper reported another Kickapoo incident in 1908 when an Interior Department agent was suspended for entering Sonora without permission and bringing 125 "kicking Kickapoos" back to the United States under false pretenses. It was also reported that year that Creek Indians purchased land north of Durango in exchange for their Oklahoma land. Mexico's El Paso consul claimed they decided to emigrate because they were really of the Black race, and there was much prejudice against them in the United States. The consul did not mention Mexican prejudice against blacks in his recommendation that the Creeks not be allowed to emigrate. He warned, however, that it would probably be unwise to allow rich foreigners, who had no intention of establishing businesses or farming, to move to Mexico.[55]

Constantly fearing United States hegemony on its northern states, Mexican officials read a March 1905 article published in the *San Antonio Express* with alarm. The paper accused an American named John Dwyer of supporting Yaqui rebels in Sonora for the purpose of annexing that state to the United States. Six months later Mexico received a confidential letter from a Captain Goodrich in San Antonio, warning that many Americans sympathized with the Yaquis. In addition, Arizona's *Daily Star* alleged that Mormon colonists in northeast Sonora were giving aid to Yaquis, citing as proof the fact that no Mormons had been killed by the Indians.[56]

Whether annexationists or not, Americans accused Mexico of minimizing the Yaqui threat while failing to end the revolt, which threatened Sonora's mining interests. The Yaquis had renewed their war against the Mexican government in 1899 and 1900, complaining that the government had not returned their land and was attempting to give them worthless land outside their fertile valley. The Yaqui war engaged one-fourth of the government's troops and cost Mexico enormous sums.[57]

Numerous complaints about Yaquis from United States citizens living in Sonora were forwarded directly to Mexico's secretary of war. United States Secretary of State Elihu Root declared that Yaquis were killing Americans in Sonora in addition to disrupting mining. In April 1905, the *San Francisco Chronicle* pronounced Yaqui country unsafe for Americans.[58]

Mexico continually refuted stories of the Yaqui rebellion in America's press. The *San Francisco Bulletin* accused Sonora's governor Rafael Izábal of murdering Yaqui and Seri Indians on Tortuga Island near Guaymas, alleging that Seris had taken fourteen right hands cut from Yaqui warriors to Izábal in a futile effort to obtain mercy. An article in the *San Francisco Chronicle*, illustrated with a large color picture of a Japanese samurai warrior next to a Yaqui, claimed that Mexico planned to use samurai to defeat the Yaqui Indians. Mexico's secretary of war termed stories in the American press regarding the Yaqui revolt false and sensational.[59]

Mexico countered that Sonora was winning the battle against the Yaquis while important mines remained open. Mexico City's *El Imparcial* pointed out that the Mexican government warned foreigners that Yaqui country was unsafe, but that foreigners went there anyway, while refusing Mexican protection.[60]

In April 1905 the *San Francisco Examiner* quoted Herbert L. Miller, a would-be miner, who claimed to be the sole survivor of a Yaqui massacre in Sonora. Miller alleged that Sonora's governor Izábal had tried to bribe him into denying that Yaquis killed his party and, when that failed, accused him of murdering his four companions. That same month, Mexico denied Miller's accusations. The *Tucson Citizen* blamed Miller for his companions' deaths because he had dismissed his Mexican escorts.[61]

The *Citizen* compared Mexico's Yaqui war to the Apache menace of some thirty years before. Claiming that Mexico was only trying to protect Americans in Sonora, Mexico's *El Imparcial* quoted an American businessman who said the Yaqui war differed from the Apache conflict because Yaqui labor was so sought after that it precluded extermination.[62]

Utilization of Yaqui labor, primarily to meet a worker shortage on Mexico's henequen (sisal fiber) plantations, was the main reason Yaquis were deported from Sonora beginning in 1903. Yaquis were employed in every capacity in Sonora, and their mechanical abilities were highly praised. It is unknown how many Yaquis had been deported when the policy terminated in 1908; estimates range from five to fifteen thousand. American investors protested the deportation, and Arizona eagerly offered Yaquis jobs until the 1907 depression reduced the labor demand.[63]

Mexico protested it was not to blame for Yaqui raids in Sonora; after all, the Indians allegedly bought their arms in Arizona. Mexico had no suspects, but investigated all leads, like the report in Tucson's *El Fronterizo* that a shoemaker known to be associated with the Yaquis had papers in English and six hundred dollars in "grinbaks" in his possession. Mexico's vice-consul in Douglas said Yaqui arms entered Mexico through an American ranch that extended into Mexican territory.[64]

Determined to discover the culprits, in December 1905 Díaz approved the Tucson consul's proposal to hire a detective at a hundred dollars a month to investigate. That month the Tucson consul announced his discovery of two Mexicans selling arms to Yaquis.[65]

Yaquis continued to purchase arms, however, prompting Mexico to ask United States officials to prevent arms sales to the Indians. Mexico's Yuma consul said Arizona had a law preventing arms sales to the Indians, but that it was difficult to apprehend Yaqui buyers because they dressed like Mexican workers. In addition to requesting the cooperation of American officials, Yuma's consul offered a bonus to police discovering Yaquis purchasing arms.[66]

Tucson's *Daily Citizen* reported that the district attorney would enforce the Arizona law prohibiting arms sales to Indians. In July 1906 President Theodore Roosevelt ordered United States marshals and customs collectors to stop the sale of arms to Yaquis, and Arizona's governor agreed to cooperate. As a result, Yaquis resorted to buying arms in California; in November 1906 Mexico asked California's governor to prevent arms sales.[67]

Mexico also tried to prevent Yaquis from entering the United States. When Mexico received information that Yaquis were going to cross the border in April 1906, Arizona's acting governor W. F. Nichols placed rangers in border towns to stop them. Mexico's Tucson consul reported that the detective in his pay had captured two Yaquis, who would be deported. Mexico also asked United States immigration officials to deport Yaquis.[68]

After trying to obtain United States cooperation in the Yaqui war, Mexico was dismayed by a report that an American was directing the campaign against the Yaquis in Sonora. Of all the fantastic stories concerning the Yaquis, the *San Francisco Chronicle* published one of the best in May 1906; it alleged that Mexico had commissioned a United States soldier of fortune to defeat the Yaquis. The *Chronicle* claimed that Lorenzo Boido's force consisted of about forty-five Americans and between six and eight hundred

Pimas and Opatas. The *Los Angeles Times* said that Sonora's government had hired Boido to fight Yaquis because Mexico's troops were composed of criminals and vagabonds, unable to march or shoot. The paper even supplied a photo of "Dr. Boido coaching his Indian scouts" and suggested that Sonora had retained Boido because warring Yaquis were rampant in the districts of Hermosillo, Ures, Sahuaripa, and north Guaymas. The next day the *Los Angeles Times* ran a story entitled "Red Raiders of Sonora's Hills," which complained that the Mexican government was deporting peaceful Yaqui workers to Yucatán and leaving the "bronco" Yaquis to halt Sonora's mining.[69]

Alarmed by these allegations, on May 15 Mexico's secretary of foreign relations asked Mexican consuls in border cities to investigate the charges. The San Diego consul responded on May 24 with articles from other United States papers in border states calling the *San Francisco Chronicle's* report that Sonora had hired a United States soldier of fortune irresponsible. A few days later, however, Tucson's consul informed the minister that the Pima County, Arizona, register listed Lorenzo Boido as a United States citizen and a Tucson voter.[70]

Faced with this revelation, the Mexican government reprimanded Sonora's governor, telling him that Boido, a United States citizen, should not be commanding forces in Sonora. The governor defended his actions, saying Boido claimed to be from Guaymas, and born of an Italian father and a Mexican mother. The governor did say that he had ordered Boido to the capital to explain his citizenship and that, if proven an American citizen, he would be relieved of his command.[71]

Although Mexico would not tolerate an American citizen commanding Sonoran forces, the state's governor, Rafael Izábal, welcomed aid from armed United States volunteers. Mexican troops were not close enough to respond quickly to Colonel William Greene's urgent request for help to put down the June 1, 1906, strike at his Cananea Consolidated Copper Company in Sonora. Captain Tom Rynning of the Arizona Rangers reached the border first with over two hundred armed volunteers ready to assist at Cananea.

Rynning disbanded his force after meeting Governor Izábal at the border town of Naco. The Bisbee, Arizona, volunteers then crossed into Sonora individually with Izábal's approval. Once on Mexican soil, the men were sworn into the Mexican army as volunteers and allowed to proceed to Cananea by train.

The Bisbee volunteers made a show of force at Cananea on June 2 and then waited back on their train. Just before sunset that same afternoon,

Colonel Emilio Kosterlitzky and his Rurales arrived and restored order, declaring martial law. The Arizona volunteers, no longer needed, were sent home via train that night without having fired a shot.

Governor Izábal defended his actions, denying that the armed Americans belonged to the United States military, but Mexican eyewitnesses maintained that the Arizona volunteers were really an organized force. Izábal was criticized not only for his support for the Cananea Consolidated Copper Company but also for his persecution of the Yaquis, including the deportation of many to Yucatán.[72]

In 1906, a year during which Mexico suppressed both strikers and Yaquis, it is interesting that Mexico also did everything possible to secure justice for an unknown Indian killed in Yuma, Arizona. The controversy began when a Yuma sheriff from a prominent, wealthy family shot and killed a Cucapá Indian from Sonora, alleging the Indian had a bottle of wine in his possession. When the justice of the peace, a *compadre* of the sheriff's father, found the sheriff innocent, more than five hundred Cucapás gathered in Yuma to seek justice. Warning that Yuma's citizens would not be able to defend themselves against five hundred hostile Indians, Mexico's Yuma consul asked permission to hire an attorney to prosecute the powerful sheriff.[73]

The consul said he wanted to show the American authorities, who had such little respect for Mexican life, that Mexico would prosecute anyone who murdered a Mexican citizen, even if that citizen were only a poor, defenseless Indian. Mexico hired an American attorney to prosecute the case, and the jury returned a guilty verdict. Arizona's governor pardoned the sheriff, however, claiming that the man's epilepsy would make him unfit for prison.[74] Although unsuccessful, Mexico had attempted to obtain justice from the United States for one Mexican Indian in an era during which both countries usually cooperated to kill hostile Indians in the name of order and progress.

EIGHT

River Pilots and Pony Soldiers

✝

Although the Yaqui and Apache campaigns had ended by 1910, border hostilities continued for another decade. The overthrow of the Mexican dictator Porfirio Díaz in 1910 initiated the Mexican Revolution. During the social revolution that followed, the United States served as a haven for political refugees and plotters. An arms trade flourished from the United States into Mexico, and there was concern in Mexico that the northern states might become incorporated into the United States.

Tensions between the two countries increased in 1913 when the United States ambassador Henry Lane Wilson was implicated in the assassination of the revolutionary president Francisco I. Madero. Victoriano Huerta took over the presidency after Madero's demise. Newly elected president Woodrow Wilson denied his ambassador's recommendation for recognition of the usurper Huerta.

Mexican opposition to Huerta centered in the northern and southern states. The northern Constitutionalists were led by Coahuila governor Venustiano Carranza; "First Chief" of the army, Chihuahua's Pancho Villa; and Alvaro Obregón in Sonora. In the south, Emiliano Zapata fought from Morelos. Chaos continued when Huerta fled, and Villa, Obregón, and Zapata occupied Mexico City. The civil war continued as Villa, Zapata, and Carranza disagreed over who should serve as interim president.[1]

After Huerta's fall, Villa assumed he would be favored by the United States. Only Villa had failed to criticize the United States when President Wilson authorized the seizure of Veracruz to prevent arms shipments from reaching Huerta. When Wilson granted de facto recognition to Carranza on October 19, 1915, in hope he would restore peace to the border and protect U.S. investments, Villa felt betrayed.[2]

Villa's initial good relations with the United States were based on his reluctance to impose high taxes on U.S. companies in addition to his unwillingness to protest the American occupation of Veracruz. After Villa's decisive defeat at Celaya in April 1915, President Wilson's support shifted to Venustiano Carranza. Wilson recognized Carranza and allowed him to transport troops across the U.S. territory via Douglas, Arizona, to confront Villa's army.

Villa was bitter toward the United States after his attack on Carranza's troops at Agua Prieta, Sonora, ended in a rout in November 1915. Revenge against the United States was not the only motive for Villa's March 9, 1916, attack on Columbus, New Mexico. Villa's unfounded conviction that Wilson and Carranza had concluded an agreement making Mexico a United States protectorate is another possible rationale for the raid. Although Germany considered using Villa to provoke U.S. intervention in Mexico as a distraction from the European war, German intrigue was probably not a factor in the Columbus attack. Villa may have wanted to even the score with Sam Ravel, a Columbus merchant who had cheated him. He may have just wanted to loot the town.

After Villa's attack on Columbus, Major Frank Tompkins pursued him across the border. Villa's force of approximately 450 fought civilians and members of the Thirteenth Cavalry, leaving dead, wounded, and destroyed property. Seventeen Americans, nine of them civilians, and more than one hundred Mexicans were killed.

On the day of the Columbus raid, Secretary of State Robert Lansing asked Mexico to reinstate the reciprocal agreement for "hot pursuit" across the border.[3] Carranza replied that he would be willing to sign a new crossing agreement only if another similar raid should be repeated on the border. He maintained he could police the border without United States interference. As proof of his intentions, Carranza cited the fact that he had sent twenty-five hundred men under General Luis Gutíerrez after Villa long before the Columbus raid. Now fearing an immediate United States invasion, Carranza dispatched a telegram warning generals Gutíerrez and Augustín Millán, the Veracruz commander.[4]

Failure to sign a new reciprocal crossing agreement for Villa's capture led both nations to the brink of war in 1916. To avoid full-scale intervention, the United States readied a so-called "punitive expedition" against Villa. Wilson wanted to avoid war and hoped that Carranza would at least tolerate the expedition even if he would not cooperate. Secretary of War New-

ton D. Baker prepared to send the small, mobile force into Mexico under
General John J. "Black Jack" Pershing. It would be withdrawn when Carranza controlled northern Mexico. The expedition was ordered into Mexico on March 15, 1916.

Like Geronimo, Villa became a renegade sought by two countries. He
was often described as being everywhere, but could not be found anywhere.
In fact, the Mexicans compared the chase after Villa to "buscar el gato en el
garbanzal," or hunting a needle in a haystack.[5]

The unilateral order to send Pershing across the border received the
same Mexican rejection as did Ord's Order of 1877. Even after Pershing
crossed the border, Carranza tried to negotiate a compromise, requesting a
reciprocal "hot pursuit" of no more than one thousand men in unpopulated
areas. His plan specified that the pursuing force would organize not more
than three days after a raid and would be allowed to stay no more than
fifteen days. Wilson refused these limitations. As a result, not only Villa,
but also Carranza now opposed Pershing.[6]

Blond and blue-eyed Pershing personified the ideal American soldier. He
loved fine horses, yet his expedition was destined to be the end of the
cavalry era. Trucks, tanks, and airplanes began replacing what had been the
traditional army during the Pershing campaign. He entered Mexico with
192 officers and 4,800 enlisted men. His large expedition, which included
some Indian scouts, differed from the small forces that had entered Mexico
under the nineteenth-century crossing agreements.

Pershing's force consisted of four cavalry regiments, two infantry regiments, and two artillery batteries. The Signal Corps put up telegraph lines
while engineers built roads. Pershing was supported by mule packtrains,
wagon and truck companies, and even an air squadron. Flying was in its
infancy, and although Pershing received eight biplanes, referred to as
"crates," the aircraft flew less than two months in Mexico.

General Hugh L. Scott ordered Pershing to disperse Villa's troops
and chase them from the border, although popular American opinion proclaimed the mission was to capture Villa. By the time Pershing entered
Chihuahua, Villa already had gained a seven-day advantage. Pershing did
not have permission to use Mexican railroads. Local sympathies were with
Villa, and the Chihuahua citizenry aided him. Pershing's failure to capture
Villa only enhanced the renegade's image as a Mexican folk hero.

With Pershing facing such strong Mexican resistance, a clash seemed
inevitable. As early as April 12, a column from the Thirteenth Cavalry
under Colonel Frank Tompkins faced a riot by unwisely entering Parral.
Realizing Mexican resentment would continue to hinder Pershing, on April

30 generals Hugh Scott and Frederick Funston began negotiations with Carranza's General Alvaro Obregón. Carranza rejected any agreement not specifying immediate withdrawal of Pershing's forces. Instead of withdrawal, Wilson began a mobilization of the National Guard in May.

On Cinco de Mayo, Mexican bandit depredations in Glenn Springs and Boquillas, Texas, in the Big Bend prompted another expedition into Mexico. Major George T. Langhorne decided to lead the pursuit of the marauders in his Cadillac, along with Colonel Frederick W. Sibley and members of the Eighth and Fourteenth Cavalries. Although the Cadillac covered no more than nine miles in two hours, the expedition traveled some 160 miles south during a sixteen-day chase and killed or wounded some of the raiders.

Reacting to this unauthorized crossing, Carranza told Obregón to reject a tentative agreement reached three days earlier with U.S. negotiators for Pershing's withdrawal. On June 16, Carranza ordered Chihuahua's commander General Jacinto B. Treviño to resist any movements of Pershing's forces south with force.

Mexico's lack of cooperation with the United States contrasted with previous combined efforts of both nations to defeat rebellious border Indians in the late nineteenth century. Generals Ord and Gerónimo Treviño worked together to end Rio Grande raids in the 1870s, and Brigadier General Miles and Sonora's governor Torres acted in close alliance to effect Geronimo's surrender.

Instead of planning to leave Mexico as Carranza demanded, Pershing wanted to take command of the city and state of Chihuahua. He was convinced that Carranza had no more control over the border "than if he lived in London."[7]

Another clash between the Mexicans and the U.S. forces was inevitable. It occurred on June 21 at Carrizal. Captain Charles T. Boyd ill-advisedly entered the town with members of the Tenth Cavalry. In the fight that ensued, Boyd, Mexican general Félix U. Gómez, and others were killed. War was narrowly averted only when Carranza ordered the American prisoners captured at Carrizal returned to El Paso. Neither side could afford a war and, on September 6, a Joint High Commission convened to negotiate a solution.

It was only on February 5, 1917, that Pershing's total withdrawal was ordered. Pershing's eleven-month-long expedition went 350 miles below the border and cost $130 million. Although Villa was never found, Pershing's expedition provided valuable experience for the coming European war. "Leaders of two World Wars, Black Jack Pershing and George Patton, had won their spurs."[8]

After the withdrawal of the punitive expedition, border raids by Villa and others continued for the next several years. The most serious was the June 14 and 15, 1919, Villista attack on Cuidad Juárez. The killing or wounding of several soldiers and civilians in El Paso prompted the local El Paso commander Brigadier General James B. Erwin to give chase, but he returned to the United States on June 17.

With Villa's whereabouts still unknown, the task of finding him was given to the "river-pilots," members of the Army Air Service Border Patrol. Although the Big Bend ranchers called the aviators "river pilots," the "pony soldiers" of the cavalry ridiculed them with the name "big chickens."[9]

The Border Air Patrol consisted of squadrons fresh from European combat. The air patrol was instructed to search for bandits along the entire length of the border and to report how many were seen, what they were doing, and how much livestock they possessed. A report accompanied by a map was to be dropped at the closest outpost of the Eighth Cavalry. In addition, pilots located water and camping sites for troops.[10]

According to pilot Stacy Hinkle, the planes had orders not to cross the border, although he admits they did fly into Mexico without filing a report. The flights that did enter Mexico took photographs, Hinkle explains, but "no official action was taken," because from 10,000 feet it could not be determined within five miles which side of the border the planes transversed.[11]

The pilots knew they could not capture Villa, but they held out the hope that they might spot him and shoot him from the air. Lieutenants Russel Cooper and Frank Estill did manage to shoot bandit Jesús Rentería's horse out from under him with a Lewis machine gun. Rentería, nicknamed "fiend" and "pegleg," was being pursued after capturing two U.S. lieutenants for ransom after their plane went down in Mexico.[12]

Captain Leonard F. Matlack of the Eighth Cavalry was selected to deliver the fifteen thousand dollars in ransom money. Matlack, a dead shot with his two Colt six-guns, was the law in river country. He managed to rescue Lieutenants Harold G. Peterson and P. H. Davis while paying only half the money. The rescued aviators had little time to rest. They were ordered to return to Mexico to guide Matlack and his troops to the bandits.[13]

On August 18, 1919, Secretary of War Newton D. Baker ordered units of the Fifth and Eighth Cavalries to cross into Mexico in pursuit. General Manuel M. Diéguez, commander of Chihuahua's federal troops, did not impede the American forces. Objecting to this new punitive expedition, on August 21, Carranza ordered all American troops out of Mexico in a protest to the State Department. Two days later the War Department complied.[14]

According to pilot Hinkle, Mexican military commanders cooperated in the release of pilots forced to land in Mexico. Hinkle claims, "It was the politicians, the newspapers, and the labor unions in Mexico City who accused us of violating their territorial rights when lost planes and search planes flew over Mexico." In fact, Major General Robert L. Howze and his Fort Bliss staff provided "courtesy flights" over El Paso and Juárez for Mexican officials.[15]

In spite of such cooperation, the Border Air Patrol was terminated on July 1, 1921. Although the Border Air Patrol ended as raids diminished, racial tension on the border is a lasting legacy. Mexican raids led to reprisals by Texas Rangers and vigilantes, fostering racial conflict in south Texas that remains today.

The United States is currently faced with new border problems such as the entrance of undocumented workers. The most recent attempt at cooperation, the North American Free Trade Agreement, may help lessen these border problems by creating new jobs and bringing new prosperity to the United States–Mexico border region.

NINE

Conclusion

✝

When the United States and Mexico failed to work jointly to end raids by Villa and others, full-scale war between these two neighbors, a war that neither side could afford, almost resulted. Yet, when both nations cooperated in the 1880s to defeat border Indians, they were ultimately successful. In spite of differing Indian policies, Mexico and the United States signed an agreement in 1882 allowing regular troops of both nations to cross the border in "hot pursuit" of hostile Indians.

This period of unprecedented cooperation between the two nations lacks comparative studies of United States and Mexican Indian policies. Most United States scholars of Indians on the border during the years 1848–1911 have relied on English language sources. Mexican studies of Indians during the second half of the nineteenth century have concentrated on either the Yaquis or the Mayas. No other researcher has explored this topic in Mexico City by extensively consulting correspondence and newspapers in the Porfirio Díaz papers and the Secretaría de Relaciones Exteriores archive. This study makes an important contribution by emphasizing Mexico's perception of border Indian conflicts during this period.

Although the United States and Mexico concluded that cooperation was their only hope for success against warring Apaches in the 1880s, each country blamed the other for continuing hostilities. Recrimination and distrust are a lasting legacy often characterizing relations between the United States and Mexico.

The United States alleged, often without proof, that the raiders were Mexican Indians and that Mexico either was unable or unwilling to end hostilities. United States forces felt justified in repeatedly crossing into

·

Mexico without permission to punish alleged raiding Indians and bandits. Intrusions such as Mackenzie's 1873 raid and General Pershing's pursuit of Villa in 1916 created lasting resentment in Mexico. Unable initially to obtain a formal agreement with Mexico, the United States arrogantly announced that its troops would cross into Mexico in pursuit of raiding Indians. Mexico resented these United States intrusions and feared that they might be a pretext to the annexation of northern Mexico.

Although the United States accused Mexico of neglecting its duty to police the border, both countries failed to provide resources to adequately protect the frontier. The United States' policy was one of federal control using federal troops. Díaz permitted Mexican states to direct their own Indian campaigns with federal subsidies. Mexican state and federal forces often had more success against hostile Indians than did United States troops, sometimes earning grudging praise from U.S. commanders. Mexico was concerned enough about defending its position to hire an American to write a book justifying Mexico's role in the border Indian wars.

Mexico blamed the United States reservation system for the raids, even suspecting that reservation Indians were encouraged to raid in Mexico while they remained at peace with the United States. There was sometimes proof that the raiders came from United States reservations, a fact that even U.S. officials occasionally admitted with reluctance. Mexico distrusted United States intentions to the point of employing a spy on the San Carlos reservation in order to keep informed of Apache movements.

Before the campaigns against the Indians had ended, Mexico had sacrificed unknown numbers of Indians and soldiers and had spent millions of dollars in the name of order and progress. Most of Mexico's resources went toward pacification efforts, whereas in the United States there were more expenditures in a conscious effort to "civilize" the Indians. During the Porfiriato, Indians were considered obstacles to peace, progress, and prosperity. Therefore, Mexico sought ways to regenerate and assimilate, and when that failed, to exterminate Indians.

Many educated Mexicans believed that mestizos would eventually absorb the Indians and thereby unify the nation. The same Mexicans believed European immigration would hasten the process of mestizaje. Some looked to education for the Indians' "regeneration," but others doubted the Indians' ability to learn and improve their status. During the Díaz presidency, Indian education was primarily limited to the teaching of Spanish to Indians. Funds were concentrated in major cities, although by the end of the Porfiriato, legislation had been enacted for primary education for rural Indians.

Interest in Indian education was primarily intellectual rhetoric. Just as ephemeral were the precursors of *indigenismo* during the Díaz period. The first Indianist societies began during the Porfiriato and archaeological work started in earnest; but, ironically, this incipient indigenismo glorifying Mexico's indigenous cultures began in a society that did little to better the deplorable socioeconomic conditions of the Indians.

Porfirian Mexico did not concern itself with social welfare. Indeed, welfare was considered antiliberal and unscientific because nature had decreed that only the fittest should survive. Even the church neglected the Indians and charity remained an individual duty.

Mexican Indian policy demanded maximum economic exploitation of Indian labor and the country's land for the capitalistic modernization of the nation. During the Porfiriato, population growth and rapid commercial expansion, especially in the north and south, created new demands for Indian land and labor. Mexico's capitalist elite created defensive stereotypes to justify exploitation of "inferior" Indians.

The forced labor system of debt peonage facilitated exploitation of Indian workers. When the Yaqui rebellion threatened Sonora's mining interests, Governor Izábal deported Yaquis into slavery on Yucatán's henequen plantations. Although the Yaquis fought to defend their lands, in the end they lost out to the hacendados.

Indian communal holdings were divided up when Indians could not produce clear titles to their lands. Mexico's railroad development was closely linked to the denouncing and seizure of communal lands. Property belonged to those strong enough to obtain it, and the fact that the Indian lost his land suggested he was less than deserving. There were few attempts to protect Indians from economic exploitation during the Porfiriato, a period when no federal indigenista legislation was enacted. A Chihuahua law designed to protect Tarahumaras was never implemented.

Economic callousness during the Porfiriato was a major cause of the social revolution that would follow. Antecedents for revolution intensified during the Díaz regime when quantitative, material advances, especially in transportation and communication, were valued as the visible measures of progress. Díaz's científico advisors were in the mainstream of world opinion when they claimed Mexico's drive to modernize required more roads, railroads, and bridges.

Díaz's efforts to transform Mexico into a modern, industrial nation heightened the capitalist confrontation with noncapitalistic Indian societies. Indians reacted with rebellion to usurpation of their lands and the resultant social dislocations alienating them from their social ties. Not benefiting from Díaz's modernization policy, Indians developed a resentment that was transformed into mass revolutionary movements whose goal was to change the entire social structure. Indian rebellions played a major part in the social revolution that abruptly ended the Porfiriato.

Meanwhile, it was necessary to control hostile Indians in order to achieve internal peace and integrate the nation. Díaz's plan for Mexico's development and modernization required that the Positivist motto of "order and progress" become a reality.

Whereas usurpation of land and enslavement of Indians precipitated the Mayo and Yaqui rebellions, the seminomadic border Indians provided capitalists with neither land nor labor. Mexico's deportation policy directed toward maximum exploitation of Indian labor was not applicable to border Indians. New policies were needed to defeat hostile Indians in the frontier states, which led to joint military action with the United States to defeat the Apaches.

In 1848 hostile Indians on the frontier became a United States responsibility under provisions of the Treaty of Guadalupe Hidalgo. Unable to end border raids, the United States abrogated this responsibility with the 1853 Gadsden Purchase and Treaty. Although the United States increased military pressure against Mescalero Apaches from Fort Stanton, New Mexico, in 1870–71, Mescaleros continued to raid in Sonora and Chihuahua. Brigadier General Howard's 1872 pact with Cochise temporarily ended Chiricahua raiding in the United States, but did not prevent Chiricahua Apaches from continuing hostilities in Mexico. Comanches no longer threatened the border after their decisive defeat in 1874–75. Kickapoo depredations diminished after 1873, but Texas continued to protest raids by Kickapoos and Lipan Apaches receiving protection in Coahuila. Mexico found it difficult to reconcile U.S. Indian policy aimed at protecting Arizona and New Mexico at Mexico's expense with the constant Texas complaints of raids from Coahuila.

Mexico blamed American Indians for the continuing raids, and the United States was convinced that Mexican Indians depredated the frontier. Unauthorized border crossings by troops from both nations in pursuit of hostiles were quietly settled until 1877, when the United States declared, through the Ord order, that American troops would give chase across the border. Mexico resented Ord's order and only agreed to cooperate with the United States to defeat the hostiles when the order was revoked in 1880 after conditions had improved on the Rio Grande.

Additional appropriations for new posts and more troops on the Rio Grande enabled Ord to state in his annual report dated October 1, 1879, that he had a large reserve of troops ready to cross the border. In fact, Ord urged abrogation of the order in 1879. After the order was rescinded, Mexico agreed to sign an agreement for reciprocal troop crossing. This pact was directed against the Chiricahua menace, which had grown significantly in the late 1870s.

The area of conflict shifted west to Chihuahua, Sonora, Arizona, and New Mexico, where Chiricahua Apaches raided unhindered. In 1874 Apaches were transferred from the jurisdiction of the War Department to the Bureau of Indian Affairs. They became pawns in a struggle between these two bureaucracies for their control. Concentration of Apaches on the San Carlos Reservation exacerbated problems, and in 1877 Chiricahua and Warm Springs Apaches fled the reservation. The United States began a formal campaign against the Warm Springs Apaches in 1879. Victorio, the able leader of the Warm Springs band, was killed by Mexican forces in 1880, but the Apache threat was not over. Mescaleros fled New Mexico to join the remnants of Victorio's band in Chihuahua.

The new American and Mexican desire to work together to defeat this enemy resulted in the 1882 reciprocal crossing agreement, allowing regular troops of both nations to cross the border in "hot pursuit" of hostiles. Allowed to lapse when Geronimo surrendered in 1886, the agreement, slightly changed, was revived in 1890, 1892, and 1896 in response to a threat from Apache Kid. Although not renewed after 1896, the crossing agreement was cited by Venustiano Carranza as a precedent for General John Pershing's 1916 punitive expedition against Pancho Villa.[1]

Although the United States and Mexico were forced to sign the reciprocal crossing pact because it was their only hope for a successful campaign against the Apaches, distrust and recrimination characterized the two countries' relations. Mexico believed that U.S. reservation Indians received passes to raid in Mexico. Chiricahuas, however, fled the San Carlos reservation in resistance to corruption, the concentration policy, demoralizing rationing, white encroachment on their land, and the squabbles between the army and the Bureau of Indian Affairs.

Copper miners disregarded reservation boundaries on the east, and to the west silver, gold, and copper were found. "Large pieces of what had been the reservation were sliced off for Anglo use and mines went into operation. The federal government did nothing to interfere with the encroachments."[2] Mormon settlements expanded into Arizona at the same time. Mormon farmers pressed onto the reservation from the west, and on the southeast Mormons diverted Gila water from the reservation's irrigation projects. According to Spicer, "the agent at San Carlos and the Commissioner of Indian Affairs in Washington not only permitted the encroachments and allowed the boundaries of the reservation to be surveyed in favor of the mining and agricultural interest, but they themselves even invested in the new mines."[3]

Never trusting the United States reservation system, Mexico employed a spy on the San Carlos reservation to monitor movements of Apaches and United States troops. Mexico's criticism of American reservations increased when Geronimo returned to his United States home with stolen Mexican stock in 1884. Mexico also disliked the Americans' use of Apache scouts, accusing them of depredations in its territory. Claiming scouts were in violation of the 1882 agreement, Mexico blamed Captain Crawford's 1886 death on United States scouts having been mistaken for hostiles. The new crossing pacts specified that only two scouts could be used by each company as guides.

An official Mexican publication dated 1905 listed extermination, deportation, and colonization of Indians as policies of the Díaz government. Although never a federal policy, Chihuahua and Sonora had Apache extermination policies that carried scalp bounties. Such policies did not exist in the United States.[4]

Both Mexico and the United States took Indian lands that were valuable for farming or mining. In the United States, western votes passed the 1887 Dawes Act, which was designed to break up reservations via land allotment. Between 1883 and 1894, Mexico passed colonizing laws, accelerating the growth of large estates at the expense of Indian ejido communities. Land-grabbing hacendados received Mexican government protection, defended on the grounds that the state should not intervene in private enterprise.

Removal of Indians from their lands was practiced in both nations, but only in Mexico was this deportation policy directed toward maximum exploitation of Indian laborers such as the Yaquis. Although Mexico did not consider the United States reservation policy viable, Sonora attempted to concentrate Yaquis in guarded ranchería settlements. Yaqui labor continuing to be of primary importance, the Indians were permitted to leave their confinement in order to work in mines and on haciendas.

United States policy was consistently one of federal control with federal troops. During the Porfiriato, both federal and state troops were used. Federal presidios and colonias militares proved ineffective on the frontier, so Díaz allowed border states to direct their Indian campaigns with special federal subsidies.[5]

As commander of the army, Díaz made the ultimate decisions, giving orders through the secretary of war to commanders of Mexico's twelve military zones. After ridding Mexico of local bosses, or *caudillos*, Díaz controlled the country with loyal governors, a large percentage of them generals.[6] When governors and commanders of military zones quarreled over policy decisions, Díaz mediated disputes. The division and overlapping of supreme authority in the states worked to Díaz's advantage because governors and commanders were eager to show their loyalty by reporting any infractions on the part of their rivals. Díaz granted considerable autonomy to the states but was quick to reprimand abuses, such as Sonora's governor's hiring of an American soldier of fortune to direct the Yaqui campaign.

Mexican troops and officers served well in the joint Apache campaign, having notable successes against Victorio, Juh, and Nana. Mexican officials cooperated with their U.S. counterparts. Generals Ord and Treviño worked together to end Rio Grande raids in the 1870s. General Miles and Sonora's governor Torres acted in close alliance to effect Geronimo's surrender. Only when both nations combined their efforts were they finally able to defeat hostile border Indians.

Both the United States and Mexico cited peaceful assimilation of Indians as their ultimate goals. Mexico sought political incorporation of Indians, but United States reservation policy kept Indians isolated and provided little experience in local United States government. In reality, the primary goal of Indian policy in both countries was economic exploitation. Indians lost their traditional ranges on both sides of the border as settlers encroached on their lands. Railroad, mining, and agricultural interests grew at the Indians' expense. Mexican railroad development from 1877 to 1884 was closely linked to the denouncing and seizure of Indian communal lands. The United States federal government granted railroads a right of way through Indian reservations. Individual Indian assimilation and detribalization resulted from policies of infiltration and colonization in both nations. Solidarity of Native American groups such as the Yaquis and Chiricahuas, however, intensified through warfare.[7] Because both nations were insensitive to the consequences of their actions, the social ills that their policies created or exacerbated haunt present generations.

Notes

AHS: Arizona Historical Society, Tucson

Archivo de Sonora: Archivo General de Sonora, Ramo Relaciones Exteriores, Legajo 11, Museo Regional de Sonora, Hermosillo

Barker THC: Eugene C. Barker Texas History Center, University of Texas at Austin

CPD: Colección Porfirio Diaz, Sala Francisco Xavier Alegre, Universidad Ibero-americana

Correspondence Sheridan and Crook: Correspondence Between Lieutenant General P. H. Sheridan and Brigadier General George Crook Regarding Apache Indians, Gatewood Collection, Box 1, Folder 19, Arizona Historical Society, Tucson

Official Records: Official Records of the Department of Arizona, Communications During Field Operations Against Apache Indians, 8/29/86–10/11/86, Gatewood Collection, Box 1, Folder 5, Arizona Historical Society, Tucson

RE: Archivo Histórico Genaro Estrada, Secretaría de Relaciones Exteriores, Mexico, D.F.

PROLOGUE

1. The title "Bureau of Indian Affairs" (BIA) is used throughout for consistency, although most historical documents do not use this terminology. Secretary of War John C. Calhoun created the Bureau of Indian Affairs in 1824. However, commissioners of Indian affairs headed their annual reports "Office of Indian Affairs" until 1947, when "Bureau of Indian Affairs" was officially adopted. The National Archives and Records Service adopted the current title, although historically "Office of Indian Affairs," "Indian Department," and "Indian Service" were all used inconsistently. Francis Paul Prucha, *The Great Father: The United States Government and*

the American Indian. (Lincoln and London: University of Nebraska Press, 1984), vol. 2, pp. 1227–29.

2. Only in 1953 did the Tarahumaras receive substantial aid; Instituto Indigenista Interamericano, *Legislación Indigenista de México* (México: III Ediciones Especiales, No. 38, 1958), n.p.

3. Richard N. Adams, "Nationalization," in *Social Anthropology*, vol. 6 of *Handbook of Middle American Indians*, ed. Manning Nash, gen. ed., Robert Waughope (Austin: University of Texas Press, 1967), p. 476; and Frederick Starr, *In Indian Mexico* (Chicago: Forbes, 1908), p.v.

4. Francisco Bulnes, *El porvenir de las naciones latinoamericanos antes las conquistas recientes de Europa y los EEUU* (México: Mariano Nava, 1899), pp. 5–7, 19, 150.

5. Francisco Pimentel, *Memoria sobre las causas que han originado la situación actual de la raza indígena de México* (México: Andrade y Escalante, 1864), pp. 222, 226, 234, 238.

6. Antonio García Cubas, *Discursos sobre la decadencia de la raza indígena* (México: Tip. Literaria de Filomento Mata, 1880), pp. 167–69; and T. G. Powell, "Mexican Intellectuals and the Indian Question," *Hispanic American Historical Review* 48, no. 1 (1968): 21, 33; and John Coatsworth, "Railroads, Landholding, and Agrarian Protest in the Early Porfiriato, "*Hispanic American Historical Review* 54, no. 1 (1974): 49–50, 55.

7. Salomón Nahmad, "Las ideas sociales del positivismo en el indigenismo de la época pre-revolucionaria en México," *América Indígena* 33, no. 4 (1973): 1170–72; Leopoldo Zea, *El positivismo en México* (1943–44; rpt. México: Fondo de Cultura Economíca, 1968), pp. 119, 294, 408; Antonio Peñafiel, ed., *Códice Martínez Gracida de Jamiltepec, Estado de Oaxaca, Códice Mixteca, Lienzo de Zacatepec* (México: Secretaría de Fomento, 1900), p. 1; and Charles C. Cumberland, *Mexico: the Struggle for Modernity* (New York: Oxford University Press, 1968), pp. 201–2.

8. Carlos R. Menéndez, ed. *Historia del infame y vergonzoso comercio de indios* (Mérida: la Revista de Yucatán, 1923), pp. 106, 127, 133, 207, 276, 329, 347–64, 373–79.

9. Ricardo García Granados, *Historia de México desde la restauración de la república en 1867 hasta la caida de Huerta*, vol. 1 (México: Editorial Jus, 1923; rpt. 1956), p. 412; John Kenneth Turner, *Barbarous Mexico* (Chicago: C. H. Kerr, 1911; rpt. Austin: University of Texas Press, 1969) p. 106; Moisés González Navarro, *El Porfiriato: La vida social*, in vol. 5 of *Historia moderna de México*, ed. Daniel Cosío Villegas (México: Hermes, 1957), pp. 247, 249; Alfonso Villa Rojas, "The Maya of Yucatán," *Ethnology*, part 1, in *Handbook of Middle American Indians*, ed. by Robert Wauchope (Austin: University of Texas Press, 1969), p. 247; and Ireneo Paz, *Album de la paz y el trabajo* (México: Ireneo Paz, 1910), n.p.

10. Jack D. Forbes, "Historical Survey of the Indians of Sonora 1821–1910," *Ethnohistory* 4, no. 1 (1957): 335; Evelyn Hu-Dehart, "Development and Rural Rebellion: Pacification of the Yaquis in the Late Porfiriato," *Hispanic American Historical Review* 54, no. 1 (February, 1974): 73, 76; and Francisco Paso y Troncoso,

Las guerras con los tribus Yaqui y Mayo del estado de Sonora (México: Tip. del Departamento del Estado Mayor, 1905) p. 342.

11. Alfonso Fábila, *Los tribus Yaquis de Sonora, su cultura y anhelada autodeterminación* (México: Departamento de Asuntos Indigenas, 1940) pp. 88, 96, 98; Francisco R. Almada, *La revolución e el estado de Sonora* (México: Institución Nacional de Estudias Históricas de la República Méxicana, 1971), p. 20; and Paso y Troncoso, *Las guerras*, p. 79.

12. Paso y Troncoso, *Las guerras*, p. 317; Moisés González Navarro, "Instituciones indígenas en México independiente," *Métodos y resultados de la política indigenista en México*, vol. 6 (Memorias del Instituto Nacional Indigenista, 1954) p. 163; and Hu-Dehart, "Development," pp. 80–89, 92.

13. Edward H. Spicer, "The Yaqui and Mayo," in *Ethnology*, part 2 of *Handbook of Middle American Indians*, ed. Evan. Voyt (Austin: University of Texas Press, 1969) p. 833.

14. Francisco R. Almada, *Juárez y Terrazas: Aclaraciones históricas* (México: Libros Mexicanos, 1958), p. 313.

15. Luis Torres to José G. Carbó, 23 July and 14 August 1885, CPD, Legajo 10, Box 16, Sala Francisco Xavier Alegre, Universidad Iberoamericana, México, D.F.

16. Paso y Troncoso, *Las guerras*, p. 342.

17. Daniel Gutiérrez Santos, *Historia militar de México, 1876–1914* (México: Ediciones Ateneo, 1955), pp. 20–21; and Jorge Alberta Lozoya, "Un guión para el estudio de los ejércitos mexicanos del siglo diecinueve," *Historia Mexicana* 17 (April–June 1968), no. 4, pp. 553–68.

18. Sec. of Gobernación Corral to Foreign Relations, 2 July 1906, RE, LE 2250, pt. 1, México, D.F.

CHAPTER I

1. Robert M. Utley, *Frontier Regulars: The United States and the Indian, 1866–1891* (New York: Macmillan, 1973), p. 214.

2. Francis B. Heitman, *Historical Register and Dictionary of the United States Army, from its Organization, September 29, 1789, to March 2, 1903*, vol. 2 (Washington, D.C.: Government Printing Office, 1903), p. 626; and Edward H. Spicer, *Cycles of Conquest: The Impact of Spain, Mexico, and the United States on the Indians of the Southwest, 1533–1960* (Tucson: University of Arizona Press, 1976), p. 248.

3. Donald E. Worcester, "The Apaches in the History of the Southwest," *New Mexico Historical Review* 50 (January 1975): 9; Francisco R. Almada, *Diccionario de historia, geografía y biografía chihuahuenses* (Chihuahua, Chihuahua: Universidad de Chihuahua, Departmento de Investigaciones Sociales, Sección de Historia, 1928; 2nd ed. Cuidad Juárez, Chihuahua: En Impresora de Juárez, 1968) p. 430; and Daniel Cosío Villegas, ed., *Historia moderna de México*, vol. 3 of *La república restaurada: La vida social*, eds. Luis González y González et al. (Mexico: Hermes, 1957),

p. 190. Hereafter referred to as Cosío Villegas, *Historia moderna: República restaurada, vida social.*

4. John Bret Harte, "The San Carlos Indian Reservation, 1872–1886: An Administrative History" (Ph.D. dissertation, University of Arizona, 1972), pp. 9, 11, 13–14; and Max L. Moorehead, *The Presidio: Bastion of the Spanish Borderlands* (Norman: University of Oklahoma Press, 1975), pp. 243, 260, 262–63.

5. Albert H. Schroeder, *A Study of the Apache Indians, Parts IV and V* (New York and London: Garland, 1974), p. 515; Herbert Howe Bancroft, *History of Arizona and New Mexico, 1530–1888* (San Francisco: The History Company, 1889; rpt. Albuquerque: Horn and Wallace, 1962), p. 403; Joseph F. Park, "The Apaches in Mexican-American Relations, 1848–1861: A Footnote to the Gadsden Treaty," *Arizona and the West* 3 (Summer, 1961): 134; A. B. Bender, "Frontier Defense in the Territory of New Mexico, 1846–1853," *New Mexico Historical Review* 9, no. 3 (July, 1934): 251; Almada, *Diccionario*, p. 38; William B. Griffen, *Utmost Good Faith: Patterns of Apache-Mexican Hostilities in Northern Chihuahua Border Warfare, 1821–1848* (Albuquerque: University of New Mexico Press, 1988), pp. 11–12, 28; and Héctor A. Pesqueira, "Una Muerte Llamada Gerónimo," *Temas Sonorenses A Través de los Simposios de Historia* (Hermosillo: Gobierno del Estado de Sonora, 1984), p. 242.

6. Dan L. Thrapp, *Victorio and the Mimbres Apaches* (Norman: University of Oklahoma Press, 1974), p. 19; Moisés González Navarro, "Instituciones indígenas en México independiente," p. 139; and González Navarro, *El Porfiriato: La vida social*, p. 145.

7. Schroeder, *Apache Indians IV*, pp. 129, 131, 516; Bancroft, *History of Arizona and New Mexico*, p. 407; Griffen, *Utmost Good Faith*, pp. 51, 58; William C. McGaw, *Savage Scene: The Life and Times of James Kirker, Frontier King* (New York: Hastings House, 1972), p. 91; Ralph A. Smith, "The Scalp Hunt in Chihuahua—1849," *New Mexico Historical Review* 40, no. 2 (April 1965): 117; Almada, *Diccionario*, p. 38; and Francisco R. Almada, *Gobernadores del estado de Chihuahua*, 2nd ed. (Chihuahua: Centro Librero La Prensa, 1980), p. 85.

8. Almada, *Diccionario*, p. 302; Almada, *Gobernadores*, p. 93; McGaw, *Savage Scene*, pp. 136, 150–51, 192; and Fernando Jordán, *Crónica de un país bárbaro*, 2nd ed. (México: B. Costa-Amic, 1965), p. 229.

9. González Navarro, *El Porfiriato: La vida social*, p. 246; and José Fuentes Mares, *Y México se refugió en el desierto: Luis Terrazas, historia y destino* (México: Editorial Jus, 1954), p. 134.

10. Fuentes Mares, *Y México se refugió*, p. 135; and Ministerio de Relaciones de la Republica Mexicana, *Traducción del dictamen de Mr. Wadsworth, sobre las reclamaciones mexicanas procedentes de depredaciones de los indios* (México: Imprenta del gobierno, en Palacio, 1873), p. 28. Hereafter referred to as Ministerio de Relaciones, *Dictamen*.

11. Almada, *Diccionario*, p. 282; and John C. Cremony, *Life Among the Apaches* (New York: John H. Carmany Co., 1868; rpt. Glorieta, New Mexico: Rio Grande Press, 1969), pp. 38–41.

12. Fred Rippy, "The Indians of the Southwest in the Diplomacy of the United States and Mexico, 1848–1853," *Hispanic American Historical Review* 2 (Baltimore: Williams and Wilkins, 1919), p. 364. Hereafter referred to as Rippy, "Indians."

13. Charles I. Bevans, *Treaties and Other International Agreements of the United States of America, 1886–1949*, vol. 9, Department of State publication 8615 (Washington, D.C.: U.S. Government Printing Office, 1972), pp. 774–75.

14. Rippy, "Indians," p. 365.

15. Even after final pacification, the border continued to divide tribes, for there are Chiricahua Apaches living in Mexico today. Spicer, *Cycles*, pp. 245–46, 346; and Rippy, "Indians," pp. 364–65, 375.

16. Rippy, "Indians," p. 370.

17. Rippy, "Indians," pp. 367, 372–73, 377–79.

18. Rippy, "Indians," pp. 368–69, 375, 395.

19. Cosío Villegas, *Historia moderna: República restaurada, vida social*, p. 192; and Rippy, "Indians," pp. 380, 382–83, and 391.

20. Rippy, "Indians," pp. 384, 386, 389; and Sánchez Navarro Collection, Nettie Lee Benson Latin American Collection, University of Texas at Austin.

21. Ministerio de Relaciones, *Dictamen*, pp. 19–20; and Rippy, "Indians," pp. 373, 391.

22. Fuentes Mares, *Y México se refugió*, pp. 132–33; and Rippy, "Indians," p. 394.

23. Ministerio de Relaciones, *Dictamen*, pp. 20–21; and Clarence C. Clendenen, *Blood on the Border: The United States Army and the Mexican Irregulars* (London: Collier-MacMillan, 1969), p. 19.

24. Donald Dewitt, "El acuerdo diplomático del 29 de julio de 1882: Su significado para los estados de Arizona y Sonora," trans. Leo Sandoval, vol. 2 of *Memoria III Simposio de Historia de Sonora* (Hermosillo, Sonora: Instituto de Investigaciones Históricas, 1978), p. 610.

25. RE 17-11-39; and Clendenen, *Blood*, p. 56.

26. Fuentes Mares, *Y México se refugió*, p. 136; and RE 6-2-6.

27. Cosío Villegas, *Historia moderna: República restaurada, vida social* p. 188; and Texas Adjutant General Records, 1839–1879, Box No. 20253, Statement 'C,' Barker THC.

28. Ernest Wallace, *Ranald S. Mackenzie on the Texas Frontier* (Lubbock: West Texas Museum Association, 1964), pp. 93, 95; James M. Callahan, *American Foreign Policy in Mexican Relations* (New York: Macmillan, 1932), p. 348; and Utley, *Frontier Regulars*, p. 345.

29. Cosío Villegas, *Historia moderna: República restaurada, vida social*, pp. 196–97; Robert Goldthwaite Carter, *On the Border with Mackenzie or Winning West Texas from the Comanches* (1935; rpt. New York: Antiquarian Press, 1961), pp. 432–33; and Utley, *Frontier Regulars*, pp. 345–46, 349.

30. Dorman H. Winfrey and James M. Day, eds., *The Indian Papers of Texas and the Southwest, 1825–1916* (Austin: Pemberton Press, 1906), pp. 313–33.

31. Cosío Villegas, *Historia moderna: República restaurada, vida social* p. 198.

32. Philip H. Sheridan, *Record of Engagements with Hostile Indians within the Military Division of the Missouri, from 1868–1882* (Washington, D.C.: Government Printing Office, 1882), p. 35; Carter, *On the Border*, p. 433; and Robert Goldthwaite Carter, "General R. S. Mackenzie's Raid into Mexico, 1873," *Outing Magazine* (April 1888): p. 4; Charles B. Gatewood Collection, Box 1, Folder 23, AHS.

33. Carter,"General R. S. Mackenzie's Raid," p. 46; Utley, *Frontier Regulars*, p. 349; Carl Coke Rister, *The Southwestern Frontier 1865–1881* (Cleveland, Ohio: Arthur H. Clark, 1928), p. 153; Ernest Wallace, ed., *Ranald S. Mackenzie's Official Correspondence Relating to Texas, 1871–1873*, (Lubbock, Texas: West Texas Museum Assoication, 1967), vol. 2, pp. 12, 34.

34. Rister, *Southwestern Frontier*, p. 154.

35. Cosío Villegas, *Historia moderna: República restaurada, vida social* pp. 199–200.

36. F. E. Green, ed., "Ranald S. Mackenzie's Official Correspondence Relating to Texas, 1871–1873," *The Museum Journal* 9 (Lubbock: West Texas Museum Association, 1965): 163, 171; Gastón García Cantú, *Las invasiones norteamericanos en México* (1971; rpt. México: Ediciones Era, 1974), p. 217; and Clendenen, *Blood*, pp. 81–82.

37. RE 25-20-192.

38. Texas Adjutant General Records, 1839–1879, Box 2, Q400-UT8 (1870–1876), No. 212, Barker THC.

39. Texas Adjutant General Records, 1839–1879, Box 2, Q400-UT8 (1870–1876), No. 186, Barker THC.

40. Sheridan, *Record of Engagements*, p. 48.

41. RE 25-20-191.

42. RE 15-16-8736.

43. RE 16-3-38.

44. United States Congress, House, *Mexican Border Troubles*, H.E.D. 13, 45th Cong., 1st sess., 1876.

45. United States Congress, House, *Texas Frontier Troubles*, H.R. 343, 45th Cong., 1st sess., 1876.

46. United States Congress, House, H.E.D. 33, 44th Cong., 2nd sess., 1876.

47. Heitman, *Historical Register*, p. 626; and Sheridan, *Record of Engagements*, p. 59.

CHAPTER 2

1. Superintendent Thomas J. Goree, Huntsville, Penna., 21 September 1877, notation of statement made to him by convict W. A. Bridges, Texas Adjutant General Records, 1839–1879, Box 2 Q400-UT9 (Jan.–July 1877), Barker THC; RE 11-1-20; and Rister, *Southwestern Frontier*, pp. 179, 182.

2. Minister of War to Foreign Relations, 21 December 1877, Foreign Relations to Minister of War, 27 December 1877, RE 2-1-1782; *Diario Oficial*, 13 July 1877, conversation Gerónimo Treviño with E.O.C. Ord, 30 June 1877, Hipólito Charles to Foreign Relations, 6 April 1877, RE 11-1-20.

conversation Gerónimo Treviño with E.O.C. Ord, 30 June 1877, Hipólito Charles to Foreign Relations, 6 April 1877, RE 11-1-20.

3. Louis Craig to Commanding Officer, Huachuca Mountains, A.T., 22 April 1877, Letters Received by the Office of Indian Affairs, 1824–1881, Arizona Superintendency, 1863–1880, Roll 19, Microcopy 234, United States Bureau of Indian Affairs; and Committee Foreign Relations on Relations of United States with Mexico, H.R. Rep. No. 701, 45th Cong., 2nd sess.

4. Report from Committee Military Affairs Regarding Senate Bill 53, passed unanimously 3 January 1878, S.R. No. 40, 46th Cong., 2nd sess.

5. Memorandum of Points Noticed by the Minister of the United States in Conference at the Mexican Foreign Office, signed John W. Foster, copy left at Mexican Foreign Office, 23 June 1877, H.E.D., 46th Cong., 1st sess., v. 1, No. 13.

6. Ignacio Mariscal to Foreign Relations, 7 June 1877, RE 11-1-22; and Pauline Safford Relyea, "Diplomatic Relations between the United States and Mexico under Porfirio Díaz, 1876–1910," *Smith College Studies in History* 10, no. 1 (October 1924): 31.

7. Memorandum signed Ignacio Mariscal, 7 June 1877, RE 11-1-22; and Report of Secretary of War Relative to Mexican Border Troubles, H.E.D., 45th Cong., 1st sess., v. 1, No. 13.

8. Private Mexican businessman, San Antonio, to Foreign Relations, 28 January 1878, RE 11-1-20.

9. *The London Times*, 31 May 1877, RE 11-1-22.

10. *The New Banner of the Free* (Austin), 6 August 1880, CPD, Legajo 5, Box 7; Safford Relyea, "Diplomatic Relations," pp. 31–32; Miguel Velasco Valdés, *La pre-revolución y el hombre de la calle* (México: Costa-Amie, 1964), p. 300; Fred J. Rippy, *The United States and Mexico* (New York: Knopf, 1926), p. 307; and Robert Gregg, *The Influence of Border Troubles in Relations between the United States and Mexico, 1876–1910* (Baltimore: Johns Hopkins Press, 1937), pp. 27, 46, 711.

11. Boletin Oficial (Ures), 15 February 1878, Speech by Deputy Ismael S. Quiroga, 13th current session, in *El Mensajero*, 21 December 1877, Archivo de Sonora, Biblioteca y Museo de Sonora, Universidad de Sonora, Serie Sonora, Rolls 7–8, Biblioteca del Museo de Antropología e Historia, México, D. F.; and Gonzáléz Navarro, *El Porfiriato: La vida social*, p. 245.

12. Papers Relating to the Foreign Affairs of the United States, H.E.D., 46th Cong., 2nd sess., v. 1, Part 1, No. 336, John Foster to William Evarts, 14 December 1878; and RE 11-1-22.

13. RE 11-1-22; *Diario Oficial*, 13 July 1877, Private Mexican businessman, San Antonio, to Foreign Relations, 28 January 1878, RE 11-1-20; Gregg, *Influence of Border Troubles*, p. 58; Wilbert Timmons, ed., *John F. Finerty Reports Profirian Mexico 1879* (El Paso: Texas Western Press, 1974), pp. 16–17; Cora H. Crawford, *The Land of the Montezumas* (New York: John B. Alden, 1889), p. 307; and Dan Thrapp, *General Crook and the Sierra Madre Adventure* (Norman: University of Oklahoma

Treviño married an American. In order to pacify Treviño, he was given a hacienda and made general-in-chief of the Army of Northwestern Mexico. In 1883 Ord died of yellow fever while visiting his daughter in Mexico.

14. Governor of Coahuila to Foreign Relations, 25 July 1877; Governor of Nuevo León to Foreign Relations, 1 August 1877; Governor of Tamaulipas to Foreign Relations, 2 August 1877; Governor of Chihuahua to Foreign Relations, 24 August 1877; Governor of Durango to Foreign Relations, 26 August 1877; Governor of Chihuahua to Foreign Relations, 6 and 13 September 1877; Governor of Sonora to Foreign Relations, 10 September 1877; Governor of Durango to Gobernación, 4 December 1877, RE 2-1-1786.

15. Sheridan, *Record of Engagements*, p. 75.

16. Edward Hatch to Assistant Adjutant General, 11 October 1877, Letters Received by the Office of Indian Affairs, 1824–1881, Arizona Superintendency, 1863–1880, Roll 19, Microcopy 234, United States Bureau of Indian Affairs.

17. Report from Schleicher, Committee Foreign Relations on Relations of the United States with Mexico, H.R. No. 701, 45th Cong., 2nd sess.

18. RE 1-14-1623; Claims of Texas, S.E.D. No. 19, 45th Cong., 2nd sess., v. 1; RE 1-14-1629; and 16 February 1878, RE 2-1-1771.

19. General Naranjo to Gerónimo Treviño, 16 July 1876, RE 1-14-1629; Daniel Cosío Villegas, ed., *Historia moderna de Mexico: El Porfiriato, la vida política exterior*, part 2 (México: Hermes, 1963), p. 154; México, *Las memorias diplomáticas de Mr. Foster sobre México*, Archivo Histórico Diplomático Mexicano, No. 29 (México: Secretaría de Relaciones Exteriores, 1929), pp. 123–25, hereafter referred to as *Foster sobre México*.

20. Relations between the United States and Mexico, H.R. No. 701, 45th Cong., 2nd sess., v. 3; and Committee Foreign Relations on Relations of United States with Mexico, H.R. No. 701, 45th Congs., 2nd sess.

21. Removal of Kickapoo Indians, S.M.D. No. 23, 45th Cong., 2nd sess., v. 1.

22. Governor of Coahuila to Foreign Relations, 26 April 1878; Ranald Mackenzie to William Shafter, 25 February 1878, RE 1-14-1628; and Minister of War to Foreign Relations, 17 May 1878, RE 2-1-1782.

23. Mexican consul San Antonio to Foreign Relations, 4 August 1878, RE 1-13-1524.

24. Declaration Santa Rosa, Coahuila, 20 August 1878; Governor of Coahuila to Foreign Relations, 27 September 1878, RE 1-13-1524; A. R. Moffett, 1879, RE 1-12-1160; and Papers Relating to the Foreign Relations of the United States, H.E.D. No. 1, 46th Cong., 2nd sess., part 1.

25. Minister of War to Foreign Relations, 5 November 1878, RE 1-13-1524; and George Sykes to Servando Canales, 20 November 1878; George Sykes to Servando Canales, 22 November 1878; Minister of War to Servando Canales, 23 November 1878, RE 1-14-1602.

26. Telegram Colonel Price to Assistant Adjutant General, 9 December 1878; Servando Canales to George Sykes, 25 December 1878, RE 1-14-1602.

27. Papers Relating to the Foreign Affairs of the United States, H.E.D. No. 1, 46th Cong., 2nd sess., part 1, Eleuterio Avila to John Foster, 11 November 1878.

28. Papers Relating to the Foreign Affairs of the United States, H.E.D. No. 1, 46th Cong., 2nd sess., part 1.

29. Report from Committee Military Affairs Regarding Senate Bill 53, passed unanimously 3 January 1878, S.R. No. 40, 46th Cong., 2nd sess.

30. Ibid.

31. Ibid.

32. RE 11-3-133.

33. Cosío Villegas, *Historia moderna: El Porfiriato, vida política exterior*, part 2, p. 154; México, *Foster sobre México*, pp. 123–25; and Gregg, *Influence of Border Troubles*, p. 105.

34. Annual Message of Rutherford B. Hayes, 1 December 1879, H.E.D. No. 1 46th Cong., 2nd sess., part 1.

35. Janos customs officer to Foreign Relations, 2 and 20 February 1879, RE 1-15-1654; and Dan L. Thrapp, *Juh: An Incredible Indian*, University of Texas at El Paso Southwestern Studies, 39 (El Paso: Texas Western Press, 1973), p. 26.

36. Gobernación to Foreign Relations, 6 March 1879, RE 5-15-8389; 11 March 1879, RE 29-15-45; Servando Canales to Porfirio Díaz, 13 March 1879, CPD, Legajo 4, Box 1; Janos customs officer to Foreign Relations, 28 May 1879, RE 1-15-1654; and Governor of Nuevo León to Gobernación, 7 May 1879, RE 1-15-8389.

37. RE 6-1-18.

38. United States Department of Interior to United States Secretary of State, 31 May 1879, RE 29-15-45; and C. L. Sonnichsen, *The Mescalero Apaches* (Norman: University of Oklahoma Press, 1958, rpt. 1973), pp. 136, 158, 160–61, 166–67.

39. Clendenen, *Blood on the Border*, p. 94; Minister of War to Foreign Relations, 25 June 1879, RE 1-15-8389; Janos customs officer to Foreign Relations, 11 June 1879, RE 1-15-1654, and Schroeder, *Apache Indians IV*, p. 259.

40. Worcester, "The Apaches in the History of the Southwest," p. 34.

41. August V. Kautz to Adjutant General, 12 February 1877; L. A. Abbott to Assistant Adjutant General, 21 August 1877; August V. Kautz, Endorsement of Abbot, 22 September 1877, Letters Received by the Office of Indian Affairs, 1824–1881, Arizona Superintendency, 1863–1880, Roll 19, Microcopy 234, United States Bureau of Indian Affairs.

42. John Foster to Foreign Relations, 10 July 1879, RE 1-15-1654; John Foster to Miguel Ruelas, Foreign Relations, 18 July 1879 and John Foster to Foreign Relations, 22 July 1879, RE 6-1-18.

43. RE 11-1-22.

44. Mexico's General-in-Chief of Northern Division to Foreign Relations, 10 August 1879, RE 6-1-18; Gobernación to Foreign Relations, 15 August 1879 and Foreign Relations to Minister of War, 1 September 1879, RE 1-15-1654.

45. Carlos Ortiz to Foreign Relations, 12 September 1879, RE 13-14-44; and Minister of War to Foreign Relations, 22 September 1879, RE 17-11-38.

46. E.O.C. Ord to Gerónimo Treviño, 29 September 1879, RE 5-15-8389.

47. H.R. No. 432, 46th Cong., 2nd sess., v. 2, part 1; Gregg, *Influence of Border Troubles*, p. 105; México, *Foster sobre México*, pp. 123–25.

48. Heitman, *Historical Register*, p. 445; RE 11-1-42; RE 5-15-8389; and Schroeder, *Apache Indians IV*, p. 264. Victorio was also called "Vitoyo," "Vitorio," and "Victoria." The Chihennes (Warm Springs) are sometimes referred to as "Mimbreños."

49. Gerónimo Treviño to Foreign Relations, 20 December 1879, RE 5-15-8389; Janos customs officer to Foreign Relations, RE 1-15-1654; *El Diario Oficial*, 8 January 1880, RE 20-23-60; and Archivo de Sonora.

50. Zamacona to Foreign Relations, 5 February 1880, RE 1-13-1539.

51. Telegram United States War Department, 13 January 1880; Minister of War to Foreign Relations, 6 February 1880; Foreign Relations to Minister of War, 7 February 1880, Luis Terrazas to Foreign Relations, 26 February 1880, RE 1-13-1539; RE 5-15-8389; and *El Monitor Republicano*, 14 October 1880, Inclosure 5, Ex. Doc. No. 121, 47th Cong., 1st sess., 1881–1882, v. 1, For. Rel., No. 1, part 1.

52. Rippy, *The United States and Mexico*, p. 310; Alberto María Carreño, *La diplomacia extraordinaria entre México y los Estados Unidos, 1789–1947* (México: Jus, 1961); Porfirio Díaz, *Archivo del general Porfirio Díaz* (México: Elede, 1947), p. 194; Clendenen, *Blood on the Border*, p. 85; and Coded Telegram, 22 October 1879, RE 11-1-21.

53. Ricardo Rodríguez, *Historia auténtica de la administración del Sr. Gral. Porfirio Díaz*, vol. 2 (México: Oficina Tip. de la Secretaría de Fomento, 1904), pp. 66, 74, 90–94; Gordon C. Baldwin, *The Warrior Apaches: A Story of the Chiricahua and Western Apaches* (Tucson: Dale Stuart King, 1965), p. 38; P. H. Morgan to Evarts, 16 October 1880; José Fernández to P. H. Morgan, 21 September 1880, Inclosure 1 in no. 121, Ex. Doc., 47th Cong., 1st sess., 1881–1882, v. 1, Foreign Relations, no. 1, part 1.

54. *El Monitor Republicano*, 13 October 1880, Inclosure 4; 15 October 1880, Inclosure 3; 24 October 1880, Inclosure 2, no. 121, Ex. Doc., 47th Cong., 1st sess., 1881–1882, v. 1, Foreign Relations, no. 1, part 1.

55. Office of the Secretaries of the Chamber of Senators of the Congress of the Union, Section 1, Secret Bureau, to the Chief Clerk in Charge of the Department of Foreign Affairs, 29 May 1880; Fernández to Morgan, 15 October 1880, Inclosure 6; Morgan to Evarts, 16 October 1880, Ex. Doc. no. 121, 47th Cong., 1st sess., 1881–1882, v. 1, Foreign Relations, no. 1, part 1, no. 439.

56. Eugene A. Carr, Colonel 6th Cavalry Commanding, Fort Bowie, to [General George Crook?], 29 August 1880, field operations in Southern Arizona, 1 October 1879–29 August 1880, Folder 22, G258c, Box 1, Gatewood, AHS; RE 5-15-8389; and Sheridan, *Record of Engagements*, p. 94.

57. Colonel Martin L. Crimmins, "Colonel Buell's Expedition into Mexico in 1880," *New Mexico Historical Review* 10 (1935): 135, 142; RE 5-15-8389; Governor of Chihuahua to Porfirio Díaz, 9 September 1880, CPD Legajo 5, Box 7 and Box 8; and Sonnichsen, *Mescalero Apaches*, p. 210.

58. *Periódico Oficial*, 20 October 1880, CPD, Legajo 5, Box 8; RE 5-15-8389; and Crimmins, "Colonel Buell's Expedition," p. 142.

59. H.E.D. No. 1, 46th Cong., 2nd sess.; Francisco Almada, *Juárez y Terrazas*, p. 316; Dewitt, "El acuerdo diplomático," p. 614; and RE 5-15-8389.

CHAPTER 3

1. Annual Report of Brigadier General George Crook, U.S. Army Commanding Department of Arizona 1885, Gatewood, G258c, Box 2, Folder 19, pp. 5–6, AHS.

2. Foreign Relations to Secretary of War, 13 January 1881, and War to Foreign Relations, 25 January 1881, RE 5-15-8389.

3. Evarts to Morgan, Department of State, 4 February 1881, and Evarts to Navarro, Department of State, 3 January 1881, Ex. Doc., 47th Cong., 1st sess., v. 1, Foreign Relations, no. 1, pt. 1.

4. *Arizona Daily Star*, 24 February 1881; *Arizona Daily Journal*, 31 January 1881, Ex. Doc., 47th Cong., 1st sess., v. 1, Foreign Relations, no. 1, pt. 1, no. 496.

5. Zamacona to Blaine, 19 April 1881, and Terrazas to Minister of Foreign Affairs, 28 April 1881, Ex. Doc., 47th Cong., 1st sess., v. 1, Foreign Relations, no. 1, pt. 1, no. 498.

6. Blaine to Morgan, 28 April 1881, Ex. Doc., 47th Cong., 1st sess., v. 1, Foreign Relations, no. 1, pt. 1, no. 451.

7. Blaine to Zamacona, 26 July 1881, Ex. Doc., 47th Cong., 1st sess., v. 1, Foreign Relations, no. 1, pt. 1, no. 507; *El Progresista* [El Paso], 8 July 1881; Ignacio Mariscal, Foreign Relations, to Tucson Consul, 13 April 1881; Mariscal to Governor of Chihuahua, 13 April 1881; and Terrazas to Foreign Relations, 9 May 1881, RE 5-15-8389.

8. War to Foreign Relations, 15 April 1881; War to Foreign Relations, 18 June 1881; Mariscal to Mexican Legation, 30 June 1881; and Mariscal to War, 7 June 1881, RE 5-15-8389.

9. Zamacona to Blaine, 19 April 1881, Ex. Doc., 47th Cong., 1st sess., v. 1, Foreign Relations, no. 1, pt. 1, no. 498.

10. Captain Baylor to Consul Escobar, 10 May 1881, Ex. Doc., 47th Cong., 1st sess., v. 1 Foreign Relations, no. 1, pt. 1.

11. Zamacona to Blaine, 18 July 1881, Ex. Doc., 47th Cong., 1st sess., v. 1, Foreign Relations, no. 1, pt. 1, no. 505; Governor of Chihuahua to Foreign Relations, 5 February 1881, RE 25-20-193; *El Paso Herald*, 13 July 1881, RE 5-15-8389; and *New York World*, July 1881, RE 25-20-193.

12. *New York Times*, 17 August 1881, RE 5-15-8389; Governor of Chihuahua to

Foreign Relations, 5 September 1881, RE 25-20-193; Governor of Chihuahua to Foreign Relations, 2 December 1881, and Foreign Relations to Mexican Legation, 3 November 1881, RE 5-15-8389; Zamacona to Blaine, 18 August 1881, Ex. Doc., 47th Cong., 1st sess., v. 1, Foreign Relations, no. 1, pt. 1, no. 515; Mexican Legation to Foreign Relations, 28 September 1881, RE 5-15-8389 and Zamacona to Foreign Relations, 7 October 1881, RE 13-14-44.

13. Zamacona to Blaine, 8 August 1881, Ex. Doc., 47th Cong., 1st sess., v. 1, Foreign Relations, no. 1, pt. 1, no. 509; Sheridan, *Record of Engagements*, p. 100, Gatewood, G258c, Box 1, Folder 31, AHS, 6 August 1881; and *New York Herald*, 13 August 1881 and 26 September 1881, RE 5-15-8389.

14. *Chicago National Republican*, 8 August 1881, Ex. Doc., 47th Cong., 1st sess., v. 1, Foreign Relations, no. 509; and *New York Herald*, 8 August 1881, RE 5-15-8389.

15. Zamacona to Blaine, 18 August 1881, Ex. Doc., 47th Cong., 1st sess., v. 1, Foreign Relations, no. 1, pt. 1, no. 515; *Chicago National Republican*, 16 August 1881; *New York Herald*, 13 August 1881; and El Paso consul to Foreign Relations, 17 August 1881, R 13–14–44.

16. Harte, "San Carlos Indian Reservation," pp. 648–49; and Blaine to Morgan, 31 August 1881; Frémont to Kirkwood, 20 August 1881, Ex. Doc., 47th Cong., 1st sess., v. 1, Foreign Relations, no. 1, pt. 1, no. 474.

17. Zamacona to Blaine, 25 July 1881, Ex. Doc., 47th Cong., 1st sess., v. 1, Foreign Relations, no. 1, pt. 1, no. 506; and Tucson consul to Foreign Relations, 25 February 1881; Terrazas to Foreign Relations, 27 April 1881, RE 11-2-101.

18. Matamoros to Foreign Relations, 17 May 1881; *El Diario Oficial*, 1 May 1881; *San Antonio Daily Express*, 14 May 1881; Eagle Pass consul to Fort Duncan commander, 16 May 1881; Commander Ft. Duncan to Eagle Pass consul, 23 May 1881; *New York Times*, 29 May 1881; and Eagle Pass consul to Foreign Relations, 8 June 1881, RE 11-2-97.

19. *New York Sun*, 13 October 1881; Ortiz to Foreign Relations, 12 September 1881; Secretary of War to Reyes, 5 October 1881; and Treviño to Foreign Relations, 12 October 1881, RE 13-14-44.

20. Dewitt, "El acuerdo diplomático," p. 615; and Reyes to Carbó, 31 May 1881, CPD, Legajo 6, Box 2.

21. *New York Herald*, 26 and 18 September 1881, RE 5-15-8389; and Harte, "San Carlos Indian Reservation," p. 627.

22. *New York Herald*, 5 November 1881; *New York Times*, 10 December 1881; M. de Zamacona to Foreign Relations, 9 November 1881; Mariscal to Zamacona, 21 November 1881; and Zamacona to Foreign Relations, 12 December 1881, RE 13-14-68.

23. *New York Herald*, 25 December 1881; and *New York Sun*, 26 December 1881, RE 5-15-8389.

24. Tucson consul to Foreign Relations, 7 January 1882, RE 13-14-68; M. de Zamacona to Frederick T. Frelinghuysen, 18 February 1882, no. 225; Frelinghuysen to Romero, 13 March 1882, no. 227; and Romero to Frelinghuysen, 6 April

1882, no. 229, Ex. Doc., 2nd sess., 47th Cong., v. 1, Foreign Relations, no. 1, pt. 1; José Otero to Carbó, 23 January 1882; Otero to Carbó, 6 February 1882, CPD, Legajo 7, Box 1; and H. Price, Office of Indian Affairs, to S. J. Kirkwood, Secretary, Department of the Interior, 7 March 1882, Ex. Doc., 47th Cong., 2nd sess., v. 1, Foreign Relations, no. 1, pt. 1, no. 228.

25. General Irvin McDowell to General Drum, Military Division of the Pacific and Department of Calif., 23 March 1882, Ex. Doc., 47th Cong., 2nd sess., v. 1, Foreign Relations, no. 1, pt. 1, no. 233; Mexican Legation to Foreign Relations, 17 April 1882; General W. T. Sherman to R. T. Lincoln, Sec. of War, 11 April 1882, RE 13-14-68 and Memorandum signed by George D. Ruggles, Acting Adjutant General, Ex. Doc., 47th Cong., 2nd sess., v. 1, Foreign Relations, no. 1, pt. 1, no. 214.

26. *El Fronterizo* [Tucson], 28 April 1882, RE 5-15-8389; Tucson consul to Foreign Relations, 23 April 1882, El Paso consul to Foreign Relations, 28 April 1882, RE 13-14-69; and Brownsville consul to Foreign Relations, 29 April 1882, RE 20-23-60.

27. *New York Herald*, 27 April 1882, RE 13-14-68; *New York Herald*, 12 May 1882, RE 11-1-42; Sheridan, *Record of Engagements*, p. 101, Gatewood, Box 1, Folder 31, AHS; Prefecto de Moctezuma to Srio. de Estado, Hermosillo, 4 May 1882; Col. Lorenzo García to General Reyes, *La Constitución* [Hermosillo], 23 May 1882, 4, No. 25, Ramo Relaciones Exteriores, Archivo de Sonora; and George A. Forsyth, *Thrilling Days in Army Life* (New York: Harper and Brothers, 1900), pp. 119–20.

28. *New York Times*, 1 May 1882; M. Romero to Foreign Relations, 2 May 1882, and *New York Herald*, 30 April 1882 and 2 May 1882, RE, LE 2242, pt. 1; and Heitman, *Historical Register*, p. 626.

29. Mariscal to Morgan, 2 May 1882, Ex. Doc., 47th Cong., 2nd sess., v. 1, Foreign Relations, no. 1, pt. 1, no. 211; Mariscal to Secretary of War, 4 May 1882, RE, LE 2242, pt. 1; Matías Romero to Foreign Relations, 23 May 1882, and *Washington Evening Star*, 23 May 1882, RE 13-14-44.

30. Wm. J. Ross to Colonel Terrazas, 4 June 1882, Archivo de Sonora; M. Romero to Foreign Relations, 20 June 1882, RE 5-15-8389; *Arizona Daily Star*, 24 June 1882; and Reyes to Carbó, 2 July 1882, CPD, Legajo 7, Box 2.

31. *Washington Evening Star*, 23 May 1882, RE 13-14-44.

32. *Tucson Sun*, 6 May 1882, RE 13-14-44; and P. H. Sheridan to Drum, 4 May 1882, Ex. Doc., 47th Cong., 2nd sess., v. 1, Foreign Relations, no. 1, pt. 2, no. 236.

33. Memorandum signed by George D. Ruggles, Acting Adjutant General, Ex. Doc., 47th Cong., 2nd sess., v. 1, Foreign Relations, no. 1, pt. 1, no. 297; President Díaz's message to Congress, 16 September 1882, Dispatches from U.S. Consuls in Mexico City, 1822–1906, vol. 17 (Jan. 2, 1880–March 31, 1883), U.S. National Archives, U.S. Embassy, Mexico; and *El Diario Oficial*, 15 August 1882, 7, No. 194, Biblioteca Lerdo de Tejada, Mexico, D.F.

34. M. Romero to Foreign Relations, 12 September 1882; Secretary of War to Foreign Relations, 3 August 1882; Secretary of War to Foreign Relations, 5 September 1882; War to Foreign Relations, 17 October 1882, RE 13-14-68;

M. Romero to Foreign Relations, 7 May 1882, RE 11-1-42; Mariscal to Mexican Legation, 3 November 1881, RE 5-15-8389; and Romero to Foreign Relations, 14 July 1882; Mariscal to Foreign Relations, 5 July 1882, RE 13-14-68.

35. El Paso Consul to Foreign Relations, 1 June 1882, and Mexican Legation to El Paso consul, 17 June 1882, RE 13-14-68.

36. Romero to Foreign Relations, 12 September 1882, RE 13-14-68.

37. *New York Tribune*, 2 September 1882; *New York Herald*, 23 May 1882; and Mexican Legation to Foreign Relations, 14 June 1882, RE 13-14-68.

38. General Pope to Commander-in-Chief, United States Army, 23 May 1882, RE 13-14-44.

39. *New York World*, 19 May 1882, Dispatch General Sheridan to General Sherman, RE 13-14-44; and *San Francisco Morning Call*, 15 October 1882, RE 11-1-42.

40. *La Constitución*, 25 July 1881, 3, No. 35, Archivo de Sonora, Museo de Antropología e Historia, México, D.F.

41. Carlos Pacheco to Díaz, 14 March 1882; Carlos Ortiz to Pacheco, 25 January 1882; and Ortiz to Díaz, 26 January 1882, CPD, Legajo 7, Box 1.

42. [Carbó?] to Pacheco, 9 February 1882; [Carbó?] to Secretary of War, 6 February 1882; [José G. Carbó?] to Pacheco, 9 February 1882; Francisco Naranjo, Secretary of War, to Carbó, 24 February 1882, CPD, Legajo 7, Box 1; and Carbó to Secretary of War, 3 February 1882, CPD, Legajo 7, Box 2.

43. [Ramón Corral?] to Pacheco and Secretary of War, 9 February 1882, CPD, Legajo 7, Box 1; García to Carbó, 21 February 1882, CPD, Legajo 7, Box 2; and Yzábal [*sic*] to Carbó, 1 February 1882, CPD, Legajo 7, Box 1.

44. García to Carbó, 2 and 9 February 1882; García to Carbó, 15 and 16 February 1882, CPD, Legajo 7, Box 2; García to Carbó, 18 February 1882, CPD, Legajo 7, Box 3; and Reyes to Carbó, 26 February 1882, CPD, Legajo 7, Box 2.

45. Pacheco to Díaz, 23 February and 14 March 1882, CPD, Legajo 7, Box 1.

46. Pacheco to Díaz, 15 March 1882 and [Díaz?], Oaxaca, to Ortiz, 21 March 1882, CPD, Legajo 7, Box 1; and *La Constitución*, Periódico Oficial del Gobierno de Sonora, 12 April 1882, CPD, Legajo 7, Box 1.

47. García to Carbó, 2 March 1882, CPD, Legajo 7, Box 2; Corral to Carbó, 7 March 1882, CPD, Legajo 7, Box 1; and González to Reyes, 7 March 1882, CPD, Legajo 7, Box 2.

48. Secretary of War Francisco Naranjo to Carbó, 17 April 1882; Reyes to Carbó, 20 April 1882; Secretary of War to Carbó, 26 May 1882; Reyes to Carbó, 5 May 1882; Reyes to Carbó, 2 April 1882, CPD, Legajo 7, Box 2; and García to Carbó, 12 August 1882, CPD, Legajo 7, Box 3.

49. Reyes to Carbó, 3 and 7 July 1882, CPD, Legajo 7, Box 2.

50. Reyes to Carbó, 6 May 1882; González to Carbó, 10 July 1882, CPD, Legajo 7, Box 2; and González to Carbó, 15 July 1882, CPD, Legajo 7, Box 3.

51. Reyes to González, 1 September 1882; Reyes to Carbó, 15 October 1882; and Reyes to Carbó, 3 August 1882, CPD, Legajo 7, Box 3.

52. Decoded message [no name or date], 1882, CPD, Legajo 7, Box 2; and Reyes to Carbó, 3 September 1882, CPD, Legajo 7, Box 3.

53. González to Carbó, 4 September 1882; García to Carbó, 14 October 1882, CPD, Legajo 7, Box 3.

54. *La Constitución*, 12 October 1882, 4, No. 51, Archivo de Sonora, Museo de Antropología e Historia, México, D.F.

55. Daniel Cosío Villegas, *The United States versus Porfirio Díaz*, trans. Nettie Lee Benson (Lincoln: University of Nebraska Press, 1963), p. 207.

56. Dewitt, "El acuerdo diplomático," pp. 615–20; 28 September 1882, RE, LE 2242, pt. 1; *El Diario Oficial*, 25 August 1882, 7, No. 203, Biblioteca Lerdo de Tejada, México, D.F.; and Ex. Doc., 47th Cong., 2nd sess., v. 1, Foreign Relations, no. 1, pt. 1, no. 216, Enclosure no. 309.

57. Sheridan, *Record of Engagements*, pp. 103–4, Gatewood, Box 1, Folder 31, AHS.

CHAPTER 4

1. Dewitt, "El acuerdo diplomático," p. 620; and George Crook, *Annual Report of Brigadier General George Crook, U.S. Army, Commanding Department of Arizona*, 1883, Official Records of the Department of Arizona, Gatewood, Box 2, Folder 19, p. 3, AHS.

2. Prefecto de Arizpe to Srio. de Estado, Hermosillo, Sonora, 29 March, 1883, Archivo de Sonora, Legajo 12; Harte, "San Carlos," p. 2; and Crook, *Annual Report*, 1883, p. 10,

3. *Tombstone Daily Epitaph*, 17 January 1883, RE 5-16-8768; S. M. Barrett, ed., *Geronimo's Story of His Life* (New York: Duffield, 1906), pp. 133–34; and Utley, *Frontier Regulars*, p. 375.

4. Utley, *Frontier Regulars*, pp. 370–71.

5. Crook, *Annual Report*, 1883, p. 9.

6. [Carbó?] to González, 27 March 1883, CPD, Legajo 8, Box 1; and Almada, *Juárez y Terrazas*, p. 314.

7. Cornelius C. Smith, *J. Emilio Kosterlitzky: Eagle of Sonora and the Southwest Border* (Glendale, Calif.: Arthur H. Clark, 1970), p. 73; Prefecto de Arizpe to Srio. de Estado, Hermosillo, 12 March 1883, Archivo de Sonora, Legajo 12; [Carbó]; to González, 27 March 1883, CPD, Legajo 8, Box 1; Corral to Carbó, 25 March 1883, CPD, Legajo 10, Box 26; and González to Carbó, 22 May 1883, CPD, Legajo 9, Box 1.

8. Corral to Carbó, 29 March [1883?]; García to Carbó, 29 March 1883, CPD, Legajo 10, Box 26; and González to Carbó, 5 March 1883, CPD, Legajo 8, Box 1.

9. Charles B. Gatewood, "When Chatto Raided into Arizona," typescript, n.d., Gatewood, Box 3, Folder 6, p. 2, AHS; *Tombstone Daily Epitaph*, 17 January 1883, RE 5-16-8768; and Crook, *Annual Report*, 1883, p. 10.

10. George Crook, "The Apache Problem," typescript, n.d., Gatewood, Box 2, Folder 5, p. 15, AHS.

11. Crook, *Annual Report*, 1883, p. 4; and Gatewood, "When Chatto Raided into Arizona," p. 2.

12. Crook, *Annual Report*, 1883, pp. 4–5; Crook, "The Apache Problem," pp. 6, 11, and Jason Betzinez, *I Fought with Geronimo*, ed. by W. S. Nye, (Harrisburg, PA: Stackpole, 1959), pp. 109, 118.

13. Gatewood, "When Chatto Raided into Arizona," p. 3.

14. González to Carbó, 9 April 1883, CPD, Legajo 9, Box 1; García to Carbó, 8 April 1883; CPD, Legajo 10, Box 26.

15. Corral to Carbó, 9 April 1883, CPD, Legajo 10, Box 26; [Carbó?] to González, 27 March 1883, CPD, Legajo 8, Box 1; and Corral to Carbó, 14 May 1883, CPD, Legajo 10, Box 26.

16. Harte, "San Carlos," pp. 8, 9; and Crook, "The Apache Problem," p. 7.

17. Crook, "The Apache Problem," pp. 7, 8, 11.

18. "General Crook's Apache Campaign," *Frank Leslie's Illustrated Newspaper*, 2 June 1883, p. 233, MS 197, General George Armstrong Crook Collection, Small Collections, c949ge, AHS.

19. Dan Thrapp, *General Crook and the Sierra Madre Adventure* (Norman: University of Oklahoma Press, 1974), pp. 114–18.

20. *El Fronterizo* [Tucson], 17 February 1884, RE 5-16-8768.

21. Crook, *Annual Report*, 1883, p. 6; Romero to Foreign Relations, 25 April 1883, RE, LE 2242, pt. 1; Ralph H. Ogle, *Federal Control of the Western Apaches, 1848–1886* (Albuquerque: University of New Mexico Press, 1970), p. 219; Richard N. Ellis, ed., *The Western American Indian: Case Studies in Tribal History* (Lincoln: University of Nebraska Press, 1972), p. 92, and Almada, *Gobernadores del Estado de Chihuahua*, p. 400.

22. Mexican Legation to Foreign Relations, 23 April 1883, RE, LE 2242, pt. 1; and Corral to Carbó, 3 and 24 May 1883, CPD, Legajo 10, Box 26.

23. Naiche is also spelled Nátchez, Náchez, and Nachite; Eve Ball, "The Apache Scouts; a Chiricahua Appraisal," *Arizona and the West*, 7, No. 4 (Winter 1965), p. 323; John P. Clum, "The Capture of Geronimo," *San Dimas Press*, 21 April 1927, Gatewood Collection G258c, Box 1, Folder 27, AHS; and Tucson Consul to Foreign Relations, 8 March 1884, RE 5-16-8768.

24. Thrapp, *Crook*, pp. 176, 178.

25. Charles B. Gatewood, "Crook Was Hindered in Geronimo Hunt," *The National Tribune* [Washington, D.C.], 15 July 1926, MS 197, General George Armstrong Crook Collection, Small Collections, c948e, AHS.

26. George Crook, *Annual Report of Brigadier General George Crook, U.S. Army, Commanding Department of Arizona, 1885*, Official Records of the Department of Arizona, Gatewood, Box 2, Folder 19, p. 5, AHS.

27. Corral to Carbó, 16 July and 16 August 1883, CPD, Legajo 10, Box 26.

28. Carbó to Governor of Sonora, 22 October 1883, Archivo de Sonora, Legajo 12.

29. Secretary of War to Foreign Relations, 2 July 1883, RE, LE 2242; *La Constitución*, 14 December 1883, Biblioteca del Museo de Antropología e Historia, Archivo de Sonora; and Annual Message to Congress with Documents, President Arthur, 4 December 1883, Ex. Doc., 48th Cong., 1st sess., v. 1–11.

30. Britton Davis, "An Apache Evanescence: How Geronimo Brought His Stolen Cattle to San Carlos," typescript, n.d. Gatewood, Box 2, Folder 3, p. 3, AHS; and *El Fronterizo* [Tucson], 4 January 1884, RE 5-16-8768.

31. Davis, "An Apache Evanescence," p. 7.

32. Davis, "An Apache Evanescence," p. 10; and Affidavit signed by J. E. Clark to Britton Davis, 8 March 1884, RE 5-16-8768.

33. *Arizona Daily Star*, 12 March and 1 April 1884; Tucson Consul to Foreign Relations, 12 March 1884, RE 5-16-8768; Governor of Sonora to Foreign Relations, 21 March 1884, Archivo de Sonora, Legajo 12; Mexican Legation to Foreign Relations, 20 March 1884, RE 5-16-8768; and *El Fronterizo*, 14 and 28 March 1884, RE 5-16-8768.

34. Frelinghuysen to M. Romero, 7 April 1884, copy; RE 5-16-8768; *Diario Oficial*, 12 June 1884, RE 5-16-8768; and Srio. de Gobierno de Sonora to Prefecto de Arizpe, 30 June 1884, Archivo de Sonora, Legajo 14.

35. Prefecto de Ures to Srio. de Estado [de Sonora], 6 October 1884, Archivo de Sonora, Legajo 14; Foreign Relations to Prefecto de Ures, 16 August 1884, RE 5-16-8768; Prefecto de Moctezuma to Srio. de Estado, 8 July 1884, Archivo de Sonora, Legajo 14; and M. Romero to Foreign Relations, 8 February, 1884; Tucson Consul to Foreign Relations, 30 March 1884, RE 5-16-8768.

36. Srio. de Estado to Prefecto de Arizpe, 28 November 1884, Archivo de Sonora, Legajo 12; and Affidavit signed 15 December 1884 by L. Fielder and Pedro Ortiz, Grant County, New Mexico, copy; Fielder and Fielder, Washington, D.C. to M. Romero, 12 January 1885, copy, RE 5-16-8768.

37. M. Romero, Washington, D.C. to Fielder and Fielder, Deming, New Mexico, 19 January 1885, copy, and Foreign Relations, 28 January 1886, RE 5-16-8768.

38. *Arizona Daily Star*, 12 March 1884, RE 5-16-8768, pt. 2.

39. *Arizona Daily Citizen*, 13 and 20 March 1884, and *Arizona Daily Star*, 3 April 1884, RE 5-16-8768, pt. 2.

40. Crook, *Annual Report*, 1883, p. 5; *Arizona Daily Star*, 11, 15, 20 and 21 March and 2 April 1884; *Arizona Daily Citizen*, 7 and 20 March 1884, RE 5-16-8768, pt. 2.

41. *Daily Star*, 16 March 1884; and *Daily Citizen*, 24 March 1884, RE 5-16-8768, pt. 2.

42. *Daily Citizen*, 24 March and 4 April 1884; *Daily Star*, 28 and 30 March 1884, RE 5 16-8768, pt. 2.

43. Tombstone Consul to Foreign Relations, 3 January 1884, RE 5-16-8768.

44. Tucson Consul to Foreign Relations, 31 March 1884; Tombstone Consul to Foreign Relations, 28 March 1884, RE 5-16-8768.

45. Foreign Relations to Tucson, El Paso, and Tombstone Consuls, 15 February 1884, RE 5-16-8768.

46. Tombstone Consul to Foreign Relations, 28 March 1884, RE 5-16-8768.

47. Tucson Consul to Foreign Relations, 12 March 1884, RE 5-16-8768.

48. Tucson Consul to Foreign Relations, 12 March 1884, RE 5-16-8768; Torres to Carbó, 23 July and 14 August 1885, CPD, Legajo 10, Box 16; and Governor of Sonora to Commander of First Military Zone, 4 January 1886, Archivo de Sonora, Legajo 14.

49. Crook, *Annual Reports*, 1883, pp. 11–13; 1885, p. 4.

50. Crook, *Annual Report*, 1883, p. 14.

51. Crook, *Annual Report*, 1885, p. 3; and Harte, "San Carlos", p. 799.

52. *San Francisco Examiner*, Tombstone Dispatch, 29 February 1884, RE 5-16-8768; and Crook, *Annual Report*, 1884, pp. 2, 6.

53. Crook, *Annual Reports*, 1884, p. 3 and 1885, pp. 7–8.

54. Crook, *Annual Report*, 1884, pp. 3, 6–7; and Angie Debo, *A History of the Indians of the United States* (Norman: University of Oklahoma Press, 1970), p. 229. Kayatennae is also spelled "Kaetena."

55. Frelinghuysen, Department of State, to M. Romero, 2 July 1884; Romero to Frelinghuysen, 3 July 1884, RE 17-21-132; and García to Carbó, 11 December 1884, CPD, Legajo 10, Box 26.

56. Torres to Foreign Relations, 12 June and 10 July 1885; RE 17-21-132.

57. Governor of Chihuahua to Foreign Relations, 28 February 1885 and 9 June 1885, RE 17-21-132.

58. M. Romero to Foreign Relations, 2 October 1886, RE 11-9-7.

59. Pedro Hinojosa, Secretary of War, to Carbó, 24 June 1884, CPD, Legajo 10, Box 26.

60. González to Carbó, 7 and 12 May and 2 June 1884; Naranjo, Secretary of War, to Carbó, 26 May 1884; and González to Carbó, 31 July 1884, CPD, Legajo 9, Box 1.

61. Jesús Luna, *La carrera pública de don Ramón Corral* (México: Secretaría de Educación Pública, 1975), p. 520; Hector Aguilar Camín, *La frontera nomada: Sonora y la revolución Mexicana* (México: Siglo Veintiuno, 1977), p. 25; Antonio Manero, *El antiguo régimen y la revolución* (México: La Europa, 1911), pp. 187–88, 190; Carleton Beals, *Mexican Maze* (Philadelphia: J. B. Lippincott, 1931), pp. 185, 310; Richard N. Adams, "Nationalization," in *Social* Anthropology, Vol. 6 of *Handbook of Middle American Indians*, ed. Manning Nash, gen. ed., Robert Wauchope (Austin: University of Texas Press, 1967), p. 475; Leonidas Hamilton, *Border States of Mexico: Sonora, Sinaloa, Chihuahua and Durango* (San Francisco: Bacon and Company, 1881), p. 43; and Alfonso Fábila, *Los tribus Yaquis de Sonora, su cultura y anhelada autodeterminación* (México: Departmento de Asuntos Indígenas, 1940), p. 98.

62. Reyes to Díaz, 24 February 1885, CPD, Legajo 10, Box 4; and Hinojosa to Carbó, 17 March 1885, CPD, Legajo 10, Box 26, no. 012886.

63. J. A. Rivero, Guaymas, to Carbó, 2 February 1885, CPD, Legajo 10, Box 26, no. 012819; and Fuero to Díaz, 24 February 1885, CPD, Legajo 10, Box 3.

64. Torres to Díaz, 19 February 1885, CPD, Legajo 10, Box 5; Díaz to Torres, 10

February 1885, CPD, Copiador, v. 1, no. 241–42; and Díaz to Fuero, 21 and 25 April 1885, CPD, Legajo 10, Box 8, nos. 00393–4.

65. Osage Nation to Mexican Government, 1 November 1885; Romero, Mexican Legation, to Foreign Relations, 1 December 1885; and U.S. Indian Agent to Mexican Consul, 14 January 1885, RE 15-2-38.

66. Hinojosa to Carbó, 24 June 1885, CPD, Legajo 10, Box 27, no. 013127; and Torres to Díaz, 6 August 1885, CPD, Legajo 10, Box 18, no. 008597.

67. Torres to Díaz, 19 February 1885, CPD, Legajo 10, Box 5; Topete to Carbó, 25 February 1885, CPD, Legajo 10, Box 26, no. 012823; and Torres to Díaz, 21 February 1885, CPD, Legajo 10, Box 5.

68. Díaz to Torres, 28 February 1885, CPD, Legajo 10, Box 5; Ortiz to Díaz, 18 March 1885, CPD, Legajo 10, Box 7; Díaz to Ortiz, 27 March 1885, CPD, Copiador v. 1, no. 353; Díaz to Carbó, 4 April 1885, CPD, Copiador, v. 1, no. 402; and Díaz to Otero, 13 April 1885, Copiador, v. 1, no. 452.

69. Hinojosa to Carbó, 26 February 1885, CPD, Legajo 10, Box 26, no. 012840; *La Constitución*, 20 March 1885, 7, no. 12, Biblioteca del Museo de Antropología, Archivo de Sonora; Carbó to Díaz, 31 March 1885, CPD, Legajo 10, Box 7, no. 003382.

70. Díaz to Carbó, 24 March 1885; Hinojosa to Carbó, 12 and 30 March 1885, CPD, Legajo 10, Box 26; Carbó to Díaz, 24 March 1885, CPD, Legajo 10, Box 7, no. 003422; and Carbó to Díaz, 10 April 1885, CPD, Legajo 10, Box 8, no. 003884.

71. M. Romero to Foreign Relations, 14 and 15 April 1885, RE, LE2242, pt. 5.

72. M. Romero to Foreign Relations, 15 April 1885; and Mariscal, Foreign Relations, to Gobernación, 16 April 1885, RE, LE2242, pt. 5.

73. Hinojosa to Carbó, 27 April 1885, CPD, Legajo 10, Box 27, no. 012928.

74. Britton Davis, "A Short Account of the Chirricahua [*sic*] Tribe of Apache Indians and the Causes Leading to the Outbreak of May 1885," typescript, n.d., Gatewood, Box 2, Folder 3, p. 4, AHS.

75. Davis, "A Short Account," p. 6.

76. Davis, "A Short Account," p. 8.

77. Davis, "A Short Account," pp. 4–8 and Harte, "San Carlos," p. 805.

CHAPTER 5

1. Torres to Carbó, 22 May 1885, CPD, Legajo 10, Box 10; Fuero to Díaz, 19 May 1885, CPD, Legajo 10, Box 11, no. 005037; and Fuero to Díaz, 8 May 1885, Díaz's reply at bottom of letter, n.d., CPD, Legajo 10, Box 11.

2. Torres to Carbó, 22 May 1885, CPD, Legajo 10, Box 10; Copy of letter signed Scott, 29 May 1885, CPD, Legajo 10, Box 16; and Torres to Carbó, 30 May 1885, CPD, Legajo 10, Box 16, no. 007649.

3. Carbó to Díaz, 20 May 1885, CPD, Legajo 10, Box 12, no. 005787; Torres to Carbó, 22 May 1885, CPD, Legajo 10, Box 10; and Díaz to Carbó, 26 May 1885, CPD, Legajo 10, Box 27, no. 013115.

4. Ramón Corral to Carbó, 24 March 1885, CPD, Legajo 10, Box 26.

5. Torres to Carbó, 9 August 1885, CPD, Legajo 10, Box 16, no. 007595; Torres to Carbó, 14 August 1885, Legajo 10, Box 16, no. 007598; *La Constitución*, 7, No. 37, 21 August 1885, Archivo de Sonora, Biblioteca del Museo de Antropología e Historia, México, D.F.; and Carbó to Díaz, 2 August 1885, CPD, Legajo 10, Box 16.

6. Torres to Carbó, 25 June 1885, CPD, Legajo 10, Box 12.

7. Hinojosa to Carbó, 11 and 18 August and 2 Sept. 1885, CPD, Legajo 10, Box 27.

8. *Sociedad Indianist Mexicana Boletín*, Nos. 1–6, 8–11 (1911), p. 44; González Navarro, *Vida social*, p. 246; González Navarro, "Instituciones indígenas en México independiente," p. 147; and Rámon Corral, *Obras históricas* (Hermosillo, México; n.p., 1959), p. 212.

9. Carbó to Díaz, 20 August 1885, CPD, Legajo 10, Box 16; Carbó to Díaz, 26 August 1885, CPD, Legajo 10, Box 18; Hinojosa to Carbó, 9 September 1885 and Díaz to Carbó, 18 August 1885, CPD, Legajo 10, Box 27; Díaz to Carbó, 3 September 1885, CPD, Legajo 10, Box 18; Torres to Díaz, 12 July 1885, Legajo 10, Box 15, no. 007246; and Díaz to Torres, 20 July 1885, CPD, Legajo 10, Box 15, no. 007247.

10. Torres to Carbó, 16 June 1885, CPD, Legajo 10, Box 12; Torres to Díaz, 7 June 1885, CPD, Legajo 10, Box 13; Governor of Sonora to Moctezuma Prefect, 12 June 1885, Archivo de Sonora, Legajo 11, no. 30; and Carbó to Díaz, 2 August 1885, CPD, Legajo 10, Box 16.

11. Hinojosa to Carbó, 6 October 1885, CPD, Legajo 10, Box 27, no. 013306; *La Constitución*, 7, no. 23, 4 August 1885, Archivo de Sonora, Biblioteca del Museo de Antropología e Historia; Torres to Carbó, 11 June 1885, CPD, Legajo 10, Box 12, no. 005705; Secretary of War to Governor of Sonora, 14 June 1885, Archivo de Sonora, Legajo 13; Torres to Carbó, 4 July 1885, CPD, Legajo 10, Box 16, no. 007630; *La Constitución*, 7, no. 35, 11 August 1885, Archivo de Sonora, Biblioteca del Museo de Antropología e Historia; War to Foreign Relations, 6 Oct. 1885, RE 17-21-94; Governor of Chihuahua to Foreign Relations, 23 Oct. 1885, RE 17-21-29; and War to Foreign Relations, 29 October 1885, RE 17-21-31.

12. Gobernación to Foreign Relations, 1 July 1885; M. Romero to Foreign Relations, 6 and 7 Oct. 1885; and *Dictamen* from Foreign Relations, 27 August 1885, RE 17-21-94.

13. Montoya to Torres, 6 August 1885, CPD, Legajo 10, Box 16; and Utley, *Frontier Regulars*, p. 383

14. M. Romero to Foreign Relations, 9 June 1885, RE 11-2-30.

15. M. Romero to Foreign Relations, 9 June 1885, RE 11-2-30; Heitman, *Historical Register*, p. 447; Utley, *Frontier Regulars*, p. 383; and Henry W. Daly, Chief Packer, Q.M. Department of U.S. Army, "The Geronimo Campaign," *The United States Cavalry Journal*, 9 and 10, no. 70 (1908), p. 88, Gatewood, Box 2, Folder 13, AHS. Emmet has been spelled in different ways. The correct spelling is with one "t". Letter signed by Emmet Crawford, M1395, *Letters Received by the Appoint-*

ment, Commission and Personal Branch, Adjutant General's Office, 1871–1894, Record Group 94, ACP fiche 87, fiche 1, National Archives.

16. El Paso Consul to Foreign Relations, 10 Sept. 1885, RE 17-21-94; El Paso Consul to Foreign Relations, 13 Oct. 1885, RE, LE 2242, pt. 5; and Foreign Relations to El Paso Consul, n.d., RE 17-21-94.

17. Díaz to Carbó, 3 Oct. 1885, CPD, Legajo 10, Box 26, no. 013318; Lorenzo García to Díaz, 30 Oct. 1885, CPD, Legajo 10, Box 21, no. 010205; and Díaz to Torres, 2 Nov. 1885; CPD, Legajo 10, Box 22, no. 010878.

18. M. Romero to Foreign Relations, 17 Sept. 1885, RE, LE 2242, pt. 5; and M. Romero to Foreign Relations, 12 Dec. 1885; M. Romero to Governor of Chihuahua, 11 Dec. 1885; War to Foreign Relations, 9 Feb. 1886; Romero to Foreign Relations, 24 Feb. 1886, RE 15-2-37.

19. Romero to Foreign Relations, 6 Oct. 1885, RE 17-21-94; and (Major) Charles B. Gatewood, "Crook Was Hindered in Geronimo Hunt," The National Tribune (Washington, D.C.), 15 July 1926, George Crook Collection, Arizona Historical Society.

20. Clendenen, Blood on the Border, p. 109; Montoya to Torres, 18 August 1885, CPD, Legajo 10, Box 16; and Torres to Carbó, 25 June 1885, CPD, Legajo 10, Box 12.

21. W. E. Shipp, "Captain Crawford's Last Expedition," Cavalry Journal, 1892, rpt. The United States Cavalry Journal, 19, no. 10 (1908), p. 290; and Marion P. Maus to C. S. Roberts, 21 January 1886, Ex. Doc., 49th Cong., 2nd sess., serial 2460, Papers Relating to the Foreign Relations of the United States, 1886–87 (Washington, D.C.: Government Printing Office, 1887), p. 571. Hereafter referred to as Foreign Relations. For maps of the location of the attack, see Dan L. Thrapp, ed., Dateline Fort Bowie: Charles Fletcher Lummis Reports on an Apache War (Norman: University of Oklahoma Press, 1979), p. 140; Charles E. Herbert, Mapa oficial del estado de Sonora, 1884–1909 (Nogales, Arizona: Sonora News Company, 1909); and Paul M. Roca, Paths of the Padres Through Sonora: An Illustrated History and Guide to Its Spanish Churches (Tucson: Arizona Pioneers' Historical Society, 1967), pp. 286–89. In a letter to the author, Steve Wilson places the site southeast of Nácori Chico. The Nácori referred to in Maus to Roberts, January 27, 1886; and Mariscal to Morgan, May 19, 1886, both in Foreign Relations, 1886–87, pp. 571 and 597 respectively, is Nácori Chico on the Rio Nácori, southeast of Bacadéhuachi. Teópar, originally a Spanish mission called San José de Teópare, is some forty miles southeast of Nácori Chico, below the Rio Sátachi and northeast of Sahuaripa on a tributary of the Rio Aros (also called "Haros" or "Papigóchic"). It is near the Chihuahua border and the Devil's Backbone, the ruggedest part of the Sierra Madre.

22. Shipp, "Captain Crawford's Last Expedition," p. 291.

23. Maus to Roberts, 21 January 1886, Foreign Relations, p. 571; and Shipp, "Captain Crawford's Last Expedition," p. 299.

24. Shipp, "Captain Crawford's Last Expedition," p. 297; and Luis G. Zorrilla, *Historia de las relaciones entre México y los Estados Unidos de America, 1800–1958*, vol. 2 (México: Editorial Porrúa, 1965), p. 47.

25. Shipp, "Captain Crawford's Last Expedition," p. 298–99.

26. Jas. D. Porter, acting Secretary, to Jackson, Dept. of State, 2 Feb. 1886, *Foreign Relations*, no. 297, p. 570; Shipp, "Captain Crawford's Last Expedition," p. 292–94, 296; and Maus to Roberts, 21 Jan. 1886, *Foreign Relations*, p. 571.

27. Maus to Roberts, 23 Feb. 1886, *Foreign Relations*, p. 577; Matías Romero to Bayard, 5 May 1886, *Foreign Relations*, no. 343, p. 729.

28. Mariscal to Morgan, 19 May 1886, *Foreign Relations*, inclosure in no. 230; p. 595; and Romero to Bayard, 5 May 1886, *Foreign Relations*, no. 343, p. 729.

29. Shipp, "Captain Crawford's Last Expedition," p. 297.

30. Romero to Bayard, 29 April 1886, *Foreign Relations*, no. 341, p. 727.

31. R. Benavidez to Díaz, 2 Feb. 1886, CPD, Legajo 11, Box 3.

32. González Navarro, *Vida social*, p. 246.

33. Romero to Bayard, 5 May 1886, *Foreign Relations*, no. 343, p. 730.

34. Maus to Roberts, 23 Feb. 1886, *Foreign Relations*, p. 578; Special dispatch, Washington, D.C., 5 Feb. 1886, to *Globe-Democrat* [St. Louis, Mo.], 6 Feb. 1886, *Foreign Relations*, p. 599.

35. Mariscal to Morgan, 19 May 1886, *Foreign Relations*, inclosure in no. 230, p. 595.

36. Maus to Roberts, 21. Jan. 1886; Maus to Roberts, 23 Feb. 1886; and A. F. Perchos to Crawford, 2 Jan. 1886, Statement H, all in *Foreign Relations*, pp. 572, 579, and 584, respectively.

37. Maus to Roberts, 23 Feb. 1886, *Foreign Relations*, p. 578.

38. Shipp, "Captain Crawford's Last Expedition," p. 295.

39. Nelson A. Miles, *Personal Recollections and Observations of General Nelson A. Miles* (Chicago/New York: The Werner Co., 1896), p. 459.

40. Maus to Roberts, 21 Jan. 1886, *Foreign Relations*, p. 573; and Miles, *Personal Recollections*, p. 465. Crawford was later buried in Kearney, Nebraska.

41. Shipp, "Captain Crawford's Last Expedition," p. 298–99; *Arizona Star*, 4 Feb. 1886, RE 12-27-127; *Los Angeles Times*, 6 May 1886, in Dan L. Thrapp, ed., *Dateline Fort Bowie: Charles Fletcher Lummis Reports on an Apache War* (Norman: University of Oklahoma Press, 1979), pp. 123.

42. Thrapp, *Dateline Fort Bowie*, p. 162; and Britton Davis, *The Truth About Geronimo* (New Haven: Yale University Press, 1929, rpt. Lincoln: University of Nebraska Press, 1976), pp. 185–88.

43. *New York Times*, January 29 and 30, February 5, March 25, 1886.

44. Henry Jackson to Mariscal, 15 Feb. 1886 and Mariscal to Jackson, 18 Feb. 1886, *Foreign Relations*, inclosures in nos. 152 and 158, pp. 574–75.

45. Governor of Chihuahua to Díaz, 10 April 1886, CPD, Legajo 11, Box 8, Morgan to Mariscal, 13 April 1886, *Foreign Relations*, inclosure in no. 201, p. 586; and Matías Romero to Díaz, 19 April 1886, CPD, Legajo 11, Box 11.

46. U.S. National Archives, U.S. Embassy, Mexico, Dispatches from U.S. Consuls in Mexico City, 1822–1906, v. 17 (2 Jan. 1880–31 March 1883); and *Los Angeles Times*, 9 May 1886 in Thrapp, *Dateline Fort Bowie*, p. 51.

47. Mariscal to Morgan, 19 May 1886 and Deposition of Santana Pérez, 12 February 1886, *Foreign Relations*, inclosure 1 in no. 203, p. 589, 601.

48. Mariscal to Morgan, 19 May 1886, *Foreign Relations*, pp. 595, 589; Shipp, "Captain Crawford's Last Expedition," p. 288; and Maus to Roberts, 23 Feb. 1886, *Foreign Relations*, p. 577.

49. Mariscal to Morgan, 19 May 1886, *Foreign Relations*, pp. 591–92, 595; Mariscal to T.C. Manning, 28 Feb. 1887, Ex. Doc., 50th Cong., 1st sess., v. 1, serial 2532, no. 433, *Foreign Relations, 1887* (Washington, D.C.: Government Printing Office, 1887), p. 692; and Miles, *Personal Recollections*, p. 463.

50. Mariscal to Morgan, 19 May 1886, *Foreign Relations*, p. 590; Personal interview with Víctor Mendoza, 24 Sept. 1981, Chihuahua; and Juan Corredor and Pedro de la Cruz, "Corrido de Mauricio Corredor," Rio Verde de Vilaguchic y Arisiachic, Chihuahua, 1906, transcribed by Víctor Mendoza.

51. Statement D of Thomas Horn, 11 Jan. 1886 and Mariscal to Morgan, 19 May 1886, *Foreign Relations*, pp. 582, 594.

52. Mariscal to Morgan, 19 May 1886 and Bayard to Jackson, 20 March 1886, *Foreign Relations*, pp. 594, 596, and no. 301, p. 576, respectively.

53. Bayard to Jackson, 20 March 1886; Morgan to Bayard, 25 May 1886, *Foreign Relations*, no. 301, p. 575 and no. 307, p. 589.

54. Mariscal to Morgan, 19 May 1886, *Foreign Relations*, pp. 596, 593.

55. *El Fronterizo*, 16 Jan. 1886, RE 17-21-126; Mariscal to Morgan, 19 May 1886, *Foreign Relations*, pp. 595–96; and Hinojosa to Foreign Relations, 13 May 1886, RE 12-27-127.

56. Cecilio Leivas [*sic*], Guásabas, to Moctezuma Prefect, 25 Dec. 1885, and Court Witness Francisco Leyva, [26 March 1886], *Foreign Relations*, pp. 661, 673; and Davis, *The Truth About Geronimo*, p. 159.

57. Court Witness Cecilio Leiva, [26 March 1886], and Court Witness Emilio Kosterlitzky, 3 April 1886, *Foreign Relations*, pp. 672, 686; War to Foreign Relations, 11 Jan. 1886, and Mexican Legation to Foreign Relations, 25 Jan. 1886, RE 12-3-44; and *El Fronterizo*, 16 Jan. 1886, RE 17-21-126. Huásabas is also spelled "Guásabas."

58. Governor of Chihuahua to M. Romero, 5 Feb. 1886, RE 12-27-127; and Jesús G. Santa Cruz, Office of the Commissary of Nacosari, to Moctezuma Prefect, 20 Dec. 1885, *Foreign Relations*, p. 660.

59. Davis, *The Truth About Geronimo*, p. 164; Court Witness George F. Woodard, 26 March 1886, and Court Witness Ignacio Robles, 26 March 1886, *Foreign Relations*, pp. 668–69; Srio. de Gobernación to Governor of Sonora, 18 Jan. 1886, Archivo de Sonora, Legajo 14; and Court Witness Cesareo Cortés, 26 March 1886, *Foreign Relations*, p. 670.

60. Court Witness Catarino Grijalva, 26 March 1886, *Foreign Relations*, p. 671.

61. Governor of Sonora to Crispín de S. Palomares, 11 April 1886, *Foreign Relations*, p. 690.

62. Davis, *The Truth About Geronimo*, p. 198; and Crook to Lieut. Gen. P. H. Sheridan, 27 March 1886, and Sheridan to Crook, 30 March 1886. Ex. Doc., 51st Cong., 1st sess., no. 88, Letter from the Secretary of War transmitting in response to Senate resolution of March 11, 1890, correspondence regarding the Apache Indians, Correspondence between Lieut. Gen. P. H. Sheridan and Brig. Gen. George Crook Regarding the Apache Indians, Gatewood, Box 2, Folder 19, p. 2, AHS; hereafter referred to as Correspondence Sheridan and Crook.

CHAPTER 6

1. Davis, *The Truth About Geronimo*, pp. 213–14; Daly, "The Geronimo Campaign," pp. 248, 253; and Crook to Sheridan, 30 March 1886, Correspondence Sheridan and Crook, p. 3.

2. Bancroft, *History of Arizona and New Mexico, 1530–1888*, p. 573; Sheridan to Crook, 31 March and 1 April 1886, Correspondence Sheridan and Crook, pp. 4, 6; Davis, *The Truth About Geronimo*, pp. 214, 216; and P. H. Sheridan, *Personal Memoirs of P. H. Sheridan, General, U.S. Army* (1888, rpt. New York: D. Appleton and Co., 1904), vol. 2, pp. 562–63.

3. Crook to Sheridan, 1 April 1886, Correspondence Sheridan and Crook, pp. 6–7; Davis, *The Truth About Geronimo*, p. 217; M. Romero to Foreign Relations,19 Dec. 1886, RE 12-8-91; and General Orders, no. 15, Hdqrs. of the Army, Adjt. Gen.'s Office, 2 April 1886, Correspondence Sheridan and Crook, p. 10.

4. Jesús Aguirre, Arizpe Prefect, to Srio. de Estado de Sonora, 19 April and 25 June 1886, no. 25-VI-886; A. Martínez to Governor of Sonora, 9 July 1886, Archivo de Sonora, Ramo: Relaciones Exteriores, Legajo 14.

5. Nelson A. Miles, *Serving the Republic: Memoirs of the Civil and Military Life of Nelson A. Miles* (1911; rpt. Freeport, New York: Books for Libraries Press, 1971), pp. 223–24; and Dan L. Thrapp, *The Conquest of Apachería* (Norman: University of Oklahoma Press, 1967), p. 351.

6. Torres to Corral, 27 April 1886, Archivo de Sonora, Legajo 15; and Barrett, *Geronimo's Story of His Life*, p. 2.

7. Davis, *The Truth About Geronimo*, p. 219; Daly, "The Geronimo Campaign," p. 256; and Magdalena Prefect to Srio. de Estado de Sonora, 16 June 1886, Archivo de Sonora, Legajo 15.

8. L. Vega, Guaymas, to Díaz, 10 April 1886, CPD, Legajo 11, Box 9; Moctezuma Prefect to Srio. de Estado de Sonora, 1 March and 28 June 1886, Archivo de Sonora, Legajo 15; and Arizpe Prefect to Srio. de Estado, 16 August 1886, Archivo de Sonora, Ramo: Relaciones Exteriores, Legajo 14, no. 16-VIII-886.

9. Miles, *Serving the Republic*, p. 161; Utley, *Frontier Regulars*, p. 387; Heitman, *Historical Register*, p. 626; and Davis, *The Truth About Geronimo*, p. 219.

10. H. W. Lawton, 5 May 1886, typescript, Communications of Field Operations Against Apaches, 5/17/85–8/28/86, Gatewood, Box 6, v. 1, [Box 1], AHS.

11. Daly, "The Geronimo Campaign," p. 260

12. Lawton to [W. A.] Thompson, [Acting Assistant Adjutant General], 3 July 1886, and Lawton to Thompson, 27 June 1886, Gatewood, Box 6, v. 1, [Box 1], AHS.

13. Torres, Hermosillo, to Miles, Willcox, 4 May 1886, typescript, Communications of Field Operations Against Apaches, 5/17/85–8/28/86, Gatewood, Box 6, v. 1, [Box 1], AHS; and Miles to Torres, 4 May 1886, Archivo de Sonora, Legajo 14.

14. Gobernación to Governor of Sonora, 5 May 1886, and Telegram Miles, Ft. Huachuca, to Torres, 7 May 1886, Archivo de Sonora, Legajo 15.

15. Lawton to Miles, 5 July 1886; Lawton to Thompson, 31 July 1886; and Lawton to Miles, 5 July 1886, Gatewood, Box 6, v. 1, [Box 1], AHS.

16. Governor of Sonora to Commander of First Military Zone, 8 June 1886, Archivo de Sonora, Legajo 14; Telegram Miles to Torres, 5 August 1886, Archivo de Sonora, Legajo 15; and Lawton to Act. Adjt. General, S. W. District of Arizona, Fort Huachuca, Arizona, 10 June 1886, Gatewood, Box 6, v. 1, [Box 1], AHS.

17. Sahuaripa District to Srio. de Estado, Hermosillo, 5 June 1886, Archivo de Sonora, Legajo 15; and Martínez to Díaz, 13 May 1886; Torres to Díaz, 17 May 1886; Díaz to Torres, 24 May 1886, CPD, Legajo 11, Box 10.

18. Heitman, *Historical Register*, p. 447; Davis, *The Truth About Geronimo*, pp. 219–20; and Daly, "The Geronimo Campaign," pp. 257–58.

19. Davis, *The Truth About Geronimo*, p. 221; and Charles B. Gatewood, "Crook Was Hindered in Geronimo Hunt," 15 July 1926.

20. Wood to Department Commander, Ft. Huachuca, 14 July 1886; Lawton to W. A. Thompson, Acting Adjutant General, 31 July 1886; and Lawton to Adj. General, Dist. of Huachuca, 14 July 1886, Gatewood Collection, Box 6, v. 1, [Box 1], AHS.

21. Lawton to Adjt. General, Dist. of Huachuca, 14 and 27 July 1886, and Miles to Presidio of San Francisco, 21 July 1886, Gatewood Collection, Box 6, v. 1, [Box 1], AHS.

22. First Lieut. James Parker, Fourth Cavalry, Carretas, Mexico, to Acting Asst. Adjt. General, Fort Bowie, 26 July 1886; Lawton to Adjutant General, Dist. Huachuca, 8 August 1886; Lawton to Thompson, 27 June 1886 and 15 August 1886, Gatewood Collection, Box 6, v. 1, [Box 1], AHS.

23. Lawton to Adjutant General, Dist. Huachuca, 3 July 1886, Gatewood Collection, Box 6, v. 1, [Box 1], AHS.

24. Lawton to Thompson, 31 July 1886, Gatewood Collection, Box 6, v. 1. [Box 1], AHS.

25. Torres and Corral to Foreign Relations, 20 August 1886, RE 12-3-45.

26. Mariscal to War, 23 Sept. 1886; M. Romero to Foreign Relations, 8 Oct. 1886, RE 12-3-45.

27. U.S. Dept. of State to Foreign Relations, 4 Jan. 1887, RE 12-3-45.

28. Parker to Actg. Adjt. Gen'l., Fort Bowie, 26 July 1886; and 1st Indorsement [on Parker's of 5 August], N. C. Foster, Capt., 9th Infry., to Actg. Asst. Adjt. Gen'l., Dist. of Bowie, 16 August 1886, Gatewood, Box 6, v. 1, [Box 1], AHS.

29. Crook to Sheridan, 4 April 1886, Correspondence Sheridan and Crook, p. 9.

30. Davis, *The Truth About Geronimo*, pp. 222–23; Daly, "The Geronimo Campaign," p. 96; and Thomas W. Dunlay, *Wolves for the Blue Soldiers: Indian Scouts and Auxiliaries with the United States Army, 1860–1890* (Lincoln: University of Nebraska, 1982), p. 181. Kayihtah is also spelled Kayitah and Kieta.

31. Parker to Actg. Asst. Adjt. Gen'l., Fort Bowie, 26 July 1886, Gatewood, Box 6, v. 1, [Box 1], AHS.

32. George A. Forsyth, Lieut. Col., Fourth Cavalry, to Capt. Thompson, Willcox, 21 August 1886, Gatewood, Box 6, v. 1, [Box 1], AHS.

33. M. Romero to Foreign Relations, 19 Dec. 1886, RE 12-8-91; Utley, *Frontier Regulars*, p. 194, and Annual Report of Brigadier General George Crook, U.S. Army, Commanding Department of Arizona, 1883, Gatewood, Box 2, Folder 12, p. 10, AHS.

34. Miles to Lawton, 24 Aug. 1886, Gatewood, Box 6, v. 1, [Box 1], AHS.

35. Forsyth to Thompson, 18 and 21 Aug. 1886; Lieut. Thomas J. Clay, Tenth Infantry, to Post Adjutant, Fort Huachuca, 17 Aug. 1886, Gatewood, Box 6, v. 1, [Box 1], AHS.

36. Daly, "The Geronimo Campaign," p. 261.

37. Miles to W. M. Edwardy, Ures, 18 Aug. 1886, Gatewood, Box 6, v. 1, [Box 1], AHS.

38. Torres to Bowie, 18 Aug. 1886; Thomas J. Clay, 1st Lieut., 10th Inf., to Post Adjutant, Fort Huachuca, 17 Aug. 1886, Gatewood, Box 6, v. 1, [Box 1], AHS.

39. Huachuca to Willcox, 18 Aug. 1886, Gatewood, Box 6, v. 1, [Box 1], AHS; and Maj. Gen. O. O. Howard, Division of Pacific, to Adjutant General, 19 Aug. 1886, Ex. Doc., 50th Cong., 1st sess., *Foreign Relations, 1887–*, pt. 1.

40. Forsyth to Thompson, 21 Aug. 1886, Gatewood, Box 6, v. 1, [Box 1], AHS.

41. Ibid.

42. Forsyth to Thompson, 21 Aug. 1886; Miles to Lieut. Col. Wade, Apache, 28 Aug. 1886, Gatewood, Box 6, v. 1, [Box 1], AHS.

43. Torres to Bowie, 18 Aug. 1886, Gatewood, Box 6, v. 1, [Box 1], AHS; Telegram Ramón Corral to Ures Prefect, n.d., Archivo de Sonora, Legajo 15; and Gobernación to Foreign Relations, 20 Sept. 1886, RE 12-8-91.

44. Barrett, *Geronimo's Story of His Life*, p. 110.

45. Torres to Miles, 24 Aug. 1886, Gatewood, Box 6, v. 1, [Box 1], AHS.

46. Miles to Lawton, 24 Aug. 1886, Gatewood, Box 6, v. 1, [Box 1], AHS.

47. Telegram, Torres, Hermosillo, to Dr. A. A. Pesqueira, Ures, 25 Aug. 1886, Archivo de Sonora, Legajo 15.

48. Davis, *The Truth About Geronimo*, pp. 225–26.

49. Davis, *The Truth About Geronimo*, pp. 226–27; O. M. Boggess, Supt. Mes-

calero Indian Reservation, "The Final Surrender of Geronimo as Told by Apache Scouts Kayitah and Martine," 25 Sept. 1925, Gatewood, Box 1, Folder 16, p. 3, AHS; and Barrett, *Geronimo's Story*, p. 165.

50. Jack Lane, ed., *Chasing Geronimo: the Journal of Leonard Wood: May–September, 1886* (Albuquerque: University of New Mexico Press, 1970), pp. 7–8.

51. Lawton to C. O., Dist. of Huachuca, 28 Aug. 1886, Gatewood, Box 6, v. 1, [Box 1], AHS.

52. Forsyth, Huachuca, to Miles, Ft. Bowie, 30 Aug. 1886, Official Records of the Dept. of Arizona, Communications During Field Operations Against the Apache Indians 8/29/86–10/11/86, Gatewood Collection, Box 1, Folder 5, AHS (hereafter referred to as Official Records); and Miles to Torres, 31 Aug. 1886, Gatewood, Box 6, v. 1, [Box 1], AHS.

53. Torres to Miles, 31 Aug. 1836, Gatewood, Box 1, Folder 5, AHS; and Telegram, Torres to Miles, n.d., Archivo de Sonora, Legajo 15.

54. Miles to Lawton, 1 Sept. 1886, Gatewood, Box 6, v. 1, [Box 1], AHS; and Torres, Hermosillo, to Miles, Ft. Bowie, 3 Sept. 1886, Official Records.

55. Joseph C. Porter, *Paper Medicine Man: John Gregory Bourke and His American West* (Norman: University of Oklahoma Press, 1986), pp. 218, 221–22, 224.

56. Porter, *Paper Medicine Man*, p. 221; and Miles, *Serving the Republic*, p. 228.

57. *New York World*, 3 Sept. 1886; *Washington Star*, 3 Sept. 1886; *Washington Post*, 4 Sept. 1886, RE 12-8-91; and Mariscal, Foreign Relations, to M. Romero, Washington, 18 Sept. 1886; War to Foreign Relations, 29 Oct. 1886, RE 12-8-90.

58. Miles to Torres, 6 Sept. 1886, Official Records; Romero to Foreign Relations, 21 July 1886, RE 11-2-30; *Washington Post*, 21 July 1886; and *New York World*, 20 July 1886, RE 11-2-30.

59. Nelson A. Miles, *Serving the Republic: Memoirs of the Civil and Military Life of Nelson A. Miles* (1911; rpt. Freeport, NY: Books for Libraries Press, 1971), p. 228; *Tucson Daily Citizen*, 30 March 1886, George Crook Collection, Arizona Historical Society; and *New York Times*, 17 Sept. 1886, RE 12-8-91.

60. *New York Daily Tribune*, 2 Oct. 1886, RE 11-9-7; *New York World*, 6 and 9 Nov. 1886, RE 12-8-91, and Annual Message to Congress, President Cleveland, 6 Dec. 1886, Ex. Doc., 49th Cong., 2nd sess., v. 1–12, serial 2460–2471.

61. Davis, *The Truth About Geronimo*, pp. 233, 236–37; and Porter, *Paper Medicine Man*, p. 224.

62. Debo, *A History of the Indians of the United States*, pp. 233–34. General George Crook fought against the removal and imprisonment of his scouts. After Sheridan's death and his own promotion to major general, Crook openly associated with the Indian Rights Association. Alarmed by the numerous climate-induced deaths of Chiricahuas in Florida and Alabama, Crook fought to move the Chiricahuas to Fort Sill until his sudden death in 1890.

63. M. Romero, Washington, to Foreign Relations, 2 Oct. 1886, RE 11-9-7; A. Martínez, Commander of First Military Zone, to Governor of Sonora, 18 Sept. 1886, and Ayuntamiento de San Felipe to Srio. de Estado de Sonora, 16 Oct. 1886,

Archivo de Sonora, Legajo 15; and Torres to Díaz, 26 Sept. 1886, CPD, Legajo 11, Box 23.

64. *Washington Post*, 2 Oct. 1886, RE 11-9-7.

65. M. Romero, Washington, to Foreign Relations, 2 and 8 Oct. 1886; *Cincinnati Commercial Gazette*, 4 Oct. 1886, RE 11-9-7.

66. Romero to Foreign Relations, 15 and 13 Oct. 1886, RE 11-9-7.

67. *Washington Post*, 9 Oct. 1886; *El Fronterizo*, 15 Sept. 1886, RE 11-9-7; *New York Herald*, 3 Nov. 1886; and *New York Times*, 8 Nov. 1886, RE 12-8-91.

68. Srio. de Estado y del Despacho de Hacienda y Crédito Público to Foreign Relations, 29 Dec. 1886, RE, LE 2242, pts. 6 and 1; and P. Oruelas, San Antonio, to Díaz, 7 Sept. 1886; Lorenzo García, Río Yaqui, to Díaz, 17 Sept. 1886, CPD, Legajo 11, Box 20.

CHAPTER 7

1. War to Foreign Relations, 10 Jan. 1887, RE, LE 2242, pt. 6.

2. M. Romero to Foreign Relations, 5 May 1887, RE 11-9-4.

3. Telegram C. A. Pearson, Nogales, to Torres, 6 June 1887, Archivo de Sonora, Legajo 16; *New York Times*, 8 June 1887, RE 15-3-66; *Washington Post*, 13 June 1887, RE 15-3-66; Telegram Miles to Torres, 12 June 1887, Archivo de Sonora, Legajo 16; *The Washington Critic*, 27 June 1887, RE 15-3-66; and Angel Martínez, Commander of First Military Zone, to Díaz, 25 June 1887, CPD, Legajo 12, Box 11.

4. Julio Cervantes to Díaz, 10 Oct. 1887, CPD, Legajo 12, Box 19, no. 009382; and Moctezuma Prefect to Srio. de Estado [de Sonora], 26 Dec. 1887, Archivo de Sonora, Legajo 16.

5. Angel Martínez to Díaz, 12 April 1887, CPD, Legajo 12, Box 7; and Spicer, *Cycles of Conquest*, pp. 72–73.

6. *San Francisco Chronicle*, 4 March 1887, CPD, Legajo 12, Box 5, no. 002439; and *The Daily News* [Nogales, Arizona], 7 March 1887, CPD, Legajo 17, Box 5, no. 002440.

7. Torres to Díaz, 4 March 1887, CPD, Legajo 12, Box 5, no. 002457; *San Francisco Morning Call*, 8 March 1887, CPD, Legajo 12, Box 5, no. 002492; and *El Eco de la Frontera* [Nogales], 27 March 1887, CPD, Legajo 12, Box 7, no. 003338.

8. Torres to Díaz, 14 May 1887, CPD, Legajo 12, Box 9, no. 004469; Torres to Díaz, 23 May 1887, CPD, Legajo 12, Box 9, no. 004477; and *Arizona Daily Citizen*, 29 March 1888, Re 17-21-127.

9. Garza Galán to Díaz, 8 March 1888, CPD, Legajo 13, Box 5, no. 002451; *Arizona Daily Citizen*, 29 March 1888, RE 17-21-127; and Díaz to Garza Galán, 13 March 1888, CPD, Legajo 13, Box 5, no. 002461.

10. Governor of Chihuahua to Srio. de Gobierno, 22 March 1888, RE 17-21-127.

11. Foreign Relations to Governor of Chihuahua, 10 March 1888; *Washington Post*, 11 March 1888, RE 17-21-127.

12. *Washington Post*, 28 March 1888, RE 17-21-127.

13. *Arizona Daily Citizen*, 29 March 1888, RE 17-21-127.

14. U.S. Legation in Mexico to Foreign Relations, 29 May 1888; Corral to Foreign Relations, 14 Aug. 1888, RE 17-21-126.

15. El Paso Consul to Foreign Relations, 27 June 1888, RE 15-4-11; Governor of Sonora to Foreign Relations, 27 May 1890; 14 and 18 June 1888, no. 14-VII-888, Archivo de Sonora, Legajo 16; and El Paso Consul to Foreign Relations, 31 July 1881; M. Romero to Foreign Relations, 2 Aug. 1888, RE 15-4-11.

16. William M. Edwardy, "Border Troubles," *Harper's Weekly*, 18 Aug. 1888; M. Romero to Foreign Relations, 2 April 1889, RE 11-9-4.

17. Lieut. W. E. Shipp and Herbert Welsh, "Our Indian Scouts," *Harper's Weekly*, 27 Oct. 1888, p. 811, Special Collections, University of New Mexico, Albuquerque.

18. Edwardy to Romero, 8 March 1889; Romero to Foreign Relations, 2 April 1889, RE 11-9-4.

19. Edwardy to Romero, 8 March 1889; Romero to Foreign Relations, 2 and 25 April 1889, RE 11-9-14.

20. Arizpe Prefect to Srio. de Estado, Hermosillo, 14 May 1889, no. 4-XI-889; 3 Nov. 1889; and C. P. Pierson, Commander Fort Huachuca, to Corral, 4 Nov. 1889, no. 4-XI-889, Archivo de Sonora, Legajo 16.

21. Mariscal, Foreign Relations, to Governor of Sonora, 14 March 1889; 3 Nov. 1889, Archivo de Sonora, Legajo 16; and Governor of Chihuahua to Foreign Relations, 13 March 1889; M. Romero to Foreign Relations, 3 Oct. 1889; Foreign Relations to Romero, Washington, 5 Dec. 1889; Romero to Foreign Relations, 14 and 25 Jan. 1890, RE 11-9-4.

22. Ross Santee, *Apache Land* (New York: Scribner's, 1947), p. 82; Johnson, Commanding San Carlos, Arizona, 19 July 1890, Archivo de Sonora, Legajo 16; Mexico, *Tratados ratificados y convenios ejecutivos celebrados por México* (México, D.F.: Senado de la República, 1973), pp. 243–45; and Foreign Relations to Romero, 2 June 1890; Romero to Foreign Relations, 2 and 12 June 1890, RE, LE 2242, pt. 6.

23. Miles to Adjutant General, 23 August 1890 and Copy, U.S. Dept. of State to Sec. of War, 30 Aug. 1890, RE, LE 2242, pt. 6; Telegram, Mariscal, Foreign Relations, to Corral, 12 Dec. 1890, no. 2-X-890, Archivo de Sonora, Legajo 16; and Cayetano Romero to U.S. Dept. of State, 3 Sept. 1890; U.S. Dept. of State to C. Romero, 6 Sept. 1890; C. Romero to William F. Wharton, Sec. of Interior, 19 Sept. 1890, RE, LE 2242, pt. 6.

24. México, *Tratados*, p. 309; RE, LE 2242, pt. 6; *Washington Post*, 15 Oct. 1890; and Commander First Military Zone to Governor of Sonora, 2 Dec. 1892; Gobernación to Governor of Sonora, 17 Jan. 1891, Archivo de Sonora, Legajo 17.

25. Díaz to Torres, Military Commander Northern District, 11 Feb. 1891, no. 001910; Governor of Chihuahua Lauro Carrillo to Díaz, 28 Feb. 1891, no. 002237, CPD, Legajo 16, Box 4; and M. Carrillo, Guaymas, to Governor of Sonora, 21 Dec. 1891; Magdalena Prefecto to Srio. de Estado, Hermosillo, 27 June 1892; Moc-

tezuma Prefect to Srio. de Estado, 31 Aug. 1892; Telegram, Col. Noyes, Fort Huachuca, to Governor of Sonora Rafael Yzábal [Izábal], 27 Oct. 1892, Archivo de Sonora, Legajo 17.

26. C. Romero to Foreign Relations, 2 Nov. 1892, RE 42-29-94; Cayetano Romero was temporarily occupying the post of Mexico's Minister in Washington while his brother Matías was absent; *San Antonio Daily Express*, 30 March 1891; Mariscal to San Antonio Consul, 9 April 1891, RE 6-2-8; and C. Romero to Díaz, 1 Jan. 1883, no. 001129; C. Romero to Díaz, 19 Jan. 1893, no. 001140; *Washington Post*, 13 Jan. 1893, no. 001138, CPD, Legajo 18, Box 3.

27. Carrillo to Díaz, 18 Jan. 1892, CPD, Legajo 17, Box 1, no. 00271.

28. *New York Herald*, 11 Jan. 1892, CPD, Legajo 15, Box 3, no. 001177.

29. *San Francisco Morning Call*, 24 Feb. 1892, CPD, Legajo 17, Box 8, no. 003630 and CPD, Legajo 18, no. 00252.

30. Capt. U.S. Third Cavalry to General Lorenzo García, 4 March 1892, CPD, Legajo 18, Box 10, no. 003869; and Torres to Díaz, 15 March 1892, CPD, Legajo 17, Box 10, no. 004813.

31. Díaz to Torres, 8 March 1892, no. 004809; Torres to Díaz, 15 March 1892, no. 004813, CPD, Legajo 17, Box 10; and Order signed Luis Torres and Ramón Corral, 24 Aug. 1885, CPD, Legajo 10, Box 18, no. 008872.

32. *New York Evening Post*, 12 Dec. 1892; War to Foreign Relations, 28 Dec. 1892, RE 42-29-94; Cosío Villegas, *Historia moderna: República restaurada*, p. 188; *The Silver City Enterprise*, 22 Oct. 1897; Mexican Consul, Deming, New Mexico, to Foreign Relations, 12 Nov. 1897, RE 11-9-15; and Safford Relyea, "Diplomatic Relations," p. 83.

33. Telegram, Nogales Aduana to Foreign Relations, 13 Aug. 1896, RE 1-3-670.

34. Figueroa to Díaz, 13 and 15 Aug. 1896, CPD, Legajo 21, Box 28; Nogales Aduana to Foreign Relations, 13 Aug. 1896, RE 1-3-670; Almada, *Diccionario*, p. 530; and Lauro Carrillo, Governor of Chihuahua, to Díaz, 2 and 18 Jan. 1892, CPD, Legajo 17, Box 1, nos. 000262 and 00271.

35. Figueroa to Díaz, 13 Aug. 1896, CPD, Legajo 21, Box 28; and Telegram, Nogales Aduana to Foreign Relations, 13 Aug. 1896, RE 1-3-670.

36. *El Independiente* [El Paso], 21 Aug. 1896, RE 1-3-670.

37. *San Francisco Examiner*, 14 Aug. 1896, RE 1-3-670; and Figueroa, Nogales, to Díaz, 15 Aug. 1896, CPD, Legajo 21, Box 28.

38. Mariscal, Foreign Relations, to War, 18 Sept. 1896, RE 1-3-670 (I).

39. Governor of Arizona to Corral, 14 and 15 Feb. 1896, RE 7-8-19; and Corral to Foreign Relations, 21 Feb. 1896, Archivo de Sonora, Legajo 17.

40. Mariscal to Corral, 22 Feb. 1896; Corral to Governor of Arizona, 24 Feb. 1896; Governor of Arizona to Corral, 5 March 1896, RE 7-8-19.

41. Memorandum, Daniel S. Lamont, Sec. of War, to Sec. of State, 17 May 1896; Copy telegram, Wheaton, Ft. Grant, Arizona to Adjt. Gen. Col. Sumner, 17 May 1896; Copy letter, Maj. Gen. Nelson A. Miles to Army Headquarters, 2nd Endorsement to Sec. of War, 18 May 1896, RE 7-8-19.

42. Mariscal to Romero, 26 May 1896; Copy of 4 June 1896 agreement; Copy telegram, Sumner to Adjutant General, 3 June 1896, RE 7-8-19.

43. *Washington Post*, 14 June 1896, RE 7-8-19.

44. M. Covarrubias to Foreign Relations, 24 June 1896; Copy, Acting Sec. State to M. Romero, 26 Aug. 1896, Copy letter, Col. E. V. Sumner, Commander 7th Cavalry, Fort Grant, to Adjt., Gen., Dept. of Colorado, 1 Aug. 1896; Hacienda to Foreign Relations, 13 July 1896; War to Foreign Relations, 12 Aug. 1896, RE 7-8-19.

45. Copy letter, McIntosh, Fort Thomas, Ariz., to Miles, Commanding Army, 21 June 1896; Endorsement from Miles, 27 Aug. 1896, RE 7-8-19.

46. Juana Fraser Lyon, "Archie McIntosh, the Scottish Indian Scout," *The Journal of Arizona History* 7, no. 3 (Autumn 1966): 104–7, 110, 120, 122.

47. W. W. Rackhill, Acting Sec. Dept of State, to M. Romero, 2 Sept. 1896; Endorsement from Miles, 27 Aug. 1896; Copy, J. Doe, Acting Sec. of War, to Sec. of State, 1 Sept. 1896, RE 7-8-19; and Ross Santee, *Apache Land* (New York: C. Scribner's Sons, 1947), p. 92.

48. Debo, *A History of the Indians of the United States*, pp. 257–61.

49. M. Romero, Mex. Legation, to Foreign Relations, 15 April 1893; Secretary of Fomento, Colonización, Industria y Comercio to Foreign Relations, 28 April 1893, RE 15-5-100; and M. Romero to Foreign Relations, 19 Oct. 1897, RE 15-7-48.

50. *The Citizen* [Brooklyn, N.Y.], 12 July 1897, RE 17-21-37; M. Romero to Foreign Relations, 28 Dec. 1897, RE 3737-13; and Sec. of Fomento to Foreign Relations, 2 Feb. 1898, RE 3737-13.

51. San Antonio Consul to Foreign Relations, 6 Dec. 1897; Walter A. Duncan, Chairman of Cherokee Delegation, to M. Romero, 22 March 1898; Romero to Cherokee Delegation, 23 March and 30 April, 1898; *St. Louis Globe-Democrat*, 29 May 1898, RE 3737-13; and *San Antonio Daily Express*, 18 Dec. 1908, RE 27-3-122.

52. Bernardo Reyes to Ignacio Mariscal, 30 May 1899; Fomento to Foreign Relations, 10 Aug. 1899, RE 3737-12.

53. Mexican Legation to Foreign Relations, 31 Jan. 1899; *Boston Transcript*, 21 Jan. 1899; Foreign Relations to Fomento, 24 Feb. 1899, RE 15-8-66.

54. U.S. Interior Dept. to Foreign Relations, 6 May 1905; U.S. Ambassador in Mexico D. E. Thompson to Foreign Relations, 10 March 1908; U.S. Embassy in Mexico to Foreign Relations, 17 April 1908, RE 15-14-27.

55. *Daily International American* [Douglas, Ariz.], 7 May 1908; Foreign Relations to War, 2 June 1908, RE 12-5-68; and El Paso Consul to Foreign Relations, 14 Oct. 1908, RE 15-20-96.

56. Mexican Consul Laredo to Foreign Relations, 20 March 1905; *Reservada*, Mexican Consul General, San Francisco, to Foreign Relations, 13 Sept. 1905; Tucson Consul to Foreign Relations, 7 May 1906, RE, LE 2250, pt. 1.

57. Paso y Troncoso, *Las guerras*, p. 317; and Hu-Dehart, "Development and Rural Rebellion," pp. 79–83. José R. Castillo, *Historia de la revolución social de México* (México: 1915), p. 142; and González Navarro, *Vida social*, p. 257.

58. Foreign Relations to Mexican Legation, 25 Nov. 1905; Mexican Legation to Foreign Relations, 14 Nov. 1905; *San Francisco Chronicle*, 6 April 1905, RE, LE 2250. pt. 1.

59. War to Foreign Relations, 7 July 1905; *San Francisco Bulletin*, 2 July 1905; *San Francisco Chronicle*, 5 and 20 Nov. 1905; RE, LE 2250, pt. 1.

60. Sec. of Gobernación Corral to Foreign Relations, 13 Nov. 1905; *El Imparcial*, 31 June 1906, RE, LE 2250, pt. 1.

61. *San Francisco Examiner*, 4 April 1905; *Tucson Citizen*, 5 April 1905; Foreign Relations to Consul General, San Francisco, 12 April 1905; *Tucson Citizen*, 28 April 1905, RE, LE 2250, pt. 1.

62. *Tucson Citizen*, 28 April 1905; and *El Imparcial*, 26 Feb. 1906, RE, LE 2250, pt. 1.

63. Andrés Molina Enríquez, *La revolución agraria en México* (México: Museo Nacional de Arqueología, Historia y Ethnografía, 1937), p. 117; Hu-Dehart, "Development and Rural Rebellion," pp. 82, 84, 86, 88, 91; González Navarro, *Vida social*, p. 259; Edward H. Spicer, *The Yaquis: A Cultural History* (Tucson: University of Arizona Press, 1980) p. 160; and Paso y Troncosco, *Las guerras*, p. 23.

64. Foreign relations to Mex. Legation, 5 Jan. 1906; Phoenix Consul to Foreign Relations, 6 March 1906; *El Fronterizo*, 18 March 1905; Foreign Relations to War, 23 May 1905, RE, LE 2250, pt. 1.

65. War to Foreign Relations, 22 Dec. 1905; Tucson Consul to Foreign Relations, 31 Dec. 1905, RE, LE 2250, pt. 1.

66. *Reservada* Mexican Consul Yuma to Foreign Relations, 5 Jan. 1906; War to Foreign Relations, 18 April 1906, RE, LE 2250, pt. 1.

67. Tucson Consul to Foreign Relations, 15 Jan. 1906; Confidential deciphered telegram, U.S. Sec. of State to U.S. Embassy in Mexico, 21 July 1906; Los Angeles Consul to Foreign Relations, 10 Nov. 1906; Mexican Consul General to Governor of Calif., 24 Nov. 1906, RE, LE, 2250, pt. 1.

68. Mexican Consul Phoenix to Foreign Relations, 12 April 1906; Tucson Consul to Foreign Relations, 10 April 1906; Nogales Consul to Foreign Relations, 15 April 1906; Mexican lawyer to Tucson Consul, 16 April 1906; Tucson Consul to Foreign Relations, 17 April 1906; and Tucson Consul to Foreign Relations, 23 April 1906, RE, LE 2250, pt. 1.

69. *San Francisco Chronicle*, 9 May 1906; and *Los Angeles Times*, 14 May 1906, RE, LE 2250, pt. 1; and *Los Angeles Times*, 13 May 1906, RE, LE 2250, pt. 3.

70. Foreign Relations to Mexican Consuls in San Francisco, San Diego, Yuma, Tucson, Phoenix, El Paso, San Antonio, and Los Angeles, 15 May 1906; Mexican Consul San Diego to Foreign Relations, 24 May 1906; *La Nueva Centuria* [Phoenix], 26 May 1906; *El Paso Daily Evening News*, 26 May 1906; *San Diego Union*, 24 May 1906; and Mexican Consul Tucson to Foreign Relations, 29 May 1906; RE, LE 2250, pt. 1.

71. Sec. of Gobernación Corral to Foreign Relations, 2 July 1906, RE, LE 2250, pt. 1.

72. Charles Leland Sonnichsen, *Colonel Greene and the Copper Skyrocket* (Tucson: University of Arizona Press, 1974), pp. 194–200; Eduardo W. Villa, *Historia del estado de Sonora*, 3rd ed. (Hermosillo, México: Gobierno del estado de Sonora, 1984), pp. 404, 417; and Enrique Krauze, *Porfirio Díaz: Místico de la autoridad*, (México: Fondo de Cultura Económica, 1987), pp. 98–99.

73. Yuma Consul to Foreign Relations, 1 and 9 May 1906, RE 12-5-41.

74. Yuma Consul to Foreign Relations, 1 May 1906; Lovell Richey to Yuma Consul, 21 May 1906, RE 12-5-41.

CHAPTER 8

1. Paul J. Vanderwood and Frank N. Samponaro, *Border Fury: A Picture Postcard Record of Mexico's Revolution and U.S. War Preparedness, 1910–1917* (Albuquerque: University of New Mexico, 1988), p. 120.

2. Charles H. Harris III and Louis R. Sadler, "The Plan of San Diego and the Mexican-United States War Crisis of 1916: A Reexamination," *Hispanic American Historical Review* 58 (August 1978): 381, 390. Carranza offered to end raids in South Texas, many undertaken in the name of the Plan of San Diego. This document called for an uprising on February 20, 1915, to grant independence to the American Southwest. All Anglo males over sixteen years of age were to be killed by an army of Mexican-Americans, blacks, Indians, and Japanese.

3. Michael L. Tate, "Pershing's Punitive Expedition: Pursuer of Bandits or Presidential Panacea?" *The Americas* 32 (July 1975): 53; Frederick Katz, "Pancho Villa and the Attack on Columbus, New Mexico" *American Historical Review* 83 (February 1978): 102–10, 126–27; and Vanderwood and Samponaro, *Border Fury*, p. 180–82.

4. Herbert Molloy Mason, *The Great Pursuit* (New York: Random House, 1970), p. 66; and Mark T. Gilderhus, *Diplomacy and Revolution: U.S. Mexican Relations under Wilson and Carranza* (Tucson: University of Arizona Press, 1977), p. 36.

5. Florence C. and Robert H. Lister, *Chihuahua: Storehouse of Storms* (Albuquerque: University of New Mexico Press, 1966), pp. 247–48, 252.

6. Tate, "Pershing's Punitive Expedition, p. 56.

7. Dunlay, *Wolves for the Blue Soldiers*, pp. 184–85; Linda B. Hall and Don M. Coerver, *Revolution on the Border: the United States and Mexico, 1910–1920* (Albuquerque: University of New Mexico Press, 1988) p. 70; Mason, *The Great Pursuit*, p. 169; Haldeen Braddy, *Pancho Villa at Columbus: the Raid of 1916* (El Paso: Texas Western College Press, 1965), p. 6; Vanderwood and Samponaro, *Border Fury*, pp. 12, 184, 190; Gilderhus, *Diplomacy*, p. 38; and Lister, *Chihuahua*, p. 255.

8. Lister, *Chihuahua*, p. 263; and Almada, *Diccionario*, pp. 91, 228.

9. Stacy C. Hinkle, *Wings and Saddles: the Air and Cavalry Punitive Expedition of 1919* (El Paso: UTEP Texas Western Press, 1967), p. 5; Stacy C. Hinkle, *Wings Over the Border: The Army Air Service Armed Patrol of the United States-Mexico Border 1919–1921* (El Paso: UTEP Texas Western Press, 1970), p. 12; and Clarence Clen-

denen, *The United States and Pancho Villa: A Study in Unconventional Diplomacy* (Ithaca, N.Y.: Cornell University Press, 1961), pp. 310, 312

10. Hinkle, *Wings and Saddles*, pp. 8–9.

11. Hinkle, *Wings Over the Border*, pp. 11, 38.

12. Hinkle, *Wings Over the Border*, pp. 19; Hinkle, *Wings and Saddles*, p. 15; and Elton Miles, *More Tales of the Big Bend* (College Station: Texas A & M University Press, 1988), p. 179.

13. Hinkle, *Wings and Saddles*, pp. 8–19.

14. Hinkle, *Wings and Saddles*, pp. 26, 36; and Almada, *Diccionario*, p. 168.

15. Hinkle, *Wings Over the Border*, p. 54.

CHAPTER 9

1. Almada, *Juárez and Terrazas*, p. 313; and Clendenen, *The U.S. and Pancho Villa*, pp. 250, 253.

2. Spicer, *Cycles of Conquest*, p. 253.

3. Spicer, *Cycles of Conquest*, p. 254.

4. Paso y Troncoso, *Las guerras*, p. 342.

5. González Navarro, *Vida social*, p. 245.

6. Gutiérrez Santos, *Historia militar*, pp. 20–21; and Alberto Lozoya, "Un guión para el estudio de los ejércitos mexicanos," pp. 553–68.

7. Spicer, *Cycles of Conquest*, pp. 573, 577.

Sources Cited

This study is based primarily on unpublished manuscript materials contained in two major repositories in Mexico City: the Colección Porfirio Díaz in the Sala Francisco Xavier Alegre at the Universidad Iberoamericana and the Archivo Histórico Genaro Estrada at the Secretaría de Relaciones Exteriores. Two other depositories, significant for the present research, are the Charles B. Gatewood Collection at the Arizona Historical Society in Tucson and the Archivo General, Ramo de Relaciones Exteriores, at the Museo Regional de Sonora in Hermosillo.

The bulk of these materials consists of correspondence, which is fully identified in the footnotes. The bibliography of manuscript materials indicates the general archival sources from which the documents are drawn. In the bibliography of printed materials no distinction is made between contemporary source materials and modern works because many publications contain both documents and interpretation.

I. PRIMARY SOURCES

A. Manuscript materials

Arizona. General George Armstrong Crook Collection, Arizona Historical Society, Tucson.

Arizona. Charles B. Gatewood Collection, Arizona Historical Society, Tucson.

Mexico, D.F. Archivo Histórico Genaro Estrada, Secretaría de Relaciones Exteriores.

Mexico, D.F. Colección Porfirio Díaz, Sala Francisco Xavier Alegre, Universidad Iberoamericana.

Mexico, D.F. Archivo de Sonora, Biblioteca y Museo de Sonora, Universidad de Sonora, Série Sonora, Primera Série, Vol. 13, 1883–1886, Biblioteca del Museo de Antropología e Historia.

Sonora. Archivo General, Ramo de Relaciones Exteriores, Museo Regional de Sonora, Gobierno del Estado de Sonora, Legajos 10–17, Hermosillo, Sonora.

Texas. Eugene C. Barker Texas History Center, University of Texas at Austin.

Texas. Sánchez Navarro Collection, Nettie Lee Benson Latin American Collection, University of Texas at Austin.

United States. U.S. Embassy, Mexico, Dispatches from U.S. Consuls in Mexico City, 1822–1906.

United States. U.S. Embassy, Mexico, Dispatches from U.S. Ministers to Mexico, 1823–1906.

United States. U.S. National Archives, Washington, D.C., Bureau of Indian Affairs, Letters Received, 1824–1881, Arizona Superintendency, 1863–1880.

United States. Notes from the Mexican Legation in the United States to Department of State, 1876–1910.

B. Printed Documents

Bevans, Charles I. *Treaties and other International Agreements of the United States of America, 1776–1949*. Vol. 9. Washington, D.C.: Department of State Publication 8615, U.S. Government Printing Office, 1972.

Carreño, Alberto María, ed. *Archivo del General Porfirio Díaz: Memorias y documentos*. México: "Elede" and El Instituto de Historia de la Universidad Nacional Autónoma de México, 1960.

Dublán, Manuel, and José María Lozano, comp. *Legislación mexicana, o colección completa de las disposiciones legislativas expedidas desde la independencia de la República*. Vol. 31. México: Dublán y Lozano, 1876–78.

México. Archivo Histórico Diplomático Mexicano. *Las Memorias diplomáticas de Mr. Foster sobre México*. México: Secretaría de Relaciones Exteriores, 1929, No. 29.

México. *Debates del Congreso Nacional de Instrucción Pública Unico Período de Sesiones*. México: "El Partido Liberal," 1889.

México. *Derecho público mexicano*. México: Imprenta del Gobierno, 1871–82.

México. Presidente. *Informes y manifiestos de los poderes ejecutivo y legislativo de 1821 a 1904*. Vol. 2. México: Gobierno Federal, 1905.

México. Presidente. *La educación pública en México a través de los mensajes presidenciales desde la consumación de la independencia hasta nuestros días*. México: Talleres Gráficos de la Nación, 1926.

México. *Los presidentes de México ante la nación*. México: El XLVI Legislatura de la Cámara de Diputados, 1966.

México. Archivo Histórico Diplomático Mexicano. *Un siglo de relaciones internacionales de México a través de los mensajes presidenciales*. No. 39. México: Secretaría de Relaciones Exteriores, 1935.

México. *Tratados ratificados y convenios ejecutivos celebrados por México*. Vols. 2–4. México: Senado de la República, 1973.

Ministerio de Relaciones de la República Mexicana. *Traducción del dictamen de Mr. Wadsworth, sobre las reclamaciones mexicanas procedentes de depredaciones de los indios.* México: Imprenta del Gobierno en Palacio, 1873, Colección Lafragua, Biblioteca Nacional de México.

Peñafiel, Antonio, ed. *Códice Martínez Gracida de Jamiltepec, Estado de Oaxaca, Códice Mixteco, Lienzo de Zacatepec.* México: Secretaría de Fomento, 1900, Special Collections, University of New Mexico.

Tena Ramírez, Felipe. *Leyes fundamentales de México, 1800–1976.* México: Editorial Porrúa. 1976.

Wheless, Joseph. *Compendium of the Laws of Mexico Officially Recognized by the Mexican Government.* St. Louis: F. H. Thomas Law Book Company, 1910.

C. Newspapers

Arizona Daily Citizen, Tucson, 1884, 1886, 1888, 1905.

Arizona Daily Journal, Tucson, 1881.

Arizona Daily Star, Tucson, 1881–82, 1884, 1886.

Boletín Oficial, Ures, Sonora, 1878.

Boston Transcript, 1899.

Chicago National Republican, 1881.

Cincinnati Commercial Gazette, 1886.

The Citizen, Brooklyn, New York, 1897.

La Constitución, Hermosillo, Sonora, 1881–83, 1885.

Daily International American, Douglas, Arizona, 1908.

Daily News, Nogales, Arizona, 1887.

El Diario Oficial, México, 1877, 1880–82, 1884.

El Eco de la Frontera, Nogales, 1887.

El Fronterizo, Tucson, 1882, 1884, 1886, 1905.

Globe Democrat, St. Louis, Missouri, 1886, 1898.

El Heraldo de Chihuahua, Chihuahua, 1980.

El Imparcial, Mexico, 1906.

El Independiente, El Paso, 1896.

London Times, 1877.

Los Angeles Times, 1886, 1906.

El Monitor Republicano, Mexico, 1880.

National Tribune, Washington, D.C., 1926.

New Banner of the Free, Austin, Texas, 1880.

New York Daily Tribune, 1882, 1886.

New York Evening Post, 1892.

New York Herald, 1881–82, 1886, 1892.

New York Sun, 1881.

New York Times, 1881–82, 1886.

New York World, 1881–82, 1886, 1892.

La Nueva Centuria, Phoenix, 1906.
El Paso Daily Evening News, 1906.
El Paso Herald, 1881.
El Periódico Oficial, Chihuahua, 1880, 1882.
El Progresista, El Paso, 1881.
San Antonio Daily Express, 1881, 1891, 1908.
San Diego Union, 1906.
San Dimas Press, California, 1927.
San Francisco Bulletin, 1905.
San Francisco Chronicle, 1887, 1905–06.
San Francisco Examiner, 1884, 1896, 1905.
San Francisco Morning Call, 1882, 1887, 1892–93.
Silver City Enterprise, 1897.
Tombstone Daily Epitaph, 1883.
Tucson Sun, 1882.
Washington Critic, 1887.
Washington Evening Star, 1882, 1886.
Washington Post, 1881, 1886–88, 1890, 1893, 1896.

D. Interviews

Mendoza, Víctor. Personal interview, 24 September 1981.

II. SECONDARY SOURCES

A. Books

Aguilar Camín, Héctor. *La frontera nómada: Sonora y la revolución mexicana*. México: Siglo Veintiuno, 1977.
Aguirre Beltrán, Gonzalo. *Formas de gobierno indígena*. México: Imprenta Universitaria, 1953.
———. *El proceso de aculturación*. México: Universidad Nacional Autónoma de México, 1957.
Almada, Francisco R. *Juárez y Terrazas: Aclaraciones históricas*. México: Libros Mexicanos, 1958.
———. *La revolución en el estado de Sonora*. México: Instituto Nacional de Estudios Historicos de la República Mexicana, 1971.
Alva, Víctor. *Las ideas sociales contemporáneas en México*. México: Fondo de Cultura Económica, 1960.
Askinasy, Siegfried. *México indígena: Observaciones sobre algunos problemas de México*. México: Imprenta "Cosmos," 1939.
Baerlein, Henry. *Mexico: the Land of Unrest*. Philadelphia: J. B. Lippincott, 1913.

Balbás, Manuel. *Recuerdos del yaqui: Principales episodios durante la campaña de 1899 a 1901*. México: Sociedad de Edición y Librería Franco Americano, 1927.

Baldwin, Gordon C. *The Warrior Apaches: A Story of the Chiricahua and Western Apache*. Tucson: Dale Stuart King, 1965.

Ball, Eve. *In the Days of Victorio: Recollections of a Warm Springs Apache*. Narr. James Kaywaykla. Tucson: University of Arizona Press, 1970.

Bancroft, Hubert Howe. *Vida de Porfirio Díaz: Reseña histórica y social del pasado y presente*. México: La Compañía Historia de México, 1887.

——. *History of Mexico, 1861–1887*. San Francisco: The History Company, 1888.

——. *History of Arizona and New Mexico, 1530–1888*. San Francisco: The History Company, 1889; rpt. Albuquerque: Horn and Wallace, 1962.

Bannon, John Francis, S.J. *The Mission Frontier in Sonora, 1620–1687*. New York: United States Catholic Historical Society, Monograph Series XXVI, 1955.

Barocio, Alberto, et al. *México y la cultura*. México: Secretaría de Educación Pública, 1946.

Barranco, Manuel. *Mexico: Its Educational Problems, Suggestions for their Solution*. New York: Teachers College, Columbia University, 1914.

Barreda, Gabino. *Estudios*. Ed. José Fuentes Mares. México: Universidad Nacional Autónoma, 1941.

Barrera Fuentes, Florencio. *Historia de la revolución mexicana: La etapa percursora*. México: Biblioteca del Instituto Nacional de Estudios Históricos de la Revolución Mexicana, 1955.

Barrett, S. M., ed. *Geronimo's Story of His Life*. New York: Duffield, 1906.

Beals, Carleton. *Mexico: An Interpretation*. New York: B. W. Huebsch, 1923.

——. *Mexican Maze*. Philadelphia: J. B. Lippincott, 1931.

——. *Porfirio Díaz: Dictator of Mexico*. 1932; rpt. Westport: Greenwood Press, 1971.

Betzinez, Jason. *I Fought with Geronimo*. Harrisburg, Pa.: Stackpole, 1959.

Bourke, John Gregory. *On the Border with Crook*. 1891; rpt. Chicago: Rio Grande Press, 1962.

Braddy, Haldeen. *Pancho Villa at Columbus: the Raid of 1916*. El Paso: Texas Western College Press, 1965.

Brocklehurst, Thomas Unett. *Mexico Today: A Country with a Great Future*. London: John Murray, 1883.

Bulnes, Francisco. *El porvenir de las naciones latino-americanos antes las conquistas recientes de Europa y los EEUU*. México: Mariano Nava, 1899.

Calderón, Esteban B. *Juicio sobre la guerra del yaqui y génesis de la huelga de Cananea*. 2nd ed. México: Centro de Estudios Históricos del Movimiento Obrero Mexicano, 1975.

Calderón, Lisandro. *Las escuelas rudimentarias de indígenas*. Tuxtla Gutiérrez, Chiapas: n.p., 1912.

Callahan, James Morton. *American Foreign Policy in Mexican Relations*. New York: Macmillan, 1932.

Callcott, Wilfrid H. *Liberalism in Mexico, 1857–1929*. Stanford: Stanford University Press, 1931.

Campbell, Reau. *Complete Guide and Descriptive Book of Mexico*. Chicago: Robert O. Law, 1906.

Cárdenas, Lázaro. *El problema indígena de México*. México: Departmento de Asuntos Indígenas, 1940.

Carreño, Alberto María. *México y los Estados Unidos de América*. México: Imprenta Victoria, 1913.

———. *La diplomacia extraordinaria entre México y los Estados Unidos, 1780–1947*. 2 Vols. México: Editorial Jus, 1961.

Carter, Robert Goldthwaite. *On the Border with Mackenzie or Winning West Texas from the Comanches*. 1935; rpt. New York: Antiquarian Press, 1961.

Casasola, Gustavo. *Historia gráfica de la revolución mexicana, 1900–1960*. México: Editorial F. Trillas, 1965.

Caso, Alfonso, and M. G. Parra. *Densidad de la población de habla indígena en la república mexicana*. México: Instituto Nacional Indigenista, Memoria I., 1950.

Castillo, José R. *Historia de la revolución social de México*. México: n.p., 1915.

Castro, Lorenzo. *The Republic of Mexico*. New York: Thompson and Moreau, 1882.

Chapultepec. Colegio Militar de México. *El triunfo de la república: Nuestra carta magna, 1867–1917*. México: Senado de la República, 1967.

Clendenen, Clarence C. *The United States and Pancho Villa: A Study in Unconventional Diplomacy*. Ithaca, N.Y.: Cornell University Press, 1961.

———. *Blood on the Border: The United States Army and the Mexican Irregulars*. London: Collier-MacMillan, 1969.

Cline, Howard F. *The United States and Mexico*. Cambridge: Harvard University Press, 1953.

Clum, Woodworth. *Apache Agent: The Story of John P. Clum*. Boston and New York: Houghton Mifflin, 1936.

Coerver, Don M. *The Porfirian Interregnum: The Presidency of Manuel González of Mexico, 1880–1884*. Fort Worth, Tex.: Texas Christian University, 1979.

Comas, Juan. *Ensayos sobre indigenismo*. México: Instituto Indigenista Interamericano, 1953.

———. *La antropología social aplicada en México: Trayectoria y antología*. México: Instituto Indigenista Interamericano, 1964.

Corral, Ramón. *Memoria de la administración pública del estado de Sonora presentada a la legislatura del mismo por el gobernador*. 2 Vols. Guaymas, Sonora: E. Gaxiola, 1891.

———. *Obras históricas*. Hermosillo, México, n.p., 1959.

Cosío Villegas, Daniel. *El porfiriato: La vida política exterior*. Part 2, Vol. V of *Historia moderna de México*. México: Editorial Hermes, 1963.

———. *The United States Versus Porfirio Díaz*. Trans. Nettie Lee Benson. Lincoln: University of Nebraska Press, 1963.

Cosío Villegas, Emma, ed. *Diario personal de Matías Romero*. México: El Colegio de México, 1960.

Crawford, Cora Hayward. *The Land of the Montezumas*. New York: John B. Alden, 1889.

Cumberland, Charles Curtis. *Mexico: The Struggle for Modernity*. New York: Oxford University Press, 1968.

Dabdoub, Claudio. *Historia de el valle del yaqui*. México: Manuel Porrúa, 1964.

Dávila, F. T. *Sonora histórico y descriptivo*. Nogales, Arizona: R. Bernal, 1894.

Davis, Britton. *The Truth About Geronimo*. New Haven: Yale University Press, 1929; rpt. Lincoln: University of Nebraska Press, 1976.

Debo, Angie. *A History of the Indians of the United States*. Norman: University of Oklahoma Press, 1970.

Duclos Salinas, Adolfo. *The Riches of Mexico and its Institutions*. St. Louis: Nixon-Jones, 1893.

Dunlay, Thomas W. *Wolves for the Blue Soldiers: Indian Scouts and Auxiliaries with the United States Army, 1860–1890*. Lincoln: University of Nebraska Press, 1982.

Ellis, Richard N., ed. *The Western American Indian: Case Studies in Tribal History*. Lincoln: University of Nebraska Press, 1972.

Espino Barrios, Eugenio, comp. *Album gráfico de la república mexicana, 1910*. 2nd ed. México: D. F. Müller, 1910.

Fábila, Alfonso. *Las tribus yaquis de Sonora: Su cultura y anhelada autodeterminación*. México: Departmento de Asuntos Indígenas, 1940.

Faulk, Odie B. *The Geronimo Campaign*. New York: Oxford University Press, 1969.

——. *Crimson Desert: Indian Wars of the American Southwest*. New York: Oxford University Press, 1974.

Flores, Blas M. *Relación histórica de la campaña contra los salvages*. Monterrey: Imprenta del Gobierno, en Palacio, 1881.

Forsyth, George A. *Thrilling Days in Army Life*. New York: Harper and Brothers, 1900.

Frazer, Robert W. *Forts of the West: Military Forts and Presidios and Posts Commonly Called Forts West of the Mississippi River to 1898*. Norman: University of Oklahoma Press, 1965.

Fuentes Mares, José. *Y México se refugió en el desierto: Luis Terrazas, historia y destino*. México: Editorial Jus, 1954.

Fyfe, Henry Hamilton. *The Real Mexico, a Study on the Spot*. New York: McBride, Nast, 1914.

Galván Rivera, D. Mariano. *Colección de las más antiguo Galván desde su fundación hasta el 30 de junio de 1924*. México: Antigua Imprenta de Murguia, 1926.

Gamio, Manuel. *Consideraciones sobre el problema indígena*. México: Instituta Indigenista Interamericano, 1948.

——. *Arqueología e indigenismo*. México: Secretaría de Educación Pública, 1972.

García Cantú, Gastón. *Las invasiones norteamericanas en México*. 2nd ed. México: Ediciones Era, 1974.

García Cubas, Antonio. *Discursos sobre la decadencia de la raza indígena.* México: Tip. Literaria de Filomento Mata, 1880.

García Granados, Ricardo. *Historia de México desde la restauración de la república en 1867 hasta la caída de Huerta.* 2 Vols. 1923; rpt. México: Editorial Jus, 1956.

García y Alva, Federico, ed. *México y sus progresos: Album-directorio del estado de Sonora.* Hermosillo: A. B. Monteverde, 1905–07.

Gil, Carlos B., ed. *The Age of Porfirio Díaz: Selected Readings.* Albuquerque: University of New Mexico Press, 1977.

Gilderhus, Mark T. *Diplomacy and Revolution: U.S.-Mexican Relations under Wilson and Carranza.* Tucson: University of Arizona Press, 1977.

González Navarro, Moisés. *Estadísticas sociales del porfiriato, 1877–1910.* México: Dirección General de Estadística, Secretaría de Economia, 1956.

——. *El Porfiriato: La vida social.* Vol. 4 of *Historia moderna de México.* Ed. Daniel Cosío Villegas. México: Hermes, 1957.

——. *Raza y tierra: La guerra de castas y el henequén.* México: Centro de Estudios Históricos, Nueva Serie 10, El Colegio de México, 1970.

——. *Población y sociedad en México, 1900–1970.* Vol. 2. México: Universidad Nacional Autónoma de México, 1974.

González Roa, Fernando. *El aspecto agrario de la revolución mexicana.* México: Departamento de Aprovisionamientos Generales, Dirección de Talleres Gráficos, 1919.

Gooch, Fanny Chamber [Iglehart]. *Face to Face with the Mexicans.* New York: Howard and Hulbert, 1887.

Goodwin, Grenville. *Social Organization of the Western Apache.* 1942; rpt. Tucson: University of Arizona Press, 1969.

Gregg, Robert D. *The Influence of Border Troubles on Relations between the United States and Mexico, 1876–1910.* Baltimore: Johns Hopkins Press, 1937.

Griffen, William B. *Utmost Good Faith: Patterns of Apache-Mexican Hostilities in Northern Chihuahua Border Warfare, 1821–1848.* Albuquerque: University of New Mexico Press, 1988.

Griffin, Solomon Bulkley. *Mexico of Today.* New York: Harper and Brothers, 1886.

Gruening, Ernest H. *Mexico and Its Heritage.* New York and London: D. Appleton-Century-Crofts, 1928.

Gutiérrez Santos, Daniel. *Historia militar de México, 1876–1914.* México: Ediciones Ateneo, 1955.

Hall, Linda B., and Don M. Coerver. *Revolution on the Border: the United States and Mexico, 1910–1920.* Albuquerque: University of New Mexico Press, 1988.

Hamilton, Leonidas. *Border States of Mexico: Sonora, Sinaloa, Chihuahua and Durango, a Complete Description of the Best Region for the Settler, Miner and the Advance Guard of American Civilization: A Complete Guide for Travelers and Emigrants.* San Francisco: Bacon, 1881.

——. *Hamilton's Mexican Handbook: A Complete Description of the Republic of Mexico.* Boston: D. Lothrop, 1883.

Heitman, Francis B. *Historical Register and Dictionary of the United States Army, from its Organization, September 29, 1789, to March 2 1903.* 2 Vols. Washington: U.S. Government Printing Office, 1903.

Hernández, Fortunato. *Las razas indígenas de Sonora y la guerra del yaqui.* México: Talleres de la Casa Editorial "J. de Elizalde," 1902.

Hernández Luna, Juan, ed. *Ateneo de la juventud: Conferencias.* México: Centro de Estudios Filosóficos, Universidad Nacional Autónoma de México, 1962.

Hinkle, Stacy C. *Wings and Saddles: the Air and Cavalry Punitive Expedition of 1919.* El Paso: UTEP Texas Western Press, 1967.

——. *Wings Over the Border: the Army Air Service Armed Patrol of the United States-Mexico Border, 1919–1921.* El Paso: UTEP Texas Western Press, 1970.

Horowitz, Irving Louis, Josué de Castro, and John Gerassi, eds. *Latin American Radicalism: A Documentary Report on Left and Nationalist Movements.* New York: Vintage Books, Random House, 1969.

Instituto Nacional Indigenista. *Realidades y proyectos: 16 años de trabajo.* Vol. X of *Memoras.* México: INI, 1964.

Jordán, Fernando. *Crónica de un país bárbaro.* 2nd ed. México: B. Costa-Amic, 1965.

King, Charles. *Campaigning with Crook.* Norman: University of Oklahoma Press, 1964.

Krauze, Enrique. *Porfirio Díaz: Místico de la authoridad.* México: Fondo de Cultura Económica, 1987.

Lamar, Howard R. *The Far Southwest, 1846–1912: A Territorial History.* New Haven: Yale University Press, 1966.

Lane, Jack C., ed. *Chasing Geronimo: The Journal of Leonard Wood May–September, 1886.* Albuquerque: University of New Mexico Press, 1970.

Lister, Florence C., and Robert H. *Chihuahua: Storehouse of Storms.* Albuquerque: University of New Mexico Press, 1966.

López Portillo y Rojas, José. *La raza indígena.* México: Imprenta Viamonte, 1904.

Lumholtz, Carl. *New Trails in Mexico: An Account of One Year's Exploration in North-Western Sonora, Mexico, and South-Western Arizona, 1909–1910.* New York: Scribner's, 1912.

——. *Unknown Mexico.* New York: Scribner's, 1902; rpt. Glorieta, New Mexico: Rio Grande Press, 1973.

Lummis, Charles Fletcher. *The Awakening of a Nation; Mexico of Today.* New York and London: Harper and Brothers, 1902.

Luna, Jésus. *La carrera pública de don Ramón Corral.* México: Secretaria de Educación Pública, 1975.

McBride, George McCutchen. *The Land Systems of Mexico.* New York: American Geographical Society, Research Series no. 12, 1923.

McGaw, William C. *Savage Scene: The Life and Times of James Kirker, Frontier King.* New York: Hastings House, 1972.

Manero, Antonio, *El antiguo régimen y la revolución.* México: Tip. "La Europa," 1911.

Maqueo Castellanos, Esteban. *Algunos problemas nacionales.* México: E. Gómez de la Puenta, 1909.

Mason, Herbert Molloy. *The Great Pursuit.* New York: Random House, 1970.

Menéndez, Carlos R., ed. *Historia del infame y vergonzoso comerico de indios vendidos a los esclavistas de Cuba por los políticos yucatecos, desde 1848 hasta 1861.* Mérida, Yucatán: "La Revista de Yucatán," 1923.

——. *Noventa años de historia de Yucatán, 1821–1910.* Mérida: Tipográfica Yucateca, 1937.

Metz, Leon C. *Border: The U.S.-Mexico Line,* El Paso, Texas: Mangan Books, 1989.

Meyer, Jean. *Problemas campesinos y revueltas agrarias, 1821–1910.* México: Secretaría de Educación Pública, Sep Setentas, 1973.

Miles, Elton. *More Tales of the Big Bend.* College Station: Texas A & M University Press, 1988.

Miles, Nelson A. *Personal Recollections and Observations of General Nelson A. Miles.* Chicago and New York: Werner, 1896.

——. *Serving the Republic: Memoirs of the Civil and Military Life of Nelson A. Miles.* 1911; rpt. Freeport, New York: Books for Libraries Press, 1971.

Molina Enríquez, Andrés. *Los grandes problemas nacionales.* México: Imprenta de A. Carranza e Hijos, 1909.

——. *La revolución agraria en México.* México: Museo Nacional de Arqueología, Historia y Etnografía, 1937.

Moorhead, Max L. *The Presidio: Bastion of the Spanish Borderlands.* Norman: University of Oklahoma Press, 1975.

Nicoli, José Patricio. *Yaquis y Mayos: Estudio histórico.* 2nd ed. México: Francisco Díaz de León, 1885.

Ober, Frederick A. *Travels in Mexico and Life Among the Mexicans.* San Francisco: J. Dewing, 1884.

Ogle, Ralph Hedrick. *Federal Control of the Western Apaches, 1848–1886.* n.p.: The Historical Society of New Mexico, Publications in History, 1946, Vol. 9; rpt. Albuquerque: University of New Mexico Press, 1970.

Pacheco, Carlos. *Disposiciones sobre designación y fraccionamiento de ejidos de los pueblos.* México: Secretaría de Fomento, 1889.

Parkes, Henry Bamford. *A History of Mexico.* Boston: Houghton Mifflin, 1970.

Paso y Troncoso, Francisco. *Las guerras con las tribus yaqui y mayo del estado de Sonora.* México: Tipografía del Departamento del Estado Mayor, 1905.

Paz, Ireneo. *Album de la paz y el trabajo.* México: Imprenta, Litografía, Encuadernación de I. Paz, 1910.

Paz, Octavio. *The Labyrinth of Solitude.* Trans. Lysander Kemp. New York: Grove Press, 1961.

Pesqueira, Héctor A. "Una Muerte Llamada Gerónimo," *Temas Sonorenses A Través de los Simposios de Historia.* Hermosillo: Gobierno del Estado de Sonora, 1984.

Pimentel, Francisco. *Memoria sobre las causas que han originado la situación actual de la raza indígena de México y medio de remediarle.* México: Andrade y Escalante, 1864.

Porter, Jonathan C. *Paper Medicine Man: John Gregory Bourke and His American West.* Norman: University of Oklahoma Press, 1986.

Powell, T. G. *El liberalismo y el campesinado en el centro de México, 1850 a 1876.* Trans. Roberto Gómez Ciriza. México: Sep Setentas 122, 1974.

Prucha, Francis Paul. *The Great Father: The United States Government and the American Indian.* 2 vols. Lincoln and London: University of Nebraska Press, 1984.

Quirk, Robert. *Mexico.* Englewood Cliffs: Prentice-Hall, 1971.

Reed, Nelson, *The Caste War of Yucatan.* 1964; rpt. Stanford, Calif.: Stanford University, 1967.

Rice, John H. *Mexico: Our Neighbor.* New York: J. W. Lovell, 1888.

Rippy, J. Fred. *The United States and Mexico.* New York: Knopf, 1926.

Rister, Carl Coke. *The Southwestern Frontier, 1865–1881.* Cleveland, Ohio: Arthur H. Clark, 1928.

Roca, Paul M. *Paths of the Padres Through Sonora: An Illustrated History and Guide to Its Spanish Churches.* Tucson: Arizona Pioneers' Historical Society, 1967.

Rodríquez, Ricardo. *Historia auténtica de la administración del Sr. Gral. Porfirio Díaz.* 2 Vols. México: Oficina Tip. de la Secretaría de Fomento, 1904.

Romero, Matías. *Mexico and the United States: A Study Affecting Their Political, Commercial, and Social Relations, Made with a View to Their Promotion.* Vol. I. New York and London: G. P. Putnam's Sons, 1898.

Sánchez, George I. *Mexico: A Revolution by Education.* New York: Viking Press, 1939.

Santee, Ross. *Apache Land.* New York: Scribner's, 1947.

Schroeder, Albert H. *A Study of Apache Indians, Parts IV and V.* New York and London: Garland, 1974.

Sesto, Julio. *El México de Porfirio Díaz: Hombres y cosas.* Valencia: F. Sempere, 1910.

Sheridan, Philip. H. *Record of Engagements with Hostile Indians within the Military Division of the Missouri, from 1868 to 1882.* Washington, D.C.: U.S. Government Printing Office, 1882.

———. *Personal Memoirs of P. H. Sheridan, General, U.S. Army.* Vol. 2. 1888; rpt. New York: D. Appleton, 1904.

Sierra, Justo, ed. *Mexico: Its Social Evolution.* 3 Vols. México: J. Ballesca, 1900–04.

———. *Obras completas.* Vol. 13. México: Universidad Nacional Autónoma de México, 1948–49.

Smith, Cornelius C. J. *Emilio Kosterlitzky: Eagle of Sonora and the Southwest Border.* Glendale, Calif.: Arthur H. Clark, 1970.

Sonnichsen, Charles Leland. *The Mescalero Apaches.* Norman: University of Oklahoma Press, 1958; rpt. 1973.

———. *Colonel Greene and the Copper Skyrocket.* Tucson: University of Arizona Press, 1974.

Spicer, Edward H. *Cycles of Conquest: the Impact of Spain, Mexico, and the United*

States on the Indians of the Southwest, 1533–1960. Tucson: University of Arizona Press, 1976.

——. *The Yaquis: A Cultural History.* Tucson: University of Arizona Press, 1980.

Starr, Frederick. *Indians of Southern Mexico: An Ethnographic Album.* Chicago: [The Author], 1899.

——. *In Indian Mexico: A Narrative of Travel and Labor.* Chicago: Forbes, 1908.

Tannenbaum, Frank. *The Mexican Agrarian Revolution.* 1929; rpt. Hamden, Conn.: Archon Books, 1968.

Terrazas, D. Joaquín. *Memorias.* Ciudad Juárez, Chihuahua: El Agricultor Mexicano; rpt. Chihuahua, Chihuahua: Talleres de Impresos Gaytán, 1978.

Thrapp, Dan L. *The Conquest of Apachería.* Norman: University of Oklahoma Press, 1967.

——. *General Crook and the Sierra Madre Adventure.* Norman: University of Oklahoma Press, 1971.

——. *Juh: an Incredible Indian.* University of Texas at El Paso Southwestern Studies, No. 39. El Paso: Texas Western Press, 1973.

——. *Victorio and the Mimbres Apaches.* Norman: University of Oklahoma Press, 1974.

——, ed. *Dateline Fort Bowie: Charles Fletcher Lummis Reports on an Apache War.* Norman: University of Oklahoma Press, 1979.

Timmons, Wilbert H., ed. *John F. Finerty Reports Porfirian Mexico, 1879.* El Paso: Texas Western Press, 1974.

Turner, Frederick C. *The Dynamic of Mexican Nationalism.* Chapel Hill: University of North Carolina Press, 1968.

Turner, John Kenneth. *Barbarous Mexico.* Chicago: C. H. Kerr, 1911; rpt. Austin: University of Texas Press, 1969.

Tweedie, Ethel. *Mexico as I Saw It.* London and New York: Thomas Nelson, 1911.

Utley, Robert M. *Frontier Regulars: The United States Army and the Indian, 1866–1891.* New York: Macmillan, 1973.

Valadés, José. *El porfirismo.* México: Porrúa e Hijos, 1941.

Vanderwood, Paul J., and Frank N. Samponaro. *Border Fury: A Picture Postcard Record of Mexico's Revolution and U.S. War Preparedness, 1910–1917.* Albuquerque: University of New Mexico Press, 1988.

Vasconcelos, José, and Manuel Gamio. *Aspects of Mexican Civilization.* Chicago: University of Chicago Press, 1926.

Velasco Valdés, Miguel. *La prerevolución y el hombre de la calle.* México: Costa-Amie, 1964.

Villa, Eduardo W. *Historia del estado de Sonora.* 3rd ed. Hermosillo, México: Gobierno del estado de Sonora, 1984.

Villa Rojas, A. *The Maya of East Central Quintana Roo.* Washington, D.C.: Carnegie Institute, Publication 559, 1945.

Villoro, Luis. *Los grandes momentos del indigenismo en México.* México: El Colegio de México, 1950.

Wallace, Ernest. *Ranald S. Mackenzie on the Texas Frontier*. Lubbock: West Texas Museum Association, 1964.
——, ed. *Ranald S. Mackenzie's Official Correspondence Relating to Texas, 1871–1873*. 2 Vols. Lubbock, Tex.: West Texas Museum Association, 1967.
Wells, David Ames. *A Study of Mexico*. New York: D. Appleton, 1887.
Whetten, Nathan. *Rural Mexico*. 4th ed. Chicago and London: University of Chicago Press, 1964.
Winfrey, Dorman H., and James H. Day, eds. *The Indian Papers of Texas and the Southwest, 1825–1916*. Austin, Tex.: Pemberton Press, 1966.
Winter, Nevin O. *Mexico and Her People Today*. 1907; rpt. Boston: L. C. Page, 1912.
Wolfe, Eric R. *Peasant Wars of the Twentieth Century*. New York: Harper and Row, 1969.
Womack, John. *Zapata and the Mexican Revolution*. New York: Knopf, 1969.
Zayas Enríquez, Rafael de. *Los Estados Unidos Mexicanos, sus progresos en veinte años de paz, 1877–1897*. New York: H. A. Rost, 1899.
Zea, Leopoldo. *El positivismo en México: Nacimiento, apogeo y decadencia*. 1943–44; rpt. México: Fondo de Cultura Economica, 1968.
Zorilla, Luis G. *Historia de las relaciones entre México y los Estados Unidos de América, 1800–1958*. 2 Vols. México: Editorial Porrúa, 1965.

B. Articles

Adams, Richard N. "Nationalization." *Social Anthropology*. Vol. 6 of *The Handbook of Middle American Indians*. Ed. Manning Nash. Gen. ed. Robert Wauchope. Austin: University of Texas Press, 1967, pp. 469–89.
Ball, Eve. "The Apache Scouts: A Chiricahua Appraisal." *Arizona and the West* 7, No. 4 (1965): 315–28.
Beals, Ralph L. "Acculturation." *Social Anthropology*. Vol. VI of *The Handbook of Middle American Indians*. Ed. Manning Nash. Gen. ed. Robert Wauchoupe. Austin: University of Texas Press, 1967, pp. 449–68.
Bender, A. B. "Frontier Defense in the Territory of New Mexico, 1853–1861." *New Mexico Historical Review* 9, No. 4 (1934): 345–73.
Boas, Franz. "Summary of the Work of the International School of American Archaeology and Ethnology in Mexico 1910–1914." *American Anthropologist* 17 (1915): 384–95.
Bonfil Batalla, Guillermo. "Andrés Molina Enríquez y la Sociedad Indianista Mexicana: El indigenismo en víspera de la revolución." *Anales del Instituto Nacional de Antropología e Historia* 18 (1965): 217–32.
Britton, J. A. "Indian Education, Nationalism, and Federalism in Mexico 1910–1921." *The Americas* 32 (1976): 445–58.
Cano Avila, Gastón. "Las tribus indígenas en los siglos xix y principios de xx." *Memoria, Primer Simposio de Historia de Sonora*. Hermosillo: Universidad de Sonora, Instituto de Investigaciones Históricas, 1976, n.p.

Carter, Robert Goldthwaite, "General R. S. Mackenzie's Raid into Mexico, 1873," *Outing Magazine* (April 1888), p. 4, Charles B. Gatewood Collection, Box 1, Folder 23, Arizona Historical Society, Tucson.

Clum, John P. "The Apaches." *New Mexico Historical Review* 9, No. 2 (1929): 107–27.

Coatsworth, John. "Railroads, Landholding, and Agrarian Protest in the Early Porfiriato." *Hispanic American Historical Review* 54, No. 1 (1974): 48–71.

Coerver, Don M. "Federal-State Relations during the Porfiriato: the Case of Sonora 1879–1884." *The Americas* 33 (1977): 567–84.

———. "Perils of Progress: the Mexican Department of Fomento During the Boom Years 1880–1884." *Inter-American Economic Affairs* 31 (1977): 41–62.

Coffey, Frederic A. "Some General Aspects of the Gadsden Treaty." *New Mexico Historical Review* 8, No. 3 (1933): 145–64.

Crimmins, Martin L. "Colonel Buell's Expedition into Mexico in 1880." *New Mexico Historical Review* 10 (1935): 133–42.

Daly, Henry W. "The Geronimo Campaign." *The United States Cavalry Journal* 9–10 (1908): 86–103, 247–62, Charles B. Gatewood Collection, Box 2, Folder 13, Arizona Historical Society, Tucson.

Decorme, G. "Catholic Education in Mexico 1525–1912." *Catholic Historical Review* 2 (1916): 168–81.

Dewitt, Donald. "El acuerdo diplomático del 29 de julio de 1882: Su significado para los estados de Arizona y Sonora." Trans. Leo Sandoval. *Memoria, III. Simposio de Historia de Sonora.* Hermosillo: Universidad de Sonora, Instituto de Investigaciones Históricas, 1978, n.p.

Fieberger, G. J. "General Crook's Campaign in Old Mexico in 1883: Events leading Up to It and Personal Experiences in the Campaign." *Proceedings of the Annual Meeting of the Order of Indian Wars of the United States,* 20 February 1936, pp. 22–32; rpt. *The Papers of the Order of Indian Wars.* Fort Collins, Colorado: The Old Army Press, 1975.

Forbes, Jack D. "Historical Survey of the Indians of Sonora 1821–1910." *Ethnohistory* 4, No. 4 (1957): 335–68.

Fraser, Donald J. "La política de desamortización en las comunidades indígenas." *Historia Mexicana* 21, No. 4 (1972): 615–52.

García Granados, Ricardo. "El concepto científico de la historia." *Revista Positiva,* 1910.

González Navarro, Moisés. "Instituciones indígenas en México independiente." *Métodos y resultados de la política indigenista en México.* Vol. VI of *Memorias.* Ed. Alfonso Caso et al. México: Instituto Nacional Indigenista, 1954, pp. 113–69.

———. "La guerra de castas en Yucatán y venta de mayas a Cuba." *Historia Mexicana* 18, No. 1 (1968): 11–34.

González y González, Luis. "El subsuelo indígena." *La república restaurada: La vida social.* Vol. III of *Historia moderna de México.* Ed. Daniel Cosío Villegas. México: Hermes, 1957, pp. 149–325.

Green, F. E., ed. "Ranald S. Mackenzie's Official Correspondence Relating to Texas, 1871–1873." *Museum Journal* 9 (1965): 3–190.

Harris, Charles H. III, and Louis R. Sadler. "The Plan of San Diego and the Mexican–United States War Crisis of 1916: A Reexamination." *The Hispanic American Historical Review* 58 (August 1978): 381–407.

Hu-Dehart, Evelyn. "Development and Rural Rebellion: Pacification of the Yaquis in the Late Porfiriato." *Hispanic American Historical Review* 54, No. 1 (1971): 72–93.

Katz, Friedrich. "Labor Conditions on Haciendas in Porfirian Mexico: Some Trends and Tendencies." *Hispanic American Historical Review* 54, No. 1 (1974): 1–47.

———. "Peasants in the Mexican Revolution of 1910." In *Forging Nations: A Comparative View of Rural Ferment and Revolt*. Eds. Joseph Spielberg and Scott Whiteford. Lansing: Michigan State University Press, 1976, pp. 61–85.

———. "Pancho Villa and the Attack on Columbus, New Mexico." *American Historical Review* 83 (February, 1978): 101–30.

King, Arden R. "Urbanization and Industrialization." *Social Anthropology*, Vol. VI of *The Handbook of Middle American Indians*. Ed. Manning Nash. Gen. ed. Robert Wauchope. Austin: University of Texas Press, 1967, pp. 512–36.

Loyola, Mary. "The American Occupation of New Mexico 1821–1852." *New Mexico Historical Review* 14, No. 2 (1939): 143–99.

Lozoya, Jorge Alberto. "Un guión para el estudio de los ejércitos mexicanos del siglo diecinueve." *Historia Mexicana* 17, No. 4 (1968): 553–68.

Lyon, Juana Fraser. "Archie McIntosh, the Scottish Indian Scout." *The Journal of Arizona History* 7, No. 3 (Autumn, 1966): 103–122.

Mendoza, Víctor M. "Grandesa de un coloso." *Tarahumara* 15 (1980): 15, 17.

———. "Guerreros indígenas chihuahuenses: Mauricio y Vitorio." *El Heraldo de Chihuahua*, 20 September 1980, Section C, p. 1.

Nahmad, Salomón. "Las ideas sociales del positivismo en el indigenismo de la época pre-revolucionaria en México." *América Indígena* 33, No. 4 (1973): 1169–82.

Ogle, Ralph H. "The Apache and the Government— 1870s." *New Mexico Historical Review* 33, No. 2 (1958): 81–102.

Opler, Morris E. "A Chiricahua Apache's Account of the Geronimo Campaign of 1886." *New Mexico Historical Review* 13, No. 4 (1938): 360–86.

Park, Joseph F. "The Apaches in Mexican-American Relations, 1848 1861: A Footnote to the Gadsden Treaty." *Arizona and the West* 3 (Summer 1961): 129–46.

Powell, T. G. "Mexican Intellectuals and the Indian Question." *The Hispanic American Historical Review* 48, No. 1 (1968): 19–36.

Raat, William D. "Leopoldo Zea and Mexican Positivism: A Reappraisal." *The Hispanic American Historical Review* 48, No. 1 (1968): 1–18.

———. Ideas and Society in Don Porfirio's Mexico." *The Americas* 30, No. 1 (1973): 32–53.

Rippy, J. Fred. "The Indians of the Southwest in the Diplomacy of the United States and Mexico, 1848–1853." *The Hispanic American Historical Review* 2 (1919): 363–96.

Rubio Mañé, Jorge Ignacio. "La guerra de castas según un escritor anglo-americano." *Revista de la Universidad de Yucatán* 11, No. 61 (1969): 9–20.

Ruz Menéndez, Rodolfo. "La emancipación de los esclavos en Yucatán." *Revista de la Universidad de Yucatán* 12, No. 67 (1970): 19–39.

Safford Relyea, Pauline. "Diplomatic Relations Between the United States and Mexico under Porifiro Díaz, 1876–1910." *Smith College Studies in History* 10, No. 1 (1924): 5–91.

Shipp, W. E. "Captain Crawford's Last Expedition." *Cavalry Journal* (1892); rpt. *The United States Cavalry Journal* 19, No. 10 (1908): 278–300, Charles B. Gatewood Collection, Box 2, Folder 13, Arizona Historical Society, Tucson.

Shipp, W. E., and Herbert Welsh. "Our Indian Scouts," *Harper's Weekly*, 27 October 1888, p. 811.

Sims, Harold D. "Espejo de caciques: Los Terrazas de Chihuahua." *Historia Mexicana* 18 (July 1968–June 1969): 379–99.

Smith, Ralph A. "The Scalp Hunt in Chihuahua — 1849." *New Mexico Historical Review* 40, No. 2 (April, 1965): 116–40.

Sociedad Indianista Mexicana. *Boletín*, Nos. 1–6, 8–11 (1911).

Soto, Jesús S. "La población indígena de México." *Revista Mexicana de Economía* 1, No. 2 (1928): 194–213.

Spicer, Edward H. "The Yaqui and Mayo." *Ethnology*, Part 2 in *The Handbook of Middle American Indians*. Ed. Evon Z. Vogt. Gen. ed. Robert Wauchope. Austin: University of Texas Press, 1969, pp. 830–45.

Stabb, Martin S. "Indigenism and Racism in Mexican Thought 1857–1911." *Journal of Inter-American Studies* 1, No. 4 (1959): 405–23.

Tate, Michael L. "Pershing's Punitive Expedition: Pursuer of Bandits or Presidential Panacea?" *The Americas* 32 (July, 1975): 46–72.

Thrapp, Dan L. "Geronimo's Mysterious Surrender." *Los Angeles Corral of the Westerners Brand Book* 13 (1969): 16–35.

Vasconcelos, José. "Education in Mexico, Present Day Tendencies." *Bulletin of the Pan American Union* 56, No. 3 (1923): 12–42.

Villa Rojas, Alfonso. "The Maya of Yucatán." *Ethnology*, Part 1 in *The Handbook of Middle American Indians*. Ed. Evon Z. Vogt. Gen. ed. Robert Wauchope. Austin: University of Texas Press, 1969, pp. 244–75.

Worchester, Donald E. "The Apaches in the History of the Southwest." *New Mexico Historical Review* 50, No. 1 (1975): 25–44.

C. Dissertations and Theses

Carbine, Carol Lee. "The Indian Policy of Porfirio Díaz in the State of Yucatán, 1876–1910." Diss., Loyola, 1977.

Harte, John Bret. "The San Carlos Indian Reservation, 1872–1886: An Administrative History." Diss., University of Arizona, 1972.

Kaiser, Chester C. "John Watson Foster: United States Minister to Mexico, 1873–1880." Diss., American University, 1954.

Mazzaferri, Anthony J. "Public Health and Social Revolution in Mexico, 1877–1930." Diss., Kent State, 1968.

Raat, William D. "Positivism in Díaz Mexico, 1876–1910: An Essay in Intellectual History." Diss., University of Utah, 1967.

Ruiz, Ramón Eduardo. "Mexico's Struggle for Rural Education, 1910–1950." Thesis, University of California at Berkeley, 1954.

Wilson, Irma. "A Century of Educational Thought in Mexico." Diss., Columbia, 1941. New York: Hispanic Institute in the United States, 1941.

D. Bibliographies, Guides, and Maps

Almada, Francisco R. *Diccionario de historia, geografía y biografía chihuahuenses.* 2nd ed. Chihuahua, Chihuahua: Universidad de Chihuahua, Departmento de Investigaciones Sociales, Sección de Historia, 1968.

———. *Gobernadores del estado de Chihuahua.* 2nd ed. Chihuahua, Chihuahua: Centro Librero La Prensa, 1980.

Barnard, Joseph D., and Randall Rasmussen. "A Bibliography of Bibliographies for the History of Mexico," *Latin American Research Review* 13, No. 2 (1978), pp. 229–35.

Carrera Stampa, Manuel. *Archivalia mexicana.* México: Universidad National Autónoma de México, Instituto de Historia, 1952.

Colección de mapas del estado de Chihuahua. Chihuahua, Chihuahua: Centro Librero La Prensa, n.d.

Cumberland, Charles C. "The United States-Mexican Border: A Selective Guide to the Literature of the Region," *Rural Sociology* 25, No. 2, Supplement (1960), pp. 1–141.

Díaz, Agustín. *Carta general de una parte de la república mexicana.* n. p., 1868.

Diccionario Porrúa de historia, biografía y geografía de México. México: Editorial Porrúa, 1976.

García Cubas, Antonio. *Diccionario geográfico, histórico y biográfico de los Estados Unidos Mexicanos.* México: Secretaría de Fomento 1891.

García y García, J. Jesús. *Guía de archivos: Contiene material de interés para el estudio del desarrollo socioeconómico de México.* México: Instituto Investigaciones Sociales, Universidad Nacional Autónoma de México, 1972.

Herbert, Charles E. *Mapa oficial del estado de Sonora, 1884–1909.* Nogales, Arizona Territory: Sonora News Company, 1909.

Iguíñiz, Juan. *Las publicaciones del museo nacional de arqueología, historia y etnología.* México: MNAHE, 1912.

Instituto Indigenista Interamericano. *Legislación indigenista de México*. México: Instituto Indigenista Interamericano, Ed. Especiales, No. 38, 1958.

Johnson, Steven L. *Guide to American Indian Documents in the Congressional Serial Set: 1817–1899*. New York: Clearwater, 1977.

Millares Carlo, Agustín. *Repertorio bibliográfico de los archivos mexicanos y de los europeos y norteamericanos de interés para la historia de México*. México: Instituto Bibliográfico Mexicano, Biblioteca Nacional de México, 1959.

———, y José Ignacio Mantecón. *Repertorio bibliográfico de los archivos mexicanos y de las colecciones diplomáticas fundamentales para la historia de México*. México: Imprenta Aldina, 1948.

Niblo, Stephen R., and Laurens B. Perry. "Recent Additions to Nineteenth-Century Mexican Historiography," *Latin American Research Review* 13, No. 3 (1978), pp. 3–46.

Parra, Manuel Germán, and Wigberto Jiménez Moreno. *Bibliográfia indigenista de México y Centroamérica, 1850–1950*. Vol. 4 of *Memorias*. México: Instituto Nacional Indigenista, 1954.

Prucha, Francis Paul. *A Bibliographical Guide to the History of Indian-White Relations in the United States*. Chicago and London: The Center for the History of the American Indian of the Newberry Library, University of Chicago Press, 1977.

Index